"What a wonderful book. As the church seeks to know, experience and discern the person and work of the Spirit in its local and global life, these essays are a thoughtful, wise and encouraging accompaniment. They remind us of God's faithful presence among us from creation's beginning, throughout history and in the mystery of the triune life, until the final new creation. They also provide multiple entry points with which to join the wide-ranging and much-needed conversations of the church as it seeks to follow the leading of the Spirit and participate eschatologically in the triune mission of God."

Cherith Fee Nordling, associate professor of theology, Northern Seminary

"God's Spirit is present and active among his people, even amid our historical, cultural and theological differences. Thankfully this book attentively highlights this truth, not by flattening out traditions, but by seeking to listen to the past and reflect on the present. Here we are reminded of distinctions and surprising similarities, from the historic Eastern and Western emphases to how Methodist, Reformed and Pentecostal approaches often uniquely accent the person and work of the Spirit. Here we are given samples of how our pneumatology (or lack thereof) affects everything from how we read the Bible to our view of creation, from worship to soteriology, even shaping our ecclesial and social concerns. Let us not grieve the Spirit, but rather be attentive to the ways of God. This book can help us on that journey."

Kelly M. Kapic, professor of theological studies, Covenant College

Spirit of God

Christian Renewal
in the Community of Faith

Edited by **Jeffrey W. Barbeau**
and **Beth Felker Jones**

IVP Academic

An imprint of InterVarsity Press
Downers Grove, Illinois

InterVarsity Press
P.O. Box 1400, Downers Grove, IL 60515-1426
ivpress.com
email@ivpress.com

InterVarsity Press® is the book-publishing division of InterVarsity Christian Fellowship/USA®, a movement of students and faculty active on campus at hundreds of universities, colleges and schools of nursing in the United States of America, and a member movement of the International Fellowship of Evangelical Students. For information about local and regional activities, visit intervarsity.org.

While any stories in this book are true, some names and identifying information may have been changed to protect the privacy of individuals.

Cover design: Cindy Kiple
Interior design: Beth McGill
Image: "Baptism of Jesus" by He Qi/www.heqiart.com

ISBN 978-0-8308-2464-9 (print)
ISBN 978-0-8308-9775-9 (digital)

Printed in the United States of America ∞

Library of Congress Cataloging-in-Publication Data

A catalog record for this book is available from the Library of Congress.

P	23	22	21	20	19	18	17	16	15	14	13	12	11	10	9	8	7	6	5	4	3	2	1
Y	35	34	33	32	31	30	29	28	27	26	25	24	23	22	21	20	19	18	17	16	15		

For Jeffrey Greenman

Contents

Acknowledgments

Scholarship requires time. The contributors to this collection have dedicated years of research toward formulating the insights found in these essays, devoted long hours writing and reflecting on each topic and shared their time and energy in making this volume a reality. This collection includes contributions from the twenty-third annual Wheaton College Theology Conference. Yet even the task of bringing this remarkable assembly of theological experts together could not have happened without the support of many more individuals who contributed to making this project a reality. We remain grateful for the wise counsel and leadership of our administrators at Wheaton College, including Jeffrey Bingham, Jill Peláez Baumgaertner and Stan Jones. Paula Anderson, Jeannine Allen and Kristina Unzicker managed the logistics of the conference from start to finish—no small task indeed! Susanne Calhoun cheerfully prepared the index. At InterVarsity Press, morning breakfasts with Bob Fryling and David Congdon—years before the actual event—proved both encouraging and essential to our planning; their professional support and experience have made this book even better than we hoped.

The editors dedicate this collection to Dr. Jeffrey P. Greenman for his unflappable devotion to the Wheaton College community during his tenure as associate dean of the Department of Biblical and Theological Studies between 2005 and 2013. As all who have worked with him well know, Jeff has a unique capacity for biblical, theological and administrative expertise. His involvement in the planning of the conference was pivotal to its success: he championed the concept, helped configure the program and shaped the ethos of the gathering. Beyond his role in the formation of this book, however, we wish to thank him for his leadership, vision and personal devotion to people. Jeff's heart for service, perceptive mind and individual example made Wheaton College a better place, and our department grew not only in numbers but also in strength during its time under his guidance. We gratefully dedicate this collection to our friend Jeffrey Greenman.

1

Introduction

Jeffrey W. Barbeau and Beth Felker Jones

This is how we know that we live in him and he in us:
He has given us of his Spirit.

1 JOHN 4:13

During the past century, Christian churches around the world have identified a remarkable work of the Holy Spirit in the lives of everyday people. Young and old, men and women, rich and poor alike have felt the powerful and personal presence of God. Is it any surprise that Christian theology, in turn, witnessed a revival in study of the person and work of the Holy Spirit? From the phenomenal growth of Pentecostalism and the persistent invocation of the Spirit in Roman Catholicism to the Spirit-infused worship of charismatics of all denominations and ecumenical gatherings in the name of Christian unity in the Spirit, Christianity around the world continues to experience a renewal of life unlike any age since the founding era of apostolic witness.

Spirit of God: Christian Renewal in the Community of Faith contributes to the wider project of church and academy through an ecumenical collection of essays that explore biblical, historical, doctrinal and practical insights into the person and work of the Holy Spirit. The volume originated in the twenty-third annual gathering of the Wheaton College Theology Conference. Recent theology conferences at Wheaton College have explored central doctrines (Trinity, ecclesiology), major thinkers (Bonhoeffer, N. T. Wright) and other topics of wide-ranging interest (Christianity and the arts, Christianity and politics), but this gathering initiated conversations long overdue in the evangelical world.

In fact, some might argue that evangelicalism maintains a difficult relationship with pneumatology today. While noted scholars of evangelical history and theology such as Timothy Larsen have rightly highlighted the pneumatological orientation of all evangelical Christianity, tensions persist.[1] For some, evangelical commitment to biblical authority leaves contemporary reflection on the Holy Spirit's ongoing work and distribution of gifts in a subordinate position, at best, to the inspired words of Scripture. For others, the commonplace identification of some fringe Pentecostal groups (such as proponents of the so-called health-and-wealth gospel) with the Spirit's activity distorts the conversation and leaves many Christian leaders in a state of pneumatological apathy. Still others believe that pneumatology must always be subordinated to reflection on primary doctrines such as salvation or the ongoing evaluation of the person and work of Jesus Christ— it is a common claim, after all, that "the Holy Spirit prefers to go unnoticed!"

As the essays in this collection make clear, talk about the Holy Spirit is as old as talk about God. Christians believe that God has made himself known by way of the Holy Spirit from the very beginning. In the prophets, too, the Spirit's presence could be discerned in words and deeds of profound significance. The promised Messiah, Jesus Christ, was anointed for a work of proclamation and the release of those bound by various forms of oppression. And when the disciples gathered in Jerusalem after the ascension of the Lord, they experienced the Spirit's work as a diverse community of faith and gave witness to the risen Christ in the power of the Spirit.

In light of such a pervasive biblical witness to the Spirit's presence, few should be surprised that Christians in every age have continued to give testimony to the work of the Holy Spirit. Whether in creedal declarations of belief or mystical descriptions of divine renewal, the Holy Spirit continues to act in every generation—even when institutional pressures, the potential for disorder and the prevalent desire for systems threatened to domesticate

---

[1]Timothy Larsen, "Defining and Locating Evangelicalism," in *The Cambridge Companion to Evangelical Theology*, ed. Timothy Larsen and Daniel J. Treier (Cambridge: Cambridge University Press, 2007), 10–12.

the personal presence of God. The fact that the Spirit's work is directly tied to the changing face of global Christianity makes pneumatological reflection all the more important today.

Spirit of God: Christian Renewal in the Community of Faith offers timely insights that will benefit newcomers to the conversation and seasoned readers in the literature alike. Part One considers a range of biblical and historical perspectives on the Holy Spirit. The volume commences with a biblical-theological survey of the Holy Spirit. Sandra Richter's essay, "What Do I Know of Holy? On the Person and Work of the Holy Spirit in Scripture" (chap. 2), offers a bird's-eye overview of the Spirit's work throughout the grand story of redemptive history. Beginning in the opening scenes of Genesis, Richter finds the Spirit as a falcon, hovering above the primordial deep, waiting to launch the work of creation. Richter maintains that after Eden the Spirit is clothed in cloud and fire, revealing himself in glory. She finds the Spirit again at Sinai and known among the people in the tabernacle and temple of Israel. Far from an ethereal force, Richter claims that the Spirit is God's own presence manifest in the work of the judges and prophets. Indeed, she explains that the understanding of the Holy Spirit among New Testament writers stands in remarkable continuity with the Old Testament witness of the life-giving agency of the Spirit. The Spirit draws all people— frail and strong, young and old—into communion with God through the life of the church. Indeed, the New Testament provides a vision of final hope, in which the Holy Spirit brings to completion the end of exile and the final reconciliation of creation to God.

The early Christians faced serious challenges to their doctrine of the triune God, as Greg Lee explains in chapter three: "The Spirit's Self-Testimony: Pneumatology in Basil of Caesarea and Augustine of·Hippo." Through close textual analysis of central trinitarian texts in the patristic era, Lee explains that early Christian theologians such as Basil and Augustine developed theologies of the Holy Spirit in dialogue with the Scriptures, while simultaneously seeking to remain faithful to prior witnesses against new challenges to the doctrine of God. Basil's doxological confession in the East, "Glory to the Father, *and* to the Son, *and* to the Holy Spirit," affirmed the divinity and distinction of the Spirit against those who diminished the Spirit's role in salvation. Turning to the Western theological tradition and the seminal influence of Augustine, Lee maintains that a careful analysis of *De Trinitate* reveals the coherence of Augustine's pneumatological logic—a logic based on an explication of trinitarian missions, intratrinitarian relations and humanity's participation in the divine life. On the basis of a comparison of Basil and Augustine, Lee concludes that theological differences between Eastern and Western trinitarian formulations have been overstated and that common ground between the two allows for greater ecumenical dialogue than some have imagined.

In the years following Basil and Augustine, medieval Christians struggled over the divisive use of *filioque* ("of the Son") in both theological and liturgical settings to describe the eternal procession of the Holy Spirit in the Godhead. Matthew Levering ("Rationalism or Revelation? St. Thomas Aquinas and the *Filioque*") explains in chapter four both the tensions and the opportunities for fresh dialogue that surrounds a reexamination of Thomas Aquinas's discussion of the *filioque*. Levering notes the commonplace temptation to completely drop the *filioque* in the West in favor of broad, ecumenical unity. The doctrine, it is frequently claimed, simply isn't worth the trouble. At the center of so much controversy over the doctrine, Thomas Aquinas is widely praised for his theological contributions, yet when the matter of trinitarian relations arises, theologians frequently demur. Levering carefully explicates Thomas's understanding of the Spirit's procession through a detailed analysis of *Summa theologiae* 1, question 36, article 2. Thomas believes that the procession of the Spirit from both the Father and the Son not only allows Christians to distinguish between the divine persons of the Son and Spirit but also clarifies the relationship between Scripture and church traditions, with particular import for the interpretation of conciliar decisions. Levering concludes that rather than signaling the decline of Latin theology into rationalism, Thomas's theology of the Spirit marks a pivotal moment in reflection on the relationship between the Father, Son and Holy Spirit.

Turning to more recent theological constructions of the Spirit, Jeffrey Barbeau's essay, "Enthusiasts, Rationalists and Pentecost: The Holy Spirit in Eighteenth-Century Methodism" (chap. 5), examines two pivotal historical moments that exemplify the emergence of prominent and seemingly contradictory Wesleyan pneumatological traditions. Barbeau maintains that two identifiable strands of belief developed from the practical theology of John and Charles Wesley. Charles Wesley unexpectedly inculcated language of the Spirit in his own "Day of Pentecost" experience, while John Wesley's opposition to divisive tendencies in the Maxfield-Bell schism encouraged self-control and formalization in the movement. These events are indicative of a tension in the Wesleyan theological tradition—one seen in the subsequent history of the Methodist movement. On one hand, the Wesleys' own early experiences of conversion and sanctification led to vivid discussions of the works of the Spirit in everyday life. On the other hand, not only John Wesley but also theologians from Richard Watson down to the present day have attempted to set boundaries on the Spirit's work—largely in an effort to diminish criticism of the movement as little more than enthusiasm. Barbeau concludes that the Holy Spirit remains central to Wesleyan theology, most notably in the emphasis on a practical divinity marked by love in the gathered community of faith.

Oliver Crisp's essay, "Uniting Us to God: Toward a Reformed Pneumatology" (chap. 6), provides historical and constructive reflections that underscore the possibilities of a robust doctrine of the Spirit in the Reformed tradition. Crisp develops a logical argument from the person to the work of the Spirit that allows for a recovery of an avowedly pneumatological doctrine of "union with Christ" or *theosis*. He begins by reminding readers of the rich Reformed confessional heritage, in which the Spirit belongs to the extensive theological reflection on doctrines of creation, providence, salvation and eschatology. In this way, Crisp claims, the Reformed tradition upholds the Western tradition of the triune Godhead. Yet Crisp next extends the Reformed tradition with constructive reflections on the work of the Spirit. He draws out two principles: the *Trinitarian Appropriation Principle* (TAP), which affirms that the external works of God are all works of the Trinity, and the *Intention Application Principle* (IAP), which asserts that God intends his ultimate goal in creation. The first principle upholds the work of the Spirit in all times and places. The second allows Crisp to recover the doctrine of union with Christ. Crisp maintains an organic analogy in the process: even as the oak tree grows from a seed, so the church develops under the care of God and is bound across time and space by the uniting work of the Holy Spirit.

Allan Anderson's study of Pentecostalism around the world in chapter seven ("The Dynamics of Global Pentecostalism: Origins, Motivations and Future") reveals the way that experiences of the Spirit have dramatically altered global Christianity. In tracing what amounts to one of the most remarkable occurrences in the history of Christianity, Anderson maintains that Pentecostalism has bolstered the growth of Christianity as never before. Yet while the movement stands in continuity with earlier expressions of evangelical, healing and holiness churches, there is no single origin (such as Azusa Street, 1906) from which the movement flourished. Rather, Anderson explains, Pentecostalism developed out of several centers of activity and continues to expand from rapid developments in Africa, Asia and Latin America, especially. He further explains the various factors that have shaped the movement. In addition to missiological and theological factors that have reinforced a deeply personal and outward-looking understanding of Christianity, the spread of Pentecostalism has been facilitated by cultural and social as well as transnational and globalizing factors that reveal the movement as one of the most flexible expressions of Christian faith in the world today. Against predictions of modern secularity and the inevitable decline of religion, Anderson concludes that Pentecostalism has instead brought about a significant revival of global Christianity that seems unlikely to abate in the years to come.

African American Pentecostalism, one of the most significant branches of global Pentecostalism today, has proved uniquely important in the development of church practice and pneumatological reflection in the past century. In chapter eight, Estrelda Alexander ("The Spirit of God: Christian Renewal in African American Pentecostalism") traces the origins of North American Pentecostalism from the work of the Holiness preacher William Seymour. Although racial tensions threatened to undermine the reception of Seymour's teaching and associated Azusa Street Revival, Seymour's influential ministry proved successful in the formation of a wide range of African American Pentecostal churches. Alexander highlights the African and Wesleyan influences on African American Pentecostal religiosity and demonstrates the rich heritage of the movement. She further examines the theology of these churches through a detailed sociological description and analysis of African American Pentecostal "liturgy." Acts of corporate worship such as singing, dancing and tarrying shed light on Pentecostal belief in the baptism in the Holy Spirit and, indeed, on salvation itself. Alexander asserts that the collective presence of key elements of belief—oral transmission of culture, the reality of the spirit world, blurring of sacred and profane, and communal solidarity—reveals the distinct nature of African American Pentecostalism as well as the contribution of these churches to the contemporary Christian understanding of the person and work of the Holy Spirit.

Part Two of *Spirit of God: Christian Renewal in the Community of Faith* builds on the biblical and historical insights of Part One through an exploration of doctrinal and practical perspectives on the Holy Spirit. In chapter nine, Kevin Vanhoozer's essay ("The Spirit of Light After the Age of Enlightenment: Reforming/Renewing Pneumatic Hermeneutics via the Economy of Illumination") responds to one of the most pressing questions facing Christianity today: where is the Holy Spirit in the process of biblical interpretation? Vanhoozer highlights recent contributions of evangelical biblical exegetes and systematic theologians, noting how each has attempted to solve the riddle of biblical interpretation in the modern age. He surveys, too, the recent contributions of Pentecostal scholars and explains that while many evangelicals are content to recover the original author's intention through critical procedures, Pentecostals seek to preserve the original experience of the Spirit. Vanhoozer concludes that the problem of modern biblical hermeneutics can hardly be pinned on Reformed theology. In fact, drawing on a "Johannine trio"—John Calvin, John Owen and John Webster—Vanhoozer recovers resources toward a Reformed theology of illumination by the Spirit. The Spirit communicates light and life into the hearts of believers, conforming us into the divine image and transforming both individuals and the community.

In chapter ten, Amos Yong offers a prolegomena to a theology of creation by asking how a pneumatological approach to the doctrine might shape methodological considerations that have so often left Christians adrift in the modern world ("*Creatio Spiritus* and the Spirit of Christ: Toward a Trinitarian Theology of Creation"). Yong maintains that a pneumatological (and thereby fully trinitarian) theology of creation leads to a renewal of Christian beliefs and practices. Divine action takes place by, through and in Word and Spirit (the two "hands" of God). Thus the works of creation, redemption and final consummation are always fully trinitarian works of God. On this basis, Yong develops a pneumatological-eschatological approach to a renewed theology of creation. Such an approach has methodological, existential and performative applications that binitarian approaches have often overlooked. Pneumatological consideration of the doctrine of creation reveals not only the "what" of creation but also the "how" of Christian practice. The Spirit redeems the many languages of creation—even the languages of disciplines that might otherwise be deemed beyond the Spirit's reach. Applied to the landscape of modern scholarship—including the natural sciences—a pneumatological and trinitarian doctrine of creation encourages disciplinary pluralism on the basis of teleological or eschatological hope in the final reconciliation of all things.

Few Christian doctrines are as challenging to the student of pneumatology as the doctrine of salvation, as Michael Welker explains in chapter eleven ("'Rooted and Established in Love': The Holy Spirit and Salvation"). Welker notes the ever-present temptation to shy away from the Holy Spirit in favor of simplistic appeals to the work of Christ. In part, Aristotelian notions of spirit, which identify spirit with mind and intellect, have bolstered this tendency toward reduction in the West. By comparison, Welker maintains that biblical images of outpouring allow for new relationships and outward radiations to emerge. In an age of hierarchical distinctions, the biblical witness revealed the Spirit's outpouring among women and men, young and old, and slave and free alike. The new relationships described in Scripture are salvific, Welker claims, because the Spirit reorients life to new intellectual, communicative and ethical dimensions. The Spirit, no mere power of mind, turns people toward others in order to bring about new dimensions of love, exemplified in the prophetic, priestly and kingly reign of Christ. Salvation can be known already here on earth, then, because the Holy Spirit draws us toward Christ in the present-day renewal of frail and finite life.

Liturgy offers significant historical and theological resources for the development of a contemporary doctrine of the Spirit. In chapter twelve, Geoffrey Wainwright ("The Spirit of God and Worship: The Liturgical Grammar of the Holy Spirit") offers reflections on the Holy Spirit by way of various biblical and historical examples of creeds, hymns and prayers directed to God. Wainwright maintains that such examples reveal long-standing Christian commitment to "pneumatic worship" and form a liturgical grammar of the Holy Spirit. Through Pauline pneumatology drawn from the letter to the Romans, collects for purity and early Christian reflections on doxological language, to the hymns of John and Charles Wesley, seasonal prayers to the Spirit and the eucharistic prayers of epiclesis across centuries and traditions, Wainwright finds examples of worship and witness that help reframe Christian pneumatology. He maintains that reflection on such historic examples has the potential to renew faithful practice based on a common Christian baptism. In word and deed, Wainwright concludes that a shared grammar of the Spirit may illuminate authentic encounters with the triune God—perhaps most significantly in matters of ecumenical unity.

Christian commitment to acts of service has a long and venerable history. Yet some imagine that "life in the Spirit" necessarily ignores life in the community. In "Stories of Grace: Pentecostals and Social Justice" (chap. 13), Douglas Petersen shifts the conversation about the relationship between the Spirit and the church from the worshiping community to the community of action. Petersen notes that Pentecostalism, in particular, has a reputation—both within and outside the movement—for ignoring the concerns of body and mind in favor of the Spirit alone. While Pentecostals have long been active in providing assistance among the neediest members of the community, they have often remained ambivalent about articulating such commitments theologically. Petersen highlights the implicit practical theology of Pentecostal churches and maintains that a commitment to word and deed can easily be discerned in the stories that Pentecostals share. In order to illustrate the relationship between the Spirit's work and social justice, Petersen shares the stories of seven children he encountered through his work with Latin America ChildCare during more than two decades of service. Testimonies of salvation and Spirit baptism reveal a profound commitment to social change in the community—actions founded on the personal empowerment of individuals by the Holy Spirit.

If communal change finds its origins in the individual work of the Holy Spirit, then the Spirit is also responsible for the unity of the Christian churches, as Timothy George explains in chapter fourteen ("'In All Places and in All Ages': The Holy Spirit and Christian Unity"). George's biblical, historical and contemporary review of the Spirit's influence begins with the foundational insight that it is the Spirit who brings about any true fellowship among believers. Contemporary ecumenism flows from wellsprings of biblical and historical witness to the person and work of the Holy Spirit. In the Bible, perhaps no text is more significant to the interests of Christian unity than John 17, where Jesus' prayer for unity among believers is set within the larger promise of the presence of the Spirit among them. The trinitarian vision of New Testament theology found expression in the reflections of Christians in later centuries. Perhaps no judgment was as decisive as the move to excommunicate Marcion: his expulsion was an affirmation of the authority of the Old and New Testaments alike and thus an affirmation of the authority of the Holy Spirit. Indeed, more and more, Christians have come to recognize that the Spirit continues to act among the churches, not least when we read the Scriptures in communion with the wider community of faith.

The final essay in this volume, "Come, Holy Spirit: Reflections on Faith and Practice" (chap. 15), is more than an epilogue or concluding word by the editors. The essay marks a proposal and challenge for Christian faith, theological education and faithful action. The tone of the essay crosses scholarly and pastoral interests. While each essay in this volume has clear implications for the life of the church, this essay offers three proposals drawn out of pneumatology. First, we describe Christian faith as a life of fully trinitarian worship. Next, we maintain that Christian theology must take better account of global Christian witness to the Holy Spirit in the development of doctrine. Finally, we suggest several ways that scholars, pastors and laity can more effectively develop faithful Christian practice in light of the Spirit's work in the world.

Spirit of God: Christian Renewal in the Community of Faith advances the conversation in evangelical theology and contributes to the wide and ongoing discussion of the Holy Spirit in the church around the world today. Through this volume and other projects like it, we hope that all theological reflection more effectively communicates a fuller awareness of the triune God. Indeed, we pray that through such dialogue and ecumenical exchange on biblical, historical and contemporary life in the Spirit, we will truly come to know that "we live in him and he in us" for "he has given us of his Spirit" (1 Jn 4:13).

PART ONE

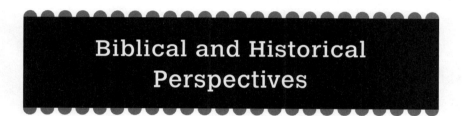

Biblical and Historical Perspectives

2

What Do I Know of Holy?

On the Person and Work of the
Holy Spirit in Scripture

Sandra Richter

Jenny Simmons, lead singer for the band Addison Road, sings a song titled "What Do I Know of Holy?"

> So what do I know of You
> Who spoke me into motion?
> Where have I even stood
> But the shore along Your ocean?
> Are You fire? Are You fury?
> Are You sacred? Are You beautiful?
> So what do I know? What do I know of Holy?[1]

Approaching this essay, I feel much the same. Decades of education, research and teaching, but what do I actually know of *Holy*? Regrettably, among his people the Lord Holy Spirit is often misunderstood or forgotten—relegated to the role of "agency" or "force" or even dismissed as some indiscernible "energy" that infuses the church or empowers his people. But the Scriptures have a different tale to tell. This "agency" is the one who moved on the waters, hurled the cosmos into being and in-filled humanity with the indefinable essence that makes us "image" as opposed to simply animate. This "force" is the thunderous theophany that shrouded Mt. Sinai in fire and storm, inhabited the temple and gave voice to the prophets. This "energy" is God himself, who

---

[1]Addison Road, "What Do I Know of Holy?" *Addison Road* (Nashville: INO Records, 2008).

called a prophet from Babylon, revealed to him the future of his nation—dead and lifeless, slaughtered on the field of battle by their own rebellion—and asked him, "Son of man, can these bones live?" (Ezek 37:3). This is the same "energy" who made good his promise when the descendants of that nation gathered on the day of Pentecost and, in response to the resurrection of the crucified Christ, were filled with a quality of life and supernatural agency of which they had only dreamed (Acts 2:4). This is the one who, when the days of this age come to a close, will invade our fallen dimension with his all-consuming fire, and a new heaven and a new earth will emerge in which there will be no temple, for the earth will be full of the knowledge of the Lord (Holy Spirit) as the waters cover the sea (Rev 21:22; Is 11:9). Who is the Holy Spirit? What does he do and why? The task of this essay is not to answer all these (enormous) questions but to lay a biblical foundation for the answering to be found in the rest of this volume. And as all biblical theology starts in Eden, let us begin at the beginning, at the foundation of all we believe.

THE HOLY SPIRIT IN THE OLD TESTAMENT

We are first introduced to our leading character in Genesis 1:2: "In the beginning, God created the heavens and the earth. The earth was formless and void [tōhû wābōhû], darkness was upon the primordial deep; and the rûaḥ ʾĕlōhîm was moving/hovering/brooding/poised like a bird of prey about to strike [mĕraḥepet][2] over the face of the waters. And then God spoke. . . ."[3] In his classic work *Images of the Spirit*, Meredith Kline interprets the rûaḥ ʾĕlōhîm in this passage as the archetypal theophanic glory of God the Holy Spirit: "the Creator Spirit . . . who makes the clouds his chariot and moves on the wings of the wind."[4] As seen in our dimension, the rûaḥ ʾĕlōhîm is "a heavenly phenomenon of light and clouds . . . expressed as light . . . as of fire or the sun, the light of divine glory that no man can approach."[5] The unique vocabulary of this first reference to the Holy Spirit in Genesis 1:2 is reiterated in Deuteronomy 32:10-11, where Yahweh finds Israel wandering in the howling waste of the wilderness (tōhû yĕlēl), and once again hovers over his fledgling people

---

[2]L. Koehler, W. Baumgartner and J. J. Stamm, *The Hebrew and Aramaic Lexicon of the Old Testament*, trans. and ed. M. E. J. Richardson, 4 vols. (Leiden: Brill, 1994–1999), (HALOT), 1219–20, s.v. "רחף."
[3]Author's translation.
[4]Meredith G. Kline, *Images of the Spirit* (Grand Rapids: Baker, 1980), 15.
[5]Ibid., 18.

until that exact moment when they are to be birthed as the people of God. He then spreads his wings to catch and carry them into the Promised Land (ʿal-gôzālāyw yĕraḥēp).[6] Kline finds this same glory cloud at the baptism of Jesus, where "at the beginning of the new creation" the Spirit once again hovers over the waters, descends "in avian form," and testifies that the One who hurled the stars into place now stands among humanity clothed in Flesh (Mt 3:16).[7] Here we find the redundant and glorious plan of God: once there was nothing, but now you have become the people of God. The kingdom is birthed out of chaos.

Hence, at the dawn of creation we find God the Holy Spirit as both actor and archetype, power and paradigm. But here also we find an echo of the creation myths of the ancient Near East. Indeed, there are several cosmologies that include wind in the creative process. In *Enuma Elish*, the creation story of Mesopotamia, the great god Anu "brought forth and begot the fourfold wind; consigning to its power the leader of the host. He fashioned . . . station[ed] the whirlwind, he produced streams to disturb Tiamat."[8] Tiamat is, of course, the primordial deep of Mesopotamian myth, and it is her battle with Marduk that results in creation as we now know it—the placing of the

---

[6]See n. 2. It has often been argued that the *nešer* ("eagle") of the biblical text does not actually "carry" its young. But in the journal *The Condor* Loye Miller, a highly regarded ornithologist, has related this account regarding the parenting practices of the golden eagle from one of his students, F. E. Schuman: "The mother started from the nest in the crags and, roughly handling the young one, she allowed him to drop, I should say, about ninety feet, then she would swoop down under him, wings spread, and he would alight on her back. She would soar to the top of the range with him and repeat the process. One time she waited perhaps fifteen minutes between flights. I should say the farthest she let him fall was 150 feet. My father and I watched this, spellbound, for over an hour" (Loye Miller, Wilson C. Hanna and Austin Paul Smith, "From Field and Study," *The Condor* 20, no. 6 [1918]: 212). This practice is also reported by famed American ornithologist Arthur Cleveland Bent (1866–1954), known particularly for his twenty-one-volume work, *Life Histories of North American Birds* (1919–1968). The story is related in "Aquila Chrysaëtos Canadensis: Golden Eagle," *United States National Museum Bulletin* 167 (1937): 302. Sir William Beach Thomas comments on the same practice of eagles with their young in *The Yeoman's England* (London: Alexander Maclehose, 1934), 135–36.

[7]Kline, *Images of the Spirit*, 19. As John Walton eloquently relates, read in its context Genesis 1 might be read: "In the beginning was the *rûaḥ*, and the *rûaḥ* was with God and the *rûaḥ* was God. All things were made by him and nothing was made without him. In him was life and that life was the light of men" (John Walton, "The Ancient Near Eastern Background of the Spirit of the Lord in the Old Testament," in *Presence, Power and Promise: The Role of the Spirit of God in the Old Testament*, ed. David G. Firth and Paul D. Wegner [Downers Grove, IL: IVP Academic, 2011], 43–44).

[8]*Enuma Elish* 1.105–10; *Ancient Near Eastern Texts Relating to the Old Testament*, ed. J. B. Pritchard, 3rd ed. (Princeton: Princeton University Press, 1969), 62; Walton, "Ancient Near Eastern Background," 39–48; James K. Hoffmeier, "Some Thoughts on Genesis 1 and 2 and Egyptian Cosmology," *Journal of the Ancient Near Eastern Society* 15 (1983): 44.

"waters above" and the "waters below" (cf. Gen 1:6-7). Similarly, in Egypt Amun is the incarnation of the four great winds of the earth, unified for one explosive creative act that separates sky and earth and fertilizes the egg that will become the sun.[9] Hence, in both Egypt and Mesopotamia, "wind" has a role to play as the great catalyst of creation (see Dan 7:2; Ex 14:21; 15:8-10). So as we circle back to Genesis 1:2 and the Holy Spirit's debut in the text, we find that his presence there seems not as transparent as we had hoped. Rather the biblical writers have chosen to portray the drama of the creation event with a broadly recognized cast of characters. But here the roles have been redefined, filled not by the anonymous forces of nature or the embodied titans of the pagan pantheons. Rather, here is the Lord Holy Spirit. Standing distinct from his creation, unencumbered by any rival, he is lord over the works of his own hands. He is wind, but he is Spirit; he is breath, but he is God.

With this first introduction to the Holy Spirit we are plunged into the essential problem of studying the person of the Holy Spirit in the Old Testament. The Hebrew word *rûaḥ* has many meanings—some natural, some supernatural. Which of the hundreds of references to *rûaḥ* as breeze, breath, wind, spirit, mind, capacity and intellect are actually references to the great God?[10] The phrase "Holy Spirit" (*rûaḥ qodšô*) only occurs three times in the Hebrew Bible. In these three instances, the LXX does indeed translate with the same expression that the New Testament uses for the third person of the Trinity, the *pneuma hagion*.[11] In these three we find David praying that God will not take his Holy Spirit from him as he did from Saul (Ps 51:11[13]), and the prophet Isaiah speaking of the great days of old when God placed his Holy Spirit in the midst of his people, saving and delivering them in spite of their grieving of the same (Is 63:9-11). Additional transparent references to the *rûaḥ* as the third person of the Trinity include the approximately one hundred times the writers speak of the "*rûaḥ* of God" and "*rûaḥ* of Yahweh." But there are hundreds more occurrences of *rûaḥ*—many of which refer to

---

[9]Mark J. Smith, *The Carlsberg Papyri 5: On the Primeval Ocean*, Carsten Niebuhr Institute of Ancient Near Eastern Studies 30 (Copenhagen: Museum Tusculanum Press, 2002), 62–33, 70–80.

[10]*HALOT*, 1197–1201, s.v. "רוח."

[11]Richard E. Averbeck, "Breath, Wind, Spirit, and the Holy Spirit in the Old Testament," in Firth and Wegner, *Presence, Power and Promise*, 26; cf. *New International Dictionary of Old Testament Theology and Exegesis*, ed. W. A. VanGemeren, 5 vols. (Grand Rapids: Eerdmans, 1997), 3:1076–7 s.v. "רוח"; W. Hildebrandt, *An Old Testament Theology of the Spirit of God* (Peabody, MA: Hendrickson, 1995), 18.

the natural forces of wind and breath, some of which are anthropomorphic references to God and his mighty acts, and many more that have little or nothing to do with the person of the Holy Spirit.[12] So we must be careful as exegetes. Illegitimate totality transfer (the practice of reading every possible translation of a term into every one of its occurrences) is not a method, it is a mistake.[13] And good exegesis demands more than lexicography. In particular, as regards an inquiry into the person of the Holy Spirit in the old covenant, there is a category more important than the lexicography of *rûaḥ*. This is the concept of God's Presence among his people. Indeed, the theologians of the Old Testament saw a commonality between the Spirit of God and the "face" or "presence" of God.[14] And for the Old Testament saints, the presence of the Presence was everything— the *means* of redemption, the *goal* of redemption and the *evidence* of redemption. "I will be their God and they will be my people and I will dwell among them" (Ex 29:45; Jer 24:7; 31:33; 32:38; Ezek 11:20; 14:11; 37:23, 27; 48:35; Jn 14:23; 2 Cor 6:16; Rev 21:3). By what means would God dwell among his people in this fallen world? *This* is the person of the Holy Spirit in the old covenant. Therefore, although *rûaḥ* is important to this discussion, the Presence of God housed among his people is more so.

Thus we return to the beginning. In Eden, God's plan was that he would share his perfectly balanced universe with his image-bearers: Adam and Eve. Here the dimensions of the divine and the human would coexist, and the cosmos would be filled with God's Presence. But with humanity's treasonous choice, Adam and Eve are cast out from the Presence, and the dimensions of human and divine habitation are separated. This "great divorce" is the most necessary and the most grievous effect of the fall. As a result,

[12]Nearly half of these references in the Old Testament can be seen transparently as references to the natural forces of wind and breath, *nepeš* and *rûaḥ*, all of which are complicated by the overlap of the semantic field in Hebrew of spirit, wind and breath (*HALOT*, 1197–1201, s.v. "רוח"; cf. Averbeck, "Breath, Wind, Spirit," 29). Sometimes this "wind" is the agency of God, perhaps even the anthropomorphized force of his hand. For example, the "wind" that brings the plague of the locusts on the Egyptians (Ex 10:13) or brings the quail to the meat-deprived Israelites in the desert (Num 11:31). Or more clearly when the "blast" (lit. "wind") of God's nostrils caused the waters of the Red Sea to pile up (Ex 15:8). The text also understands the *rûaḥ* of a person as a reference to their feelings (Judg 8:3), will, character (Prov 16:18-19), personality or even life force (Gen 45:27).
[13]See James Barr, *The Semantics of Biblical Language* (London: Oxford University Press, 1961), 218–33.
[14]Ps 139:7 offers a transparent presentation of this foundational posture: "Where can I go from your Spirit? Where can I flee from your presence?" See Jamie A. Grant, "Spirit and Presence in Psalm 139," in Firth and Wegner, *Presence, Power and Promise*, 145.

much of the task of redemption may be summarized in a single objective: reunite the Almighty with his image-bearers. Restore the relationship. Get ʾādām back into the garden.

As redemptive history progresses, a brilliant master plan unfolds. By means of ever-expanding efforts, the opportunity for cohabitation is restored. The first concrete expression of this is the building of the tabernacle (miškān). In Exodus 25:8 God speaks: "And have them make a sanctuary for me, so that I may dwell among them."[15] In the ancient Near East a "holy place" is sacred space, an area set aside for the presence of the deity and for worship. Most broadly defined, worship is that activity in which the human and divine draw near. Sacred space therefore becomes that omphalos of the universe where for one brief, shining moment, cohabitation reoccurs.[16] Hence, with the building of the tabernacle a beachhead is retaken. For the first time since Eden, God lives on earth, but unlike the animated statuary of the ancient Near East, in Israel, God dwells in the Tabernacle in the person of the Holy Spirit.[17] "I shall be their God and they shall be my people and I will dwell [škn] among them" (see Ex 29:44-46; Ezek 37:27).[18]

The irony of the tabernacle, however, is the agony of redemptive history. For in the tabernacle the Presence was housed in the holy of holies and thereby

---

[15]Author's translation. The nuance of a resultative clause here may be found in the NASB, but not the NIV. Although the consecutive perfect šakāntî would lead the grammarian to conclude the explicit consecution of an imperative and its consecutive perfect (see Thomas O. Lambdin's classic work *Introduction to Biblical Hebrew* [New York: Charles Scribner's Sons, 1971], §107b), the imperative followed by the nonconsecutive imperfect wěyiqḥû of v. 2 (ibid., §107c), in combination with the larger context that Nahum Sarna and others recognize as having wholly to do with the purpose of constructing the sanctuary, results in a resultative translation. Hence, Moses is being commanded to instruct the people to collect all these materials and build *so that* Yahweh may dwell in their midst (see Nahum Sarna, *Exodus: JPS Torah Commentary* [Philadelphia: Jewish Publication Society, 1991], 158).

[16]Jon Levenson offers an insightful and accessible discussion of the cosmic mountain as the omphalos of the universe in *Sinai and Zion: An Entry into the Jewish Bible* (San Francisco: HarperSanFrancisco, 1987), 137–51; cf. Lawrence E. Stager, "Jerusalem and the Garden of Eden," *Eretz-Israel* 26 (1999): 183–94, and Roland de Vaux, *Ancient Israel: Its Life and Institutions* (New York: McGraw Hill, 1961), 274–88.

[17]For a standard work on the animated state of "idols" in the ancient Near East, see Michael B. Dick, ed., *Born in Heaven, Made on Earth: The Making of the Cult Image in the Ancient Near East* (Winona Lake, IN: Eisenbrauns, 1999).

[18]Non-Hebrew readers should note the relationship between the verb "to dwell" (škn) and the noun "tabernacle" (miškān). Etymologically and functionally these two words should be connected in the mind of the reader. The means by which Yahweh will fulfill his promise to "dwell among" (škn) his people is by means of the "tabernacle" (miškān).

was partitioned off from those who would seek to draw near. The increasing sanctification (and therefore restriction) of the outer court, holy place and holy of holies clearly communicated that only the spiritual elite could enter there. Thus, whereas any clean, worshiping Israelite could enter the outer court, only priests could enter the holy place, and only the high priest could enter the holy of holies—and that only once per year, on the Day of Atonement.[19] This was a day of profound anxiety for the one selected as high priest, and he went through days of ritual cleansing prior to entering God's Presence. When he entered, he wore bells in order to assure all who listened outside the veil that "he had not died in the Holy Place and that he continued to minister on their behalf"[20] (see Ex 28:31-35). The increasing sanctification of the three areas of the tabernacle, the necessity of mediation and sacrifice, the restricted access and elaborate measures taken for cleansing and atonement all communicate the same message: the Holy One is here. And anyone who draws near must either be holy . . . or dead. By its very existence the tabernacle communicated God's desire for *cohabitation*, while its increasing restriction of persons commensurably communicated the legacy of sin, *separation*. In the old covenant, the typical worshiper *never* approached the Presence.

Thus the people of Israel lived for generations. The Presence (often referred to as the *kābôd*, or "glory")[21] lived in their midst, marking them as God's peculiar people and their nation as the kingdom of God. But they could only approach him via an elaborate system of mediation and sacrifice. Any who failed to heed the warning of the cherubim stationed outside the holy of holies bore the consequences. Meanwhile, the Holy Spirit continued his work in their midst as the heroes and leaders of the nation were empowered to serve the

---

[19]The increasing holiness of these areas was communicated by each area's reduced size, the quality and value of its décor, and the more limited number of individuals who might enter. Thus the tent-structure progressed from an open-air, linen-curtained courtyard to the enclosed, purple-died and embroidered wool of the Holy Place, to the perfectly square and probably elevated holy of holies, which was hung with embroidered wool and ornamented with gold. Leviticus 16 describes the Day of Atonement as an annual ritual designed to purify the sanctuary by sprinkling it with the blood of two communal sin offerings (one for the priesthood and one for the people), and to purify the people by laying their sins on a "scapegoat," who was then driven out of the camp and into the wilderness (Sandra Richter, *Epic of Eden: A Christian Entry into the Old Testament* [Downers Grove, IL: IVP Academic, 2008], 179–82).

[20]Walter C. Kaiser Jr., "Exodus," in *The Expositor's Bible Commentary* (Grand Rapids: Zondervan, 1990), 2:467.

[21]*HALOT*, 457–58, s.v. "כָּבוֹד."

kingdom. We repeatedly read that individuals are "filled with," "anointed by" or somehow have the Spirit "come upon" them in order that they might accomplish kingdom tasks. The Spirit is "placed upon" Moses' seventy elders to equip them for their new leadership positions as administrators and adjudicators (Num 11:25). Joshua is "filled with the Spirit" of wisdom in order to lead in Moses' place (Deut 34:9). Even tasks that might typically be identified as "secular" are assisted by the equipping of the Spirit. For example, Bezalel and Oholiab are "filled . . . with the Spirit of God, with wisdom, with understanding, with knowledge and with all kinds of skills" in order to facilitate the building and decoration of the tabernacle (Ex 31:3; cf. Ex 35:31).[22]

During the period of the Judges, when the sons of Israel cry out to Yahweh due to foreign oppression (foreign oppression resulting from national sin), the Spirit raises up and equips a series of champions to deliver them. In Judges 3 the Spirit was "upon" Othniel such that he was empowered as a warrior and ongoing national leader. The Spirit "clothed" *himself* with Gideon in order to empower the young leader to motivate the recalcitrant northern tribes to battle (Judg 6:34),[23] and in Judges 11:29 the Spirit "came on" Jephthah to equip him to defeat the Ammonites. In Judges 13–15 we read the saga of Samson, whom the Spirit first "stirred in" and then "came powerfully upon" such that he accomplished feats of valor against the Philistines (Judg 13:24; 14:6, 19;

---

[22]Richard Hess, "Bezalel and Oholiab: Spirit and Creativity," in Firth and Wegner, *Presence, Power and Promise*, 161–72. Setting these accounts against their ancient Near Eastern backgrounds, Hess makes the point that building the tabernacle is actually anything but a secular task. As is broadly recognized, temple-building was a divinely initiated and directed task that required divine approval and empowerment and was typically restricted to kings; see Sandra L. Richter, *The Deuteronomistic History and the Name Theology: lešakkēn šemô šām in the Bible*, Beihefte zur Zeitschrift für die alttestamentliche Wissenchaft 318 (Berlin: de Gruyter, 2002), 69–75.

[23]John Walton writes: "The terminology therefore refers to someone stepping into a persona or taking on an identity. From this we might conclude that God's power and presence went about in the guise of Gideon. The point is not Gideon's spiritual experience, but rather Gideon as Yahweh's instrument" ("Ancient Near Eastern Background," 49). Lawson G. Stone writes: "The expression used is often mistranslated as 'the spirit . . . clothed Gideon.' The verb used (*labash* [TH3847, ZH4252], 'to put on, to wear'), takes a single direct object, which is always the item put on or worn (*HALOT* 1.519, s.v. *labash*). Thus in Isa. 51:9 we read 'wake up, wake up. . . . Clothe yourself (*labash*) with strength!' Gideon thus metaphorically becomes the garment of the Spirit, an idiom with an Akkadian parallel. Akkadian texts speak of the gods as possessing a fearsome radiance, denoted by the term *pulkhu* (or the fem. *pulukhtu*). The gods 'wear' (Akkadian *labashu*) this radiance as they manifest themselves, typically through a king or warrior (*CAD* 12.503–4, 505–9)" ("Judges," in *Cornerstone Biblical Commentary*, vol. 3, *Joshua, Judges, Ruth*, ed. Joseph Coleson, Lawson G. Stone and Jason Driesbach [Carol Stream, IL: Tyndale House, 2012], 277; see Stone's forthcoming New International Commentary on the Old Testament volume on the same).

15:14).[24] Interestingly, many of these heroes were already skilled in their areas of expertise, but the Spirit empowered them to take those talents to a new level, a level desperately needed by the kingdom of God in its hour of need.

During the monarchy we learn that the Spirit "came powerfully upon" first Saul and then David to identify and equip them for their new positions of leadership (1 Sam 10:10; 16:13).[25] In these call narratives the oil of anointing serves as the physical manifestation that these individuals have been chosen and empowered to serve God's kingdom by his Holy Spirit (see Ps 2:2).

As for the prophets, they of all the Old Testament characters could explain to us the work of the Holy Spirit. For Isaiah, Jeremiah, Micaiah Ben Imlah, Amos and Ezekiel all tell us the same tale. Upon their commissioning, each is caught up into the royal throne room of God, each overhears the deliberations of his divine council and each receives their commission to speak on his behalf (Is 6:1-6; Jer 23:16-22; 1 Kings 22:19-23; Ezek 1:1–2:7; Amos 3:7).[26] Indeed Jeremiah gives voice to Yahweh's lament.

---

[24]Regarding Samson's encounter with the *rûaḥ yhwh,* the NIV translates "came powerfully upon" for the verb *ṣlḥ.* The verb *ṣlḥ* is difficult. Attempts have been made to posit two roots, one meaning "to advance; force entry into" and one meaning "to prosper" (F. Brown, S. R. Driver and C. A. Briggs, *A Hebrew and English Lexicon of the Old Testament* [Oxford: Oxford University Press, 1907], 852, s.v. "צלח"; *HALOT,* 1025–27, s.v. "צלח"). Lawson G. Stone argues against such a dual etymology, holding that the meanings of the verb are interrelated and that in contexts involving the Spirit of Yahweh the sense is "of overwhelming, even violent domination, penetrative seizure, with contextualized meanings such as 'to split, set on fire, be successful, intrude, succeed, advance, etc.'" (Lawson G. Stone, "The Phenomenon of Prophecy: A Review of Selected Biblical Evidence" [unpublished paper, 2007], 2; see also Lawson G. Stone, "Judges, Book of," in *Dictionary of the Old Testament: Historical Books,* ed. Bill T. Arnold and H. G. M. Williamson [Downers Grove, IL: InterVarsity Press, 2005], 599, 604). Stone goes on: "The LXX typically translates the verb with *ephallomai* (to spring upon, to jump). Up until now in the Book of Judges, the coming of the Spirit of Yahweh has served to authenticate the leadership of a judge. No other overt manifestations of the Spirit have been emphasized except that immediately the judge has a following of Israelites ready for battle. Here, though, the emphasis falls on superhuman acts, thus the different term is employed. In contexts involving the Spirit of Yahweh or of God, the sense of overwhelming, even violent domination appears strongly. In 1 Sam. 18:10 a 'tormenting spirit from God' seizes (*tsalakh*) Saul, and he raves like a madman. The frenzy of the Spirit impels Samson to rip apart a lion with his bare hands, to kill 30 men in Ashkelon, and to use the jawbone of an ass to slaughter a Philistine attacking force (14:6, 19; 15:14). Such a fierce and agonistic experience of the Spirit befits the note in 13:25 that the Spirit began to prod or drive Samson" ("Judges," 3:391).

[25]See n. 24.

[26]See Theodore Mullen, "Divine Assembly," in *Anchor Bible Dictionary,* ed. David Noel Freedman, 6 vols. (New York: Doubleday, 1992), 2:214–17.

But if they [the false prophets] had stood in my council,

they would have proclaimed my words to my people. (Jer 23:22)

Each of these is "raised up" by the power of the Holy Spirit and, as promised in Deuteronomy 18:18, becomes the mouthpiece of God. Isaiah repeatedly speaks of the Spirit being "upon" the Servant such that he is equipped to preach the good news of redemption (Is 42; 59; 61). Ezekiel describes this experience as having "the hand of God upon him" (e.g., Ezek 1:3; 3:14, 22; 33:22; 37:1; 40:1). Daniel Block describes this experience as both the pressure and the power of the divine will bearing down on him. In fact, Ezekiel is repeatedly "picked up" and "carried off" by the *rûaḥ* Yahweh.[27] Elijah as well is caught up in "a chariot of fire"—Meredith Kline's incarnation of the Spirit Glory Cloud.[28] Elisha's "double portion" of the Spirit equips him for miraculous acts and prophecy (2 Kings 2:7-14). Even the foreign prophet Balaam speaks of the *rûaḥ* of God "coming upon" him such that he prophesies—and this time he tells the truth (Num 24:1-9).[29]

Thus, in contrast to what many have concluded over the years, the person of the Holy Spirit is alive and well in the Old Testament. When an individual was appointed to an office of leadership, or needed special empowerment to lead, fight or preach, *the Spirit came on him or her*—the most common need being empowerment to declare the message of Yahweh. Turning our sights to the New Testament, let us consider what these same phenomena might mean there.

THE HOLY SPIRIT IN THE NEW TESTAMENT

The Gospel of John opens with the breathtaking announcement that the great hope of the Old Covenant saints has come to pass.

---

[27]Daniel I. Block, "The View from the Top: The Holy Spirit in the Prophets," in Firth and Wegner, *Presence, Power and Promise*, 182–84.

[28]Kline, *Images of the Spirit*, 62–63.

[29]Balaam's reputation as a "seer of the gods" is broadly known outside the biblical text via the mid-eighth to seventh century Deir ʿAlla inscriptions. Discovered in 1967 at the site of the same name (located in the Jordan Valley, halfway between the Sea of Galilee and the Dead Sea east of the Jordan River), this important text comes from what has been interpreted as a sanctuary and recounts Balaam's visions. As is apparent in the Bible by the fact that he is hired by the King of Moab to divine a curse against the king's opponent, and as is more apparent in the Deir ʿAlla inscriptions, in which Balaam serves a polytheistic pantheon, this divine intermediary is clearly anything but an orthodox Yahwistic prophet (see Jo Ann Hackett, "Deir ʿAlla, Tell" ABD 2:129-30; cf. Thomas L. Thompson, "Problems of Genre and Historicity with Palestine's Descriptions," in *Congress Volume Oslo 1998*, ed. by André Lemaire and Magne Sæbø, VTSupp 80 [Leiden: Brill, 2000], 322).

The Word became flesh
and made his dwelling among us [literally "tabernacled" (= Heb. *škn*)].
We have seen his glory [= Heb. *kābôd*],
the glory of the one and only Son,
who came from the Father,
full of grace and truth.[30] (Jn 1:14)

Consider again the tabernacle. The tabernacle (Heb. *miškān*) was designed to house the Presence (i.e., "glory" [Heb. *kābôd*]) in the midst of God's people. But its very structure communicated the legacy of sin—the Presence of God was forbidden to a fallen race.

But then comes Jesus. John opens his Gospel by proclaiming that the Presence has returned. But this time the means of his dwelling among us is human flesh. And this time even the most foul may approach the Presence without fear—the deformed, the wicked, the shamed. Indeed, because of the work of redemption, humanity may now behold "the exact representation of his being" (Heb 1:3), "the image of the invisible God" (Col 1:15) with no veil standing between. And rather than being consumed by their exposure to the Presence, this time they see and touch and are healed. What is the Gospel writer's message? We could not go to him, so he came to us. And the promise is fulfilled: "Behold, I will be their God, and they will be my people, and I will dwell among them."

But there are only so many people one Galilean can interact with in the course of three years of ministry. Only so many people can hear the message and be touched by his healing hand. Thus the next stage of the plan ensues. In Acts 2:1-4 we read of the dramatic event that inaugurates the ministry of the church, the ultimate game changer.

When the day of Pentecost came, they were all together in one place. Suddenly a sound like the blowing of a violent wind came from heaven and filled the whole house where they were sitting. They saw what seemed to be tongues of fire that separated and came to rest on each of them. All of them were filled with the Holy Spirit and began to speak in other tongues as the Spirit enabled them.

The imagery here is nothing new. Rather, Exodus 40:34-38 and 1 Kings 8:6-11

---

[30]There is a plethora of work available on the lexical links between John 1:14 and the tabernacle. See Raymond E. Brown, *The Gospel According to John (i–xii)*, Anchor Bible 29 (Garden City, NY: Doubleday, 1966), 32–35.

testify that both the tabernacle and the temple had also been "inaugurated" with cloud, fire and wind. These natural elements had served as the hallmarks of God's indwelling—the press release that God had approved his dwelling place and the Presence had taken up residence. The book of Acts rehearses these same hallmarks in order to communicate that the living church has now replaced the tabernacle/temple of old. Just as those structures had been set apart ("sanctified") to house the Presence, so now the church is being set apart for the same. As Paul teaches in 1 Corinthians 3:16: "Don't you know that you yourselves are God's temple and that God's Spirit dwells in your midst?" Consider as well 1 Corinthians 6:19: "Do you not know that your bodies are temples of the Holy Spirit, who is in you, whom you have received from God? You are not your own." And 2 Corinthians 6:16:

> For we are the temple of the living God. As God has said,
> "I will live with them
>   and walk among them,
>   and I will be their God,
>   and they will be my people."

The church as *individuals* and as a *community* have now become the temple (see Eph 2:19-22; 1 Pet 2:5).

What then is the church's function as the temple's successor? In the old covenant the temple was intended to house the Presence. In the new covenant the church—individually and corporately—is intended to do the same. For more than a thousand years the typical worshiper could come no closer than the outer courts of God's dwelling place. The deformed, sick, unclean or alien could not come even that close. But the gift of God in Christ Jesus is that you and I have become the dwelling place of the Spirit. The Presence from whom Adam and Eve were driven, who rested on Mt. Sinai with thunder and storm, who sat enthroned above the cherubim, now resides in the believer. It is nearly too much to apprehend.

The Israelite temple also housed the Presence in order to make God available to humanity. Here any citizen of Israel could come knowing that he or she could find God. Here the alien could do the same (1 Kings 8:41-43). Ultimately the temple stood as a testimony to the nations that Yahweh could be found in Israel. This reality offered a witness to the nations while serving to define who Israel was—God's people. So too the church. This brief biblical theology of the person of the Holy Spirit makes it crystal clear that the church is intended to be that place where saint and sinner can find God. Moreover, the restored life of the believer is God's ultimate testimony to the nations that he lives and dwells among us—in the person of the Holy Spirit. And whereas the temple was a single building that could exist in only one spot at one time, the church is an ever-expanding community that is slowly, steadily bringing the Presence to the farthest reaches of this world.

This leads us to the culmination of redemptive history, the denouement of the great story: "Behold, the tabernacle of God is with humanity, and he shall dwell among them, and they shall be his people, and God himself shall be among them" (Rev 21:3).[31] Describing heaven as the new Jerusalem, John says: "I did not see a temple in the city, because the Lord God Almighty and the Lamb are its temple. . . . The glory of God gives it light, and the Lamb is its lamp" (Rev 21:22-23). At the end of all things, God is once again with his people. Access to the Presence is restored. Adam has returned to the Garden. Redemption has been accomplished.[32]

And what of the "infilling" of the *rûaḥ* of God in Israel's national history by which her judges and theocratic officers were empowered to serve? In the New Testament this language is most frequently encountered in Luke-Acts: the history of the early church. As the Gospel of Luke opens, we are confronted with yet another unlikely hero, a young woman named Mary: "The Holy Spirit will come on you, and the power of the Most High will *overshadow* you. So the holy one to be born will be called the Son of God" (Lk 1:35). Again the *rûaḥ ʾĕlōhîm* is hovering, and again chaos is about to be dealt a mortal blow. Zachariah, Elizabeth and their unborn son John are also "filled with," have their mouths opened by or have the hand of the Holy Spirit on them (Lk 1:41, 64, 66-67). In each of these instances it is apparent that to be "filled with the Spirit" is to be empowered to declare the word of God.

When the converts of the upper room experience the outpouring of the Holy Spirit in Acts 2:4, they are also "filled with Holy Spirit" and begin to give verbal utterance, much like the elders in the book of Numbers and Saul

---

[31]Author's translation.
[32]For further reflection on this theme, see G. K. Beale, *A New Testament Biblical Theology: The Unfolding of the Old Testament in the New* (Grand Rapids: Baker Academic, 2011), 614–48, esp. 632–34.

when he receives his commission (Num 11:24-25; 1 Sam 10:9-11). When Peter attempts to explain this phenomenon to the multitude gathered in Jerusalem, he is "filled with the Holy Spirit" and powerfully delivers the inaugural address of the church (Acts 2:14-41). Here he announces the incredible news that in this new covenant the in-filling of the Holy Spirit will be the experience of every believer regardless of ethnicity, gender, rank or caste. *Everyone* will have the opportunity to be a living vessel of the Holy Spirit; everyone will have opportunity to be a part of the supernatural ministry of the Holy Spirit; and even the most coveted gift of the Old Testament—prophecy—will be extended to all.

The language of in-filling continues to be employed throughout the book of Acts. After the dramatic healing of the cripple at the Beautiful Gate in Acts 3:1-10 and the even more dramatic presentation of the gospel, Peter and John are imprisoned by the ruling class of priests. Interrogating them, the priests demand: "By what power or what name did you do this?" (Acts 4:7). Peter, "filled with the Holy Spirit," responds:

> If we are being called to account today for an act of kindness shown to a man who was lame and are being asked how he was healed, then know this, you and all the people of Israel: It is by the name of Jesus Christ of Nazareth, whom you crucified but whom God raised from the dead, that this man stands before you healed. (Acts 4:9-10)

Peter concludes by declaring: "Salvation is found in no one else, for there is no other name under heaven given to mankind by which we must be saved" (Acts 4:12). The only words I can muster in response to this apologetic masterpiece are, "Peter, you rock." Peter's sermon is surpassed only by the response of the onlookers:

> When they saw the courage of Peter and John and realized that they were unschooled, ordinary men, they were astonished and they took note that these men had been with Jesus. But since they could see the man who had been healed standing there with them, there was nothing they could say. (Acts 4:13-14)

Apparently, the evidence that Peter and John had been with Jesus was the presence of the supernatural—both the supernatural act of healing and the supernatural confidence and authority of their preaching.

Acts 4:31 reports that after Peter and John rejoin their compatriots, a prayer meeting results in which *everyone* was "filled with the Holy Spirit" such that they "spoke the word of God boldly." Similarly, Acts 9 tells us that the soon-to-be apostle Paul must be "filled with the Holy Spirit" in order that he might "proclaim my name to the Gentiles and their kings and to the people of Israel" (Acts 9:15-17). As predicted, Paul is filled and "at once he began to preach in the synagogues that Jesus is the Son of God" (Acts 9:20). In Acts 13:6-12, Paul is again "filled with the Holy Spirit" and thereby silences the magician of Salamis by locking his gaze, confronting his lie and cursing him with temporary blindness. The proconsul sees the authority behind Paul's words and is *convinced of the gospel.* In each of these contexts the filling of the Holy Spirit enables the fledgling disciples to preach the gospel with authority and accompanying signs such that the naysayer is silenced, the seeker is convinced and the kingdom is advanced.

In conclusion, having surveyed the biblical text, what *do* we know of Holy? In the beginning, the Lord Holy Spirit served as both actor and archetype, paradigm and power. The biblical writer saw him like a falcon, poised above the primordial deep, trembling with anticipation, waiting for the word to strike and to launch the miracle of creation. Because of the great rebellion, he has clothed himself in cloud and fire. He is the whirlwind. Yet this catalyst of creation has never ceased his work, ever expanding his influence over this broken world, choosing and equipping his instruments, and by his power rebuilding the kingdom of God. In these latter days the Lord Holy Spirit continues to distribute his gifts to each one individually as he wills in order to complete his work (1 Cor 12:1-11). He does not always claim the likely (1 Cor 1:26-31), but the great cloud of witnesses testifies that those who are willing to be claimed will prevail. Indeed, John the Revelator offers us a glimpse of the ultimate objective. Here in his grand description of the new Jerusalem in Revelation 22:1-5, the bondslaves of God rejoice to hear that the breach is finally healed, and that those who have been in exile in this fallen world will at last "see his face" (Rev 22:4).

We believe in the Holy Spirit who
Spoke in the law,
And taught by the prophets,
And descended to the Jordan,
Spoke by the Apostles,

And lives in the saints;
Thus we believe in him: that he is the Holy Spirit,
The Spirit of God,
The perfect Spirit,
The Spirit Paraclete,
Uncreated,
Proceeding from the Father
And receiving of the Son, in whom we believe
Amen.[33]

---

[33]The fourth-century Creed of Epiphanius, from Philip Schaff, *The Creeds of Christendom: With a History and Critical Notes*, vol. 2, *The Greek and Latin Creeds* (Grand Rapids: Baker, 1983), 37–38.

3

The Spirit's Self-Testimony

Pneumatology in Basil of Caesarea
and Augustine of Hippo

Gregory W. Lee

INTRODUCTION

Early Christian reflection on the Spirit raises a number of perplexities central to Christian theology and the shape of global Christianity. In addition to the absence of the actual word *Trinity* in Scripture, the fourth-century debates critical to the formation of trinitarian doctrine were preeminently concerned with the relation of the Son to the Father, and far less with the Spirit's relation to either.[1] One reason for this is simply that there is more biblical material to inform reflection on the second person of the Trinity than the third. Meanwhile, the Spirit's identity in Scripture can at times appear elusive and undefined. "Father" and "Son" make some sense as personal names, but who is this mysterious, ambiguous "Spirit"?

There are conceptual problems as well. The Father and the Son can be defined in terms of one another, as begetter and begotten, but it is not clear where the Spirit fits into this dynamic. What distinguishes the Spirit from the Son when both come from the Father? Is the Spirit the Son's twin? Or, stranger still, the Father's grandson?[2] The issue is not just a matter of hypothetical speculation. It bears on the most significant division in Christian history: the Great Schism of 1054 between the Eastern and Western churches, which was

---

[1]For a programmatic presentation of early Christian pneumatology, see the series of articles by Lewis Ayres and Michel R. Barnes in *Augustinian Studies* 29 (2008): 165–236.
[2]Gregory of Nazianzus, *Oration* 31.7; Augustine, *De Trinitate* 5.14.15.

prompted by the West's inclusion of the notorious *filioque* clause in the Nicene Creed to affirm the Spirit's procession from the Father "and the Son."

This apparently arcane point of contention between the East and the West is often attributed to more fundamental differences of trinitarian theology observable in the formative figures of the fourth and fifth centuries. According to a much-repeated claim, Eastern authors "began" with the persons, thus presenting a more social or relational model of the Trinity, while Western authors "began" with the divine substance and thus advanced a kind of monist deity characteristic of Western medieval theology, in which the persons are an afterthought to impersonal essence.[3] It is generally assumed that the East is superior in this regard and that Augustine is to blame for the West's woes.

In this essay, I will consider the pneumatologies of two representative figures, Basil of Caesarea from the East and Augustine of Hippo from the West, paying special attention to their use of Scripture and to their broader theological reflections on the Spirit's identity and work. For neither figure can the "forgotten person of the Trinity" be isolated from overarching questions about redemption, salvation history and participation in the divine life. By adopting a wide-angle lens, we will discover far more in common between Eastern and Western understandings of the Spirit than has often been acknowledged, and we will be reminded of the importance of reading Scripture within a received tradition. We will also understand more clearly the Spirit's unique role in directing us to Christ and completing our salvation.

BASIL OF CAESAREA

Basil of Caesarea was born in A.D. 329 or 330 and died in 378.[4] His life was thus sandwiched between the ecumenical councils of Nicaea (325) and Constantinople (381), and he missed witnessing Constantinople's affirmation of the Spirit's divinity by just under three years. Even so, his influence over that council was significant. While it cannot be demonstrated with certainty that Basil's *On the Holy Spirit* shaped the wording of the creed's third article, that treatise

---

[3]See inter alia John D. Zizioulas, *Being as Communion: Studies in Personhood and the Church* (Crestwood, NY: St. Vladimir's Seminary Press, 1985).

[4]For an excellent introduction to Basil's life and trinitarian theology, see Andrew Radde-Gallwitz, *Basil of Caesarea: A Guide to His Life and Doctrine* (Eugene, OR: Cascade, 2012). The standard biography is Philip Rousseau, *Basil of Caesarea* (Berkeley: University of California Press, 1994).

has nevertheless been received as a paradigmatic presentation of Eastern pneumatology in the years leading up to the council. A sketch of the context of Basil's controversy will be helpful before we consider his theological arguments.

The Spirit's opponents. The immediate triggers for Basil's *On the Holy Spirit*,[5] written in 375, were the Pneumatomachians, or "Spirit-fighters," who took offense at Basil's use of two doxologies at a liturgical celebration: "Glory to the Father, *with* the Son, *together with* the Holy Spirit" and "Glory to the Father, *through* the Son, *in* the Holy Spirit."[6] As Basil describes their contention, the Spirit-fighters' primary concern was not just a matter of prepositions; they sought to prove that the persons are of different substances or natures.[7] They accordingly assigned the phrase "from whom" to the Father, identifying him alone as the Creator; "through whom" to the Son, reducing him to the level of an assistant or instrument; and "in whom" to the Spirit, reducing him to only a time or place.

Basil traces this trick to an old enemy, Aetius of Antioch.[8] Aetius and his best-known colleague, Eunomius of Cyzicus, held to a rather radical doctrine of God.[9] They presumed not only to know God's essence but also to define it in such a way that the Son would summarily be dismissed from the Godhead. On their account, the essence of God is to be unbegotten. But the Son is begotten of the Father and not unbegotten. Therefore, the Father alone is God, and the Son is not. The Son is, moreover, of a different essence (*ousia*) from the Father, which means he is actually "unlike" the Father.

Basil simultaneously critiques the pneumatomachians for their captivity to inappropriate philosophical categories and for a narrow biblicism that rejects all language about God not explicitly found in Scripture.[10] Thus, at the beginning of his response to the pneumatomachians, Basil chastises them for

---

[5]For English quotations I use St. Basil the Great, *On the Holy Spirit*, trans. Stephen Hildebrand, Popular Patristics 42 (Crestwood, NY: St. Vladimir's Seminary Press, 2011). I also use Hildebrand's citation and translation of biblical passages.

[6]Basil, *On the Holy Spirit* 1.3.

[7]Basil, *On the Holy Spirit* 2.4.

[8]Basil, *On the Holy Spirit* 2.4.

[9]For a study of Eunomius's works and theology, see Eunomius, *Extant Works*, trans. Richard Paul Vaggione (Oxford: Clarendon, 1987).

[10]For a presentation of the biblical character of Basil's arguments, see Stephen M. Hildebrand, *The Trinitarian Theology of Basil of Caesarea: A Synthesis of Greek Thought and Biblical Truth* (Washington, DC: Catholic University of America Press, 2007).

applying to God categories drawn from pagan philosophers.[11] The philosophers distinguish between different kinds of causes by an appeal to common objects. There is a difference between the ways a bench, for instance, is "caused" by a person, a tool or physical material. A bench is produced "by" a carpenter, "through" an axe, "from" wood. For the pneumatomachians, the same principles apply to God. Inasmuch as each cause bears a different substance and is expressed with a different preposition, the Father, "from whom" are all things, the Son, "through whom" we receive gifts, and the Spirit, "in whom" we experience God's favor are also of different substances and require different prepositions.

The problem with this argument is that it reduces God to the level of a saw or a hammer. Basil marvels that his opponents "do not shrink from applying to the ruler of all a term ordained by pagans for lifeless instruments or for subordinate and wholly humble service."[12] Assigning human examples and distinctions to God without qualification or clarification is a fundamental category mistake—a denial of God's transcendence—the root cause of which is not just confusion but also pride. Only a fool of extraordinary arrogance could conflate Creator and creation with such clumsy incompetence.

As Basil argues, Scripture's use of prepositions is far more flexible than the pneumatomachians assume. Basil dedicates a fairly lengthy section of his text to a concrete demonstration of this phenomenon.[13] "From" can be used of both the Son and the Spirit, "through" can be used of both the Father and the Spirit, and "in" can be used of both the Father and the Son. These prepositions are in many cases interchangeable, and in at least one instance— Paul's doxology—a whole series of different prepositions is used exclusively with reference to the Son.[14] "From whom and through whom and for whom are all things" (Rom 11:36) presents an instance of praise for the cause of all existence ("from whom") and for the one who continues to preserve all things ("through whom"). The Son, who acts in accordance with the Father's will, is both of these.[15]

---

[11]Basil, *On the Holy Spirit* 3.5.

[12]Basil, *On the Holy Spirit* 3.5.

[13]Basil, *On the Holy Spirit* 4.6–5.12.

[14]Basil, *On the Holy Spirit* 5.7.

[15]Basil also acknowledges the possibility that these prepositions all refer to the Father, which would still establish his point, since "through" would then be used for the Father and not just for the Son (*On the Holy Spirit* 5.8).

Defense of the Spirit. As Basil proceeds, he develops his arguments beyond this series of cursory biblical references. Basil's defense of the Spirit's divinity focuses particularly on Scripture's presentation of the Spirit's titles and activities. The Spirit is called "the Spirit of God" (Mt 12:28), "Spirit of truth, who comes from the Father" (Jn 15:26), "Spirit of righteousness" (Ps 50:12), "directing Spirit" (Ps 50:14) and "God, the divine Spirit of wisdom, understanding, and knowledge" (Ex 31:3).[16] The Spirit also bears many names in common with the Father and the Son: "holy," "good," "Paraclete" (Jn 14:26) and even "Lord" (2 Thess 3:5; 2 Cor 3:17).[17] It was the Spirit who anointed Jesus at his baptism (Lk 3:22; Jn 1:33; Acts 10:38), sustained Jesus when he was tempted by Satan (Mt 4:1), empowered Jesus to perform miracles (Mt 12:28), came on the disciples after Jesus' resurrection (Jn 20:22-23) and established different offices and gifts in the church's order (1 Cor 12:28).[18] It is the Spirit who delivers from sin (1 Cor 6:11), restores kinship with God (Gal 4:6) and raises the dead (Ps 104:30).[19] And the Spirit will be present on the day of judgment; for "the crown of the just is the grace of the Spirit, supplied then more abundantly and more completely in proportion to virtue, when spiritual glory will be distributed to each."[20] In all this activity, the Spirit is to be ranked alongside the Father and the Son, each of whom operates inseparably with the others in every act of redemption.[21]

This emphasis on what we may call the "common operations" demands further explication. On the one hand, Basil believes "the Holy Spirit is indivisible and inseparable from the Father and the Son," and thus also affirms "the unity and indivisibility in every work of the Holy Spirit from the Father and the Son."[22] The Holy Spirit never works without the Father and the Son; anything that any one of the persons does implicates the other two in the unity of divine action. There is, moreover, only one divine will. Basil draws particular attention to passages in the Gospel of John where Jesus says he only speaks and acts according to the Father's will.[23] For Basil, these remarks cannot mean that the Son lacks freedom or self-determination or that he is

---

[16]Basil, *On the Holy Spirit* 9.22, 19.48.
[17]Basil, *On the Holy Spirit* 19.48, 21.52.
[18]Basil, *On the Holy Spirit* 16.39.
[19]Basil, *On the Holy Spirit* 19.49.
[20]Basil, *On the Holy Spirit* 16.40.
[21]Basil, *On the Holy Spirit* 24.55.
[22]Basil, *On the Holy Spirit* 16.37.
[23]Basil, *On the Holy Spirit* 8.20. The passages Basil cites are Jn 12:49-50; 14:24; 14:31.

somehow under the Father's direction or supervision. We should rather "think of a sharing of will that reaches timelessly from the Father to the Son in a way suitable for God, as for instance, some figure appears in a mirror."[24]

Still, Basil does not believe each of the persons works in exactly the same way. For each divine work, the Father is the initiator, the Son is the agent and the Spirit is the perfecter. Concerning the creation of angels, for instance, Basil writes, "The ministering spirits exist by the will of the Father, they are brought into being by the energy of the Son, and they are perfected by the presence of the Spirit."[25] This is not to say that there are three sources of activity, nor that any one of the persons is somehow imperfect in power. The Father could in principle operate alone, as could the Son. Yet the one source of activity in the Godhead, the Father, chooses to work through the Son, who concomitantly chooses to perfect his work in the Spirit. The operations are inseparable, but each divine act involves the variegated participation of the individual persons.[26]

This dynamic is cast in relief when Basil treats one of the most characteristic elements of his pneumatology—the Spirit's role in granting us knowledge of God. Basil repeatedly contrasts the Spirit with angels, whose holiness is not by nature but by choice, as they participate in the Spirit's inherent holiness. Basil compares the angels to a branding iron that burns by the infusion of fire.[27] The iron has internalized the heat, yet the fire remains extrinsic to the iron's substance, unlike the Spirit, who is fire itself and the source of all holiness. But how do the angels remain holy, even if only by choice? For Basil, angelic holiness derives from beholding the face of the Father, but the power for such perception is the Spirit's work. The Spirit is like a light that illuminates a house such that eyes may see; he is the one who teaches the seraphim to cry, "Holy, holy, holy" (Is 6:3); he is the reason the angels at Jesus' birth proclaim, "Glory to God in the highest" (Lk 2:14).

The Spirit's unique role in illumination distinguishes him from the Father and the Son, while also underscoring the unity of the persons. For the particularity of the persons does not suggest the existence of three gods, as if the divinity were "scatter[ed] . . . among a separated multitude."[28] Rather, the one

[24]Basil, *On the Holy Spirit* 8.20.
[25]Basil, *On the Holy Spirit* 16.38.
[26]Basil, *On the Holy Spirit* 8.21.
[27]Basil, *On the Holy Spirit* 16.38.
[28]Basil, *On the Holy Spirit* 18.45.

form is contemplated in both the Father and the Son as archetype and image.

> They have unity in the fact that the latter is whatever the former is, and the former is whatever the latter is. And so, with regard to the particularity of the persons, they are one and one, but with regard to the common nature, both are one thing. How, then, if they are one and one, are there not two gods? Because it is said that there is a king and the image of the king, but not two kings, for the power is not divided and the glory is not portioned out.[29]

Meanwhile, the Spirit is the Spirit of Christ and Truth and Wisdom, uniquely worthy to glorify the Son (Jn 16:14). He empowers us to perceive "the beauty of the image of the unseen God," and through the image to proceed to "the more than beautiful vision of the archetype."[30] For Basil, these distinctions between the persons are a matter of basic biblical logic. Jesus teaches, "No one knows the Father, except the Son" (Mt 11:27), while Paul writes, "No one is able to say Jesus is Lord, except in the Holy Spirit" (1 Cor 12:3).[31] The Son is thus the image of the Father, while the Holy Spirit enables us to perceive the Son.[32]

The doxologies revisited. This conceptual framework returns Basil to the original liturgical controversy with the pneumatomachians. On the one hand, the knowledge of God proceeds "from the one Spirit, through the one Son, to the one Father." On the other hand, God's gifts to us proceed "from the Father, through the Only-begotten, to the Spirit."[33] We commonly say God's gifts to us are "in" the Spirit because the Spirit brings the works of God to perfection "in" us.[34] Yet there is a difference between the way heat is "in" a fiery iron and the way heat is "with" the fire that generates it, and this difference legitimizes the two doxologies in question.[35] "Glory to the Father, *through* the Son, *in* the Holy Spirit" speaks of God's gifts to us for which we give God thanks, and is an appropriate means of praising the economic Trinity (God as he acts in time and space). "Glory to the Father, *with* the Son, *together with* the Holy Spirit" speaks of the coequal dignity of the persons

---

[29]Basil, *On the Holy Spirit* 18.45.

[30]Basil, *On the Holy Spirit* 18.47.

[31]Basil, *On the Holy Spirit* 18.47. For a similar statement see 11.27, where Basil pairs Jn 1:18 and 1 Cor 12:3 and asserts the impossibility of worshiping the Son without the Holy Spirit, and of calling upon the Father without the Spirit of adopted sonship.

[32]Basil, *On the Holy Spirit* 9.23.

[33]Basil, *On the Holy Spirit* 18.47.

[34]Basil, *On the Holy Spirit* 26.61.

[35]Basil, *On the Holy Spirit* 26.63.

for which we give God glory and is an appropriate means of praising the immanent Trinity (God as he exists apart from time and space).[36]

Still, Basil concedes, if his opponents cannot countenance "with," he will settle for "and" in imitation of the baptismal formula instituted by Christ. For Christ commanded his disciples to make disciples of all nations and to baptize them in the name of the Father *and* the Son *and* the Holy Spirit (Mt 28:19). Basil's compromise proposal is not just reluctant concession; he appeals to the baptismal formula throughout his treatise to defend the Spirit's coequal dignity with the Father and the Son.[37] Against the pneumatomachians, this formula does not indicate any kind of ranking whereby one of the persons is "after" or "under" the others.[38] There can be no "after" in the God who transcends time, nor can there be "under" in the God who fills all things. Rather, all three persons are coequal in glory, honor and dignity, despite the particularities that distinguish each person from the others.

As we consider the contemporary context and our own doxological confessions, Basil's arguments retain their force. "Glory to the Father, *and* to the Son, *and* to the Holy Spirit": to recite the *Gloria Patri* is to affirm with Basil both the divinity and the distinction of the Spirit. Against those who would forget the third person of the Trinity, we assert that the Spirit is of equal rank with the Father and the Son, crucially involved with all God does in the world, yet nevertheless distinct as the one who draws us to the Father by illuminating the Son. To understand the Spirit's role in completing our salvation is to understand the heart of Basil's pneumatology and the importance of the Spirit's work in the church today.

AUGUSTINE OF HIPPO

Augustine of Hippo wrote his great treatise on the Trinity around 400–427, some three decades after Basil's work on the Holy Spirit and in a very different context.[39] Augustine is a Latin writer, unlike the Greek Basil,

---

[36]Basil, *On the Holy Spirit* 7.16.
[37]Basil, *On the Holy Spirit* 10.24–15.36, 17.43, 18.44.
[38]Basil, *On the Holy Spirit* 6.13–15.
[39]For English translation of Augustine's work, I rely on *The Trinity*, trans. Edmund Hill, in *The Works of Saint Augustine: A Translation for the 21st Century* 1/5 (Hyde Park, NY: New City, 1991). The standard work on Augustine's trinitarian theology is Lewis Ayres, *Augustine and the Trinity* (Cambridge: Cambridge University Press, 2010).

and he admits freely—though no less remarkably—in *Confessions* that he never had much interest in learning Greek.[40] Augustine's primary influences are thus not Greek-language writers (unless in translation), but Latin pro-Nicenes in both the European and North African contexts.[41] Augustine also wrote after the primary trinitarian controversies had been settled and the decrees of Constantinople had taken root in both the East and the West. He thus begins from a somewhat more established position than Basil, operating from within a received tradition and with the ability to appeal to Catholic commentators in addition to Scripture for support of his positions.[42]

Augustine's *De Trinitate* consists of fifteen books. While the primary focus of the first seven books is the relation between the Father and the Son, the Spirit also occupies a subtle place there that flowers into a more prominent treatment in the second half of the treatise. To understand the importance of what Augustine says about the Spirit, it will be necessary to sketch a panorama of Augustine's trinitarian theology in *De Trinitate*. I will thus treat in order Augustine's remarks on the trinitarian missions, the intratrinitarian relations and the psychological analogies.[43] Only at the end of this survey will we be ready to locate Augustine's pneumatology in the broader context of his theology.

The trinitarian missions. The first four books of *De Trinitate* constitute the most obviously "biblical" section of Augustine's treatise and are primarily concerned with one overarching question: does the fact that the Son is "sent" by the Father entail that he is somehow less than the Father? Augustine's answer is, quite simply, no; but the presentation of his case will lay

---

[40]Augustine, *Confessions* 1.13.20.

[41]See Joseph T. Lienhard, "Augustine of Hippo, Basil of Caesarea, and Gregory Nazianzen," in *Orthodox Readings of Augustine*, ed. Aristotle Papanikolaou and George E. Demacopoulos (Crestwood, NY: St. Vladimir's Seminary Press, 2008), 81–99, for a survey of Augustine's use of the Cappadocian fathers. On Augustine's Latin influences see Ayres, *Augustine and the Trinity*.

[42]Augustine, *De Trinitate* 1.4.7.

[43]For other important studies of Augustine's trinitarian theology, see Luigi Gioia, *The Theological Epistemology of Augustine's* De trinitate (New York: Oxford University Press, 2008); and Maarten Wisse, *Trinitarian Theology Beyond Participation: Augustine's* De trinitate *and Contemporary Theology*, T & T Clark Studies in Systematic Theology 11 (London: T & T Clark, 2011). Two recent studies of Augustine's pneumatology include Chad Tyler Gerber, *The Spirit of Augustine's Early Theology: Contextualizing Augustine's Pneumatology*, Ashgate Studies in Philosophy and Theology in Late Antiquity (Burlington, VT: Ashgate, 2012); and Travis E. Ables, *Incarnational Realism: Trinity and the Spirit in Augustine and Barth*, T & T Clark Studies in Systematic Theology (London: T & T Clark, 2013).

the groundwork for the trinitarian superstructure he develops in the later books. For our purposes, the chief contribution of Augustine's discussion is his decision to present the activity of the economic Trinity as the epistemological basis for our understanding of the immanent Trinity and to highlight the uniquely salvific character of the sendings of the Son and the Spirit in the incarnation and Pentecost.[44]

Augustine's discussion focuses heavily on the Old Testament theophanies, or appearances of God, which might seem similar to the missions of the Son and Spirit. Against a common tendency to associate the Old Testament theophanies with the Son, Augustine does not believe the theophanies can clearly be identified with any one of the persons.[45] The most striking demonstration of this ambiguity arises in the curious story of the three men who visit Abraham by the oaks of Mamre (Gen 18).[46] These men are indistinguishable from each other and are both individually and collectively called "Lord," even after one of the men leaves and the other two proceed to destroy Sodom (Gen 19:2, 13). The appearance of three figures and not just one indicates that it was not the Son alone who was made manifest in the theophanies; all three persons could in principle have been involved.

Augustine's survey of the Old Testament material leads him to deny the possibility of determining with certainty which of the persons is represented in a given theophany, absent strong indicators from the narrative context.[47] He does, however, draw two related conclusions. First, the theophanies do not reveal the divine substance.[48] And second, the theophanies were the product of angels, who have the ability to manipulate physical objects to produce signs and wonders.[49] This latter issue raises a challenge and brings into relief how Augustine defines the trinitarian missions. Both the Old

---

[44]I am using "Pentecost" somewhat loosely here, as Augustine wrestles with the relation between Pentecost (Acts 2) and Jesus' bestowing the Spirit on the disciples in John 20:22 (see Augustine, *De Trinitate* 15.25.45–15.26.46).

[45]Gunton contrasts Augustine in this regard with Irenaeus and Tertullian (see Colin E. Gunton, "Augustine, the Trinity and the Theological Crisis of the West," in *The Promise of Trinitarian Theology* [Edinburgh: T & T Clark, 1991], 36–37).

[46]Augustine, *De Trinitate* 2.10.19–2.12.22.

[47]Augustine, *De Trinitate* 2.18.35.

[48]Augustine, *De Trinitate* 2.18.35.

[49]Augustine, *De Trinitate* 3.1.4–5, 3.9.19–3.11.21. Augustine's scriptural argument for this position is found in 3.11.22–3.11.27, where he cites Gen 22:11, 15; Acts 7:30, 53; Gal 3:19; and Heb 1:13-14; 2:1-4.

Testament theophanies and the revelations of the Son and Spirit are visible phenomena generated by manipulation of the material world, and neither set of manifestations reveals the divine substance. The physical body of Christ is not the substance of the Word whereby he is consubstantial with the Father,[50] nor is the dove or fire the substance of the Spirit whereby he is consubstantial with the Father and the Son. What, then, is the difference between the theophanies and the missions of the Son and Spirit?

Augustine's answer is that the sendings of the Son and Spirit are uniquely able to accomplish our redemption because they uniquely reveal the identity of the divine persons. God is the source of our highest knowledge, the ground of our being, and unchangingly perfect in truth, love and eternity.[51] But our love for temporal things keeps us from contemplating the eternal truth of God and binds us to this earth. Our purification must therefore be accomplished through temporal things, as we proceed from created matter to eternity, from faith to sight.[52] Christ has made this possible by adopting humanity while retaining his divinity. This "hypostatic union" leads us from faith in his humanity to the truth of his divinity whereby he is coequal to the Father. No such ascent would be available for us had the eternal Son not adopted our mortality while also remaining eternal, or if we looked toward one person in faith and another person in truth.[53]

What it means for the Son to be sent, then, is for the invisible Son to be made visible in such a way that humanity can see that he is from the Father.[54] The trinitarian missions cannot be understood as God's physically entering into the world, since God already fills heaven and earth (Jer 23:24), and he is not physical anyway.[55] The missions are rather God's redemptive mechanism for directing us toward himself through the revelation of the Son's identity in relation to the Father, and the Spirit's identity in relation to the Father and the Son. The Son is sent by the Father in time because he is begotten of the Father outside time. The Spirit is sent by the Father and the

---

[50] Augustine, *De Trinitate* 3.11.27.
[51] Augustine, *De Trinitate* 4.1.1–2.
[52] Augustine, *De Trinitate* 4.18.24.
[53] Augustine, *De Trinitate* 4.18.24.
[54] Augustine, *De Trinitate* 2.5.9.
[55] Augustine, *De Trinitate* 2.5.7.

Son because he eternally proceeds from both.[56] Since the Father is the source of all divinity,[57] the one from whom the Son is begotten and the Spirit proceeds, he is not sent.[58] Yet the Son's identity as begotten of the Father does not entail that he is less than the Father; it only means he comes from the Father even as he is coeternal and coequal with the Father.

And so the original question concerning the missions is answered: the fact that the Son is *sent* by the Father does not entail that the Son is less than the Father, but only that the Son comes from the Father. The fact that the Son *comes from* the Father does not entail that he is less than the Father, but rather that he is the eternally begotten, coequal Son of the Father, as fully God as the Father is God. And it is precisely the union of eternity and temporality in Jesus Christ that enables sinners to ascend from Christ's humanity to His divinity whereby he is coequal with the Father.

The intratrinitarian relations. *De Trinitate* 5–7 provides a fuller account of these trinitarian relations. Here Augustine's chief concern is to refute the "Arian" claim that the Father and Son are of different substances.[59] Augustine agrees with the Arians that God *is* substance or being, drawing for this point on God's revelation of the divine name to Moses: "I am who I am" or "he who is" (Ex 3:14).[60] It is unthinkable for this God to be subject to change or modification, which is why he is said *to be* in the strongest sense. Yet the conclusion the Arians draw from this notion is quite different from Augustine's. The Arians assume there are only two potential ways to speak of God: substance language and modification language. Since God is not subject to modification—for God is immutable and cannot change—they reason that every assertion we rightly make of God must concern his substance. Thus, if the Father is rightly said to be "unbegotten" and the Son is rightly said to be "begotten," then the Father and Son must be of different substances.

Augustine's response to this challenge bears strong similarities to the Cappadocian position. Besides just substance and modification language, there

---

[56]One witnesses here the roots of the *filioque* clause.

[57]Augustine, *De Trinitate* 4.20.29.

[58]Augustine, *De Trinitate* 4.20.28.

[59]For simplicity I put "Arian" in quotes, but see Michel R. Barnes ("The Arians of Book V and the Genre of 'De trinitate,'" *Journal of Theological Studies* 44 [1993]: 185–95), who argues that Augustine's opponent is not Eunomians, as is commonly supposed, but Latin Homoians.

[60]Augustine, *De Trinitate* 5.2.3.

is a third option: relationship language.[61] Substance language involves speech about something with reference to itself, while relationship language involves speech about something with reference to another. Substance language thus concerns what applies to the entire Godhead—God is good, God is eternal, God is powerful and so on—while relationship language concerns what is proper or peculiar to each person of the Trinity. The terms "unbegotten" and "begotten" are examples of relationship language. "Begotten" indicates that the second person of the Trinity derives eternally from the first. "Unbegotten" means "not the Son."[62] One cannot say that the whole Trinity is "unbegotten," or that the whole Trinity is "begotten," or that the whole Trinity is Father, or Son, or Holy Spirit.[63] The Son can be called "Image" or "Word," but the Father cannot, for the Father is not the Image or Word of anything else.[64] In this way, relationship language does not bear on the divine substance. One can affirm, against the Arians, that the Father and Son share the same substance, as does the Holy Spirit, but one can also say that they relate to each another differently and are thus irreducibly distinct.

Psychological analogies. This dynamic becomes clearer in the second half of *De Trinitate*, where Augustine pursues an "inward turn" (*modo interiore*)[65] to explore whether there is in the mind an image of the triune God. The psychological analogies of this section have often been taken to represent Augustine's trinitarian theology in its most characteristic form, namely monist, as if Augustine conceived of God as a unitary mind without doing justice to the distinction of the persons.[66] Recent scholarship has challenged this reading by questioning whether Augustine intended the psychological analogies to function as a model for the Trinity in the first place.[67] On this line, which I here affirm, the analogies do help Augustine resolve some logical difficulties pertinent to the intratrinitarian relations, but their

---

[61]Augustine, *De Trinitate* 5.5.6.

[62]Augustine, *De Trinitate* 5.6.7–5.7.8.

[63]Augustine, *De Trinitate* 5.11.12.

[64]Augustine, *De Trinitate* 5.13.14.

[65]Augustine, *De Trinitate* 8.1.1.

[66]For a prominent articulation of this argument, see Gunton, "Augustine, the Trinity and the Theological Crisis of the West."

[67]The seminal argument here is Rowan Williams, "Sapientia and the Trinity: Reflections on the *De trinitate*," in *Collectanea Augustiniana: Mélanges T. J. Van Bavel*, ed. B. Bruning, M. Lamberigts and J. van Houtem (Leuven: Leuven University Press, 1990), 317–32.

more fundamental purpose is to illustrate and enact humanity's ascent to God, whose image we bear only through participation in the divine life. More simply, the analogies are meant to facilitate our salvation and to teach us that we cannot truly understand ourselves apart from God. This ascent is especially important for our purposes because it furnishes the place where Augustine most emphatically develops his understanding of the Spirit's identity and work in the triune Godhead and economy of salvation.

Augustine's primary psychological analogy is that of memory (Father), intelligence (Son) and will (Spirit). But it may be simpler to begin, as Augustine does, with a less abstract example.[68] Suppose you are looking at a rock. There is a distinction between the rock and the image of that rock that resides in your mind. The image is identical to the rock but also derivative of it, since the image of the rock only exists because of the rock itself. The image and the rock are also coextensive in time since the image of the rock resides in your mind as long as you are actually looking at the rock. Finally, you will only look at the rock (and thus have the image of the rock in your mind) if you *will* to look at the rock and for as long as you will to look at the rock. For Augustine, the movement that emerges from these three elements—rock, image, will—is a very rough picture of the Trinity. The Father is the source of the Son, and the Spirit is the desire that directs us toward the original such that the image may arise. This is how the Spirit constitutes the union of the Father and the Son.

As Augustine progresses through his argument, he guides the reader from lower to higher analogies, with each one getting more abstract. We began with an image generated by an external object, but we can progress to an image generated by a memory of that external object.[69] This new threefold pattern is interior to the mind, but the memory is still dependent on an external thing. We thus ascend further to knowledge of our own participation in virtue, though this remains somewhat accidental in that our manifestation of virtue now, as we confront suffering and difficulty, may be different from our manifestation of virtue in the eschaton, when there will be no struggle.[70] We may finally ascend to the mind abstracted of anything

---

[68]Augustine, *De Trinitate* 11.2.2–5.
[69]Augustine, *De Trinitate* 14.8.11.
[70]Augustine, *De Trinitate* 14.9.12.

adventitious, and our mind's memory, understanding and love of itself.[71] The mind's knowledge and love of itself is absolutely contemporaneous with itself and thus seems to be the image Augustine has been seeking. Yet even this does not suffice, for the mind must not rest in remembering, understanding and loving itself but proceed to the knowledge and love of God, who made the mind.[72] The image of God is thus most fully realized in us when the movements of our mind are directed toward God.

At this final level of abstraction, Augustine does think that to some extent he has discovered an image of the Trinity in the mind. Yet this discovery does not constitute for Augustine a picture of God's very nature, and the final book of De Trinitate stridently rejects the sufficiency of the analogies as a model for the Trinity. First, the divine persons do not simplistically correspond to these mental acts, as if the Father only possessed memory, the Son only possessed understanding and the Spirit only possessed will.[73] Each person possesses all three, and is all three, and not only by dependence on the others. Second, for the human, it is the mind that remembers, understands and wills, such that the mind may be said to have memory, understanding and will. But God does not have the divine persons; he just is Father, Son, Spirit.[74] And third, the faculties of the human mind are unequal to each other, in that the content of memory may exceed what the mind currently understands. But the divine persons are absolutely equal, and unchangingly so. Thus all this speculation has only led Augustine to the deflating conclusion that we cannot see face to face, but only dimly, as through a mirror (1 Cor 13:12). Yet it is just this conclusion that enables the faithful to see the image "precisely as an image, so that they can in some fashion refer what they see to that of which it is an image, and also see that other by inference through its image which they see by observation, since they cannot see it face to face."[75] The failure to find God in the mind thus results in the triumph of humility when we realize our identity as those known and loved by God.

This is where the Spirit comes in, bringing to culmination Augustine's discussion of the missions, the relations and the analogies, and throwing into

---

[71] Augustine, De Trinitate 14.10.13.
[72] Augustine, De Trinitate 14.12.15.
[73] Augustine, De Trinitate 15.7.12.
[74] Augustine, De Trinitate 15.22.42–15.23.43.
[75] Augustine, De Trinitate 15.23.44.

relief the inextricable relation between the Son and the Spirit. It is the Spirit who directs us toward our eschatological end, when we will see God face to face, and we will even understand what the difference is between the Son's generation and the Spirit's procession, a mystery that has vexed Augustine throughout his work.[76] In the last extended section of *De Trinitate*, Augustine addresses a question he has considered briefly before: Why is the third person of the Trinity called "Holy Spirit" when both the Father and the Son are "holy" and "spirit"?[77] As best as Augustine can understand, the reason is that the Spirit is the bond of communion between the Father and the Son.[78] This is why the Spirit is called "love," both uniting the Father and the Son and igniting us to love for God and neighbor.[79] Another word for this love is "gift," which Augustine also associates with the Spirit on the basis of his favorite pneumatological verse: "The love of God has been poured out in our hearts through the Holy Spirit who has been *given* to us" (Rom 5:5).[80]

The Spirit's gift of love is the means of our ascent to God. This ascent is moral and not physical, since God is spirit, and it occurs only and ironically through Christ's prior descent. As we have seen, our ascent to the triune God proceeds from Christ's humanity to the divinity whereby he is coequal with the Father. The Spirit's gift is what enables our participation in this ascent. As Travis Ables has commented, "Augustine's pneumatology is not to be seen as portraying the Spirit as performing a second divine mission, a second work in the economy of salvation, so much as it is the excess or gratuity of God's self-giving in Christ. This gift of the Spirit . . . is not a different *work* than that of the Son, but the 'subjective' correspondence to that work in the soul."[81] Thus Christology and pneumatology coinhere for Augustine in the strongest sense, not only in the immanent relations between the Son and the Spirit but also according to their singular economic mission.

Once again, we see the importance of the wide-angle lens. Pneumatology only makes sense for Augustine within a broader theological framework that explicates the trinitarian missions, the intratrinitarian relations and

---

[76]Augustine, *De Trinitate* 15.25.45.
[77]Augustine, *De Trinitate* 5.11.12.
[78]Augustine, *De Trinitate* 15.17.27.
[79]Augustine, *De Trinitate* 15.17.31.
[80]See Ables, *Incarnational Realism*, 217 n. 54, on the importance of this verse for Augustine.
[81]Ibid., 73.

humanity's participation in the divine life. The purpose of the missions is to reveal the identities of the Son and the Spirit in relation to the Father; the relations show us how the persons can be coequal yet distinct; and the image of God in the mind directs us to the Father through the Son by the gift of the Spirit. The Spirit who proceeds eternally from the Father and the Son is thus the unique agent of the triune God, who completes our salvation by enabling us to love God and neighbor.

CONCLUSION

With these two pictures of early Christian pneumatology in mind, one from Basil and the other from Augustine, let me now suggest two conclusions of this brief survey, one more historical and the other more programmatic. First, the differences some scholars have emphasized between Eastern and Western conceptions of the Trinity have been much exaggerated. Despite Augustine's lack of direct dependence on Basil, their treatments of the Spirit bear significant similarities. Both stress the unity of the substance alongside the irreducibility of the persons. Both distinguish the persons according to the intra-trinitarian relations. And both affirm the unity of divine will and action while also acknowledging the persons' variegated contribution to the inseparable operations. These are nontrivial points of commonality that support what Lewis Ayres has called a "pro-Nicene culture" that spans East and West,[82] and they raise serious doubts about whether Augustine is indeed to blame for the medieval church's woes—and indeed, whether medieval trinitarian theology was so essentialist after all.[83]

This is not to say that the East and the West are the same in every regard. Augustine's contribution to the *filioque* clause remains a point of contention in contemporary ecumenical dialogue.[84] Yet Augustine's assertion that the

---

[82]Lewis Ayres, *Nicaea and Its Legacy: An Approach to Fourth-Century Trinitarian Theology* (Oxford: Oxford University Press, 2004), 236–40.

[83]For a relevant defense of Thomas Aquinas's trinitarian theology, see Gilles Emery, *Trinity in Aquinas* (Ypsilanti, MI: Sapientia, 2003).

[84]Other significant differences concern the privileged appellation of the Father as "God" and diverse modes of construing divine simplicity. On the former see John Behr, "Calling upon God as Father: Augustine and the Legacy of Nicaea," in Papanikolaou and Demacopoulos, *Orthodox Readings of Augustine*, 153–65. On the latter, see Andrew Radde-Gallwitz, *Basil of Caesarea, Gregory of Nyssa, and the Transformation of Divine Simplicity* (Oxford: Oxford University Press, 2009); and Lewis Ayres, "The Fundamental Grammar of Augustine's Trinitarian Theology," in *Augustine and His Critics: Essays in Honour of Gerald Bonner*, ed. Robert Dodaro and George Lawless (London: Routledge, 2000), 51–76.

Spirit proceeds from the Father and the Son also affirms that the Spirit proceeds principally (*principaliter*) from the Father,[85] and that the Father is the source (*principium*) of all divinity in the Godhead.[86] The Spirit proceeds from the Son only as the Father has given the Son to have the Spirit proceed from him. This is not necessarily to assert, as the Orthodox might countenance, that "the Spirit proceeds from the Father through the Son," but there is enough common ground here to facilitate ongoing ecumenical progress on the matter.[87] Moreover, Basil and Augustine share the same basic pneumatological concerns. Both seek to articulate the Spirit's distinct identity and work, both understand the Spirit's work to be intimately related to the Son's and both present the Spirit's perfecting work against a broader redemptive-historical frame. Again, differences between the East and the West do persist, but early writers from both can be understood as participants in a shared culture.

Second, the development of Nicene pneumatology illustrates the complex but unavoidable relation between Scripture and tradition. Even a casual perusal of Basil's and Augustine's works demonstrates the keen attention each figure dedicates to the biblical text. *On the Holy Spirit* is littered with passages that illustrate this or that point about prepositions and the divine persons, and *De Trinitate* is concerned from beginning to end to hear the canon's whole witness to the triune God. Yet each figure also finds that exploration of Scripture's testimony demands the establishment of theological categories only implicit in the text.

Basil's defense of the Spirit's divinity involves appeal to the Spirit's titles and activities but also depends critically on a series of interrelated theological concepts: the unity of the divine will, the economic and immanent Trinity, the variegated character of divine action and the Spirit's distinct epistemological role. In one striking passage,[88] Basil insists on the legitimacy of affirming unwritten traditions—though not those that enact radical innovation or depart from the scriptural witness—which have strengthened the church's faith and enhanced her worship.[89] Basil's immediate concern is

---

[85]Augustine, *De Trinitate* 15.17.29, 15.26.47–15.27.48.
[86]Augustine, *De Trinitate* 4.20.29.
[87]For discussion, see Ayres, *Augustine and the Trinity*, 263–68.
[88]Basil, *On the Holy Spirit* 27.65–68.
[89]Darren Sarisky, *Scriptural Interpretation: A Theological Account*, Challenges in Contemporary Theology (Oxford: Wiley-Blackwell, 2013), 111–28.

the pneumatomachian rejection of his doxology ("with," "together with"), whose precise form finds no explicit expression in the biblical text. Yet his arguments speak toward a broader methodological issue, namely, that his opponents' strict rejection of any doctrinal formulation without explicit biblical warrant actually produces all sorts of theological monstrosities.

If anything, Augustine's approach extends even further beyond the biblical text than Basil's. Augustine understands, for instance, that scriptural reading must be ruled, and thus sets forth a series of canonical regulations (not original to him) for passages that relate the Father and the Son: some teach the Son is equal to the Father, some describe the Son as "less" than the Father by virtue of his humanity in the incarnation and others say the Son is "less" than the Father in the sense that he derives eternally from the Father.[90] Fail to acknowledge these rules, or something like them, and the entire canon falls apart, not least as it concerns the missions of the Son and the Spirit for our salvation. The psychological analogies shed light on certain quandaries of trinitarian doctrine, even if they are not meant as models for the Trinity. And the suggestion that the Spirit is the bond of communion between the Father and the Son does not abrogate but illuminates the canonical witness as an explanation for Scripture's particular identification of the Spirit with the gift of love, its affirmation that the Spirit proceeds from the Father (and the Son) and its articulation of the *imago Dei* in humanity as a distinctly theological and not just anthropological category.

In his magisterial study of Arius, Rowan Williams suggests that the dispute between Athanasius and Christianity's arch-heretic was not simply a contest between venerable tradition and fanciful innovation. Both parties understood that something new was at stake, and Athanasius's task was to present the innovation of *homoousios* as the only way to preserve continuity with the apostolic past, to show that "strict adherence to archaic and 'neutral' terms alone is in fact a potential betrayal of the historic faith."[91] As Williams states, "There is a sense in which Nicaea and its aftermath represent a recognition by the Church at large that *theology* is not only legitimate but necessary. The loyal and uncritical repetition of formulae is seen to be inadequate as a means of

---

[90]Augustine, *De Trinitate* 2.1.3.
[91]Rowan Williams, *Arius: Heresy and Tradition*, rev. ed (Grand Rapids: Eerdmans, 2001), 235.

securing continuity at anything more than a formal level."[92] The developments we have witnessed in Basil and Augustine's pneumatology confirm Williams's judgment. Scripture demands interpretation because it advances claims about divine realities that can only be apprehended through some kind of coherent, synthesizing vision. This task of theology begins with hearing Scripture, and with it, the Spirit's testimony to Christ and himself.

---

[92]Ibid., 236 (italics his). For a fuller treatment of Scripture and tradition I take to be compatible with Williams's claims, see Kevin J. Vanhoozer, *The Drama of Doctrine: A Canonical-Linguistic Approach to Christian Theology* (Louisville, KY: Westminster John Knox, 2005).

4

Rationalism or Revelation?

St. Thomas Aquinas and the Filioque

Matthew Levering

INTRODUCTION: WAS THE *FILIOQUE* A RATIONALISTIC MISTAKE?

Does it matter whether the Holy Spirit proceeds not only from the Father but also from the Son? For Thomas Aquinas, the answer was yes, not least because of the relationship of the *filioque* to naming the Spirit "Love" and "Gift." In his *Orthodox Readings of Aquinas*, however, the Orthodox scholar Marcus Plested piles up example after example of Orthodox theologians who criticized Aquinas for the doctrine of the *filioque*, even while they often admired Aquinas's theology in other respects.[1] For instance, Plested observes that Theophanes III, metropolitan of Nicaea, showed ample and appreciative knowledge of Aquinas's theology, but "in the matter of the *filioque* any positive appreciation of Aquinas is, naturally, out of the question."[2] The same thing was true for St. Nicholas Cabasilas and many others. Indeed, in his recent comprehensive study *The Filioque*, Edward Siecienski counts Aquinas among the significant "post-schism figures on both sides whose writings contributed to the increasingly divergent views on the procession of the Holy Spirit."[3]

---

[1]Gregory Palamas firmly rejected the *filioque*, even if in his *Apodictic Treatises*, influenced by Augustine, he "allows for an 'Orthodox *filioque*' [or "co-procession"] both in respect of the eternal divine life and the manifestation of the divine *energeia* among creatures" (see Marcus Plested, *Orthodox Readings of Aquinas* [Oxford: Oxford University Press, 2012], 39).

[2]Plested, *Orthodox Readings of Aquinas*, 94.

[3]A. Edward Siecienski, *The Filioque: History of a Doctrinal Controversy* (Oxford: Oxford University Press, 2010), 14.

Reading this sad history of Orthodox appreciation for Aquinas's theology combined with strong disagreement about the *filioque*, one understands why many Catholic theologians have wondered whether the *filioque* is worth it. While supportive of the *filioque*, Hans Urs von Balthasar points out that Pope Pius XI celebrated Mass in 1925 according to the Greek rite and omitted the *filioque*, and Pope John Paul II likewise omitted the *filioque* at a Mass celebrating the 1500th anniversary of the Council of Constantinople. Balthasar cites Jean-Miguel Garrigues, Louis Bouyer and Yves Congar as examples of leading Catholic theologians who have called for the *filioque* "to be dropped for the sake of peace in the Church, emphasizing that the Greeks should have the right to adopt the contrary view, that is, the right to acknowledge the *filioque* as a possible theological interpretation of the trinitarian dogma shared by both sides, just as the Latins can allow the Greek interpretation to stand."[4]

For its part, the *Catechism of the Catholic Church*, citing the Council of Florence (1438), teaches that the Catholic Church in fact rightly affirms the *filioque*, "for the eternal order of the divine persons in their consubstantial communion implies that the Father, as 'the principle without principle,' is the first origin of the Spirit, but also that as Father of the only Son, he is, with the Son, the single principle from which the Holy Spirit proceeds."[5] Although the *filioque* does not belong to the creed confessed at the Council of Constantinople in 381, Pope Leo the Great dogmatically taught the truth of the *filioque* in 447, and "the use of this formula in the Creed was gradually admitted into the Latin liturgy (between the eighth and eleventh centuries)."[6] The catechism insists that the *filioque* controversy is simply one of "legitimate complementarity," since the Catholic Church does not deny that the Father is the "first origin of the Spirit."[7]

Under the auspices of the Faith and Order Commission of the World Council of Churches, a commission on the *filioque* that included Orthodox, Catholic and Protestant theologians convened in 1978 and 1979 at Schloss Klingenthal, France. Edward Siecienski describes this as "the single most significant dialogue on the *filioque*," and Theodore Stylianopolous similarly highlights it in his valuable essay "The Filioque: Dogma, Theologoumenon

---

[4]Hans Urs von Balthasar, *Theo-Logic*, vol. 3, *The Spirit of Truth*, trans. Graham Harrison (San Francisco: Ignatius, 2005), 208–9.
[5]*Catechism of the Catholic Church*, 2nd ed. (Vatican City: Libreria Editrice Vaticana, 1997), §248.
[6]Ibid., §247.
[7]Ibid., §248.

or Error?"[8] The Klingenthal Memorandum, signed by various Catholic and Protestant theologians, advocated removing the *filioque* from the creed, on the grounds that the Spirit has a different relationship to the Father than to the Son. Granted that the Spirit's procession from the Father presupposes the Son's coming forth from the Father, the Klingenthal Memorandum suggests replacing the *filioque* with one of the following formulae: "The Spirit proceeds from the Father of the Son; the Spirit proceeds from the Father through the Son; the Spirit proceeds from the Father and receives from the Son; the Spirit proceeds from the Father and rests on the Son; the Spirit proceeds from the Father and shines out through the Son."[9]

More recently, in 1995 the Pontifical Council for Promoting Christian Unity published a document titled "The Greek and Latin Traditions Regarding the Procession of the Holy Spirit." The pontifical council observes that "Gregory of Nazianzus . . . characterizes the Spirit's relationship of origin from the Father by the proper term *ekporeusis*, distinguishing it from that of procession *(to proienai)* which the Spirit has in common with the Son."[10] Thus, for the Cappadocians, *ekporeusis* can only characterize the Spirit's relation to the Father. The pontifical council points out in this regard that the Catholic Church now rejects the addition of "and the Son" to the creed's *Greek* form, "even in its liturgical use by Latins." After discussing the East's approval of the formula "through" *(dia)* the Son, the pontifical council remarks that the *filioque* belongs to "a theological and linguistic context different from that of the affirmation of the sole monarchy of the Father, the one origin of the Son and of the Spirit." The pontifical council lays stress on the fact that the Latin verb *procedere*, unlike the Greek term *ekporeuomenon*, does not signify solely the relation of the Spirit to the Father, but in fact signifies "the communication of the consubstantial divinity from the Father to the Son and from the Father, through and with the Son, to the Holy Spirit." The Latin West's *procedere* corresponds

---

[8]See Siecienski, *The Filioque*, 208–9; Theodore Stylianopolous, "The Filioque: Dogma, Theologoumenon or Error?," in *The Good News of Christ: Essays on the Gospel, Sacraments and Spirit* (Brookline, MA: Holy Cross Orthodox Press, 1991), 196–232.

[9]Klingenthal Memorandum, "The Filioque Clause in Ecumenical Perspective," in *Spirit of God, Spirit of Christ: Ecumenical Reflections on the Filioque Controversy*, ed. Lukas Vischer (London: SPCK, 1981), 16.

[10]Pontifical Council for Promoting Christian Unity, "The Greek and Latin Traditions Regarding the Procession of the Holy Spirit," www.ewtn.com/library/curia/pccufilq.htm. Latin has only one word for these two Greek words, namely, *procedere* ("proceed").

to the Greek East's *proienai* a point that was already made by Maximus the Confessor in his *Letter to Marinus of Cyprus*, which was written from Rome and which defended the true meaning of the *filioque*.

The pontifical council concludes by reflecting on the Spirit as "Gift of Love" who "characterizes the relation between the Father, as source of love, and his beloved Son," as is manifested in the Spirit's work in Jesus Christ. Here, in addition to numerous biblical citations, the pontifical council cites Gregory Palamas as being broadly in accord with Augustine's naming of the Spirit as "Love": "This doctrine of the Holy Spirit as love has been harmoniously assumed by St. Gregory Palamas into the Greek theology of the *ekporeusis* from the Father alone: 'The Spirit of the most high Word is like an ineffable love of the Father for this Word ineffably generated.'" The pontifical council's document was generally well received by Orthodox theologians, even if they continue to call for the excision of the *filioque* from the Latin Creed.[11]

Why, however, should we care whether the creed contains the *filioque* or suppose that we can know whether the Spirit eternally proceeds not only from the Father but also from the Son? In my view, the answer will first and foremost be a biblical one: if Scripture gives us any teachings about the distinctiveness of the Holy Spirit in the Trinity, then those teachings are well worth contemplating. Second, however, behind the *filioque* controversy lies a broader charge that the Christian West has succumbed to theological rationalism. If Western theology has been profoundly rationalistic from Augustine onward, this should be of great concern to both Catholics and Protestants.

The great Russian Orthodox theologian Sergius Bulgakov finds Thomas Aquinas's theology of the *filioque* to be the full flowering of Western theological rationalism. Bulgakov centers his attention on a relatively lengthy quotation from Aquinas's *Summa theologiae* 1, question 36, article 2. In this passage Aquinas argues that if the relation of the Son were to the Father alone and the relation of the Spirit were also to the Father alone, then these two relations would not be distinct: there would be no way of distinguishing the Son from the Spirit. In reply Bulgakov suggests that Aquinas is rationalistically attempting to pin down an ineffable mystery. Bulgakov comments: "Here, with full certainty, the doctrine of the Filioque is a logical conse-

[11]On this point, see Siecienski, *The Filioque*, 210-11.

quence postulated from the doctrine of the hypostases as relations of origination; and the source of this doctrine is not revelation but scholastic theology with its erroneous conclusions, so that one wishes to say to it: hands off!"[12] In Bulgakov's view, Aquinas supposes that he can arrive at conclusions about the Holy Spirit solely on the basis of a logical theorem that pretends to be impregnable on syllogistic grounds.

Bulgakov adds two more quotations from Aquinas, from question 36, article 4, and question 29, article 4, respectively. These quotations assure Bulgakov that Aquinas grounds his doctrine of the Holy Spirit not on revelation but on the philosophical theory of opposed relations of origin. Aquinas teaches that unlike the relations with which Aristotle was concerned, a relation in God cannot be a mere "accident" in a subject, but must be none other than the divine essence itself, since whatever is in God is God. Bulgakov finds here an exemplification of Augustinian essentialism mingled with Aristotelian rationalism. For Aquinas, Bulgakov concludes, "in the impersonal and pre-personal *Divinitas*, persons originate from relations in the capacity of substantial accidents, the ontological priority belonging to this *Divinitas*, whereas the persons appear in the capacity of accidents, although substantial ones."[13]

Even if Bulgakov's description of Aquinas's views is not technically accurate—for Aquinas the divine persons *are* the distinct relations of opposition in the order of origin, rather than originating from relations, and for Aquinas there is no divine essence outside the persons (let alone a divine essence that has "ontological priority")—nevertheless Bulgakov's concerns are well worth our attention. Although Aquinas appeals to analogous discourse and to faith seeking understanding of an ineffable mystery, Aristotelian philosophy does play a large role in Aquinas's theological reflection on the trinitarian persons constituted by divine generation and spiration. Is Thomas Aquinas's theology of the Holy Spirit's procession from the Father and the Son therefore rationalistic?

THOMAS AQUINAS ON THE *FILIOQUE*

Let me first note that Aquinas presumed a faulty understanding of the Greek word *ekporeusis* and its cognates. He thought that *procedere* adequately translated these words, whereas in fact, *ekporeusis* pertains solely to the

---

[12]Sergius Bulgakov, *The Comforter*, trans. Boris Jakim (Grand Rapids: Eerdmans, 2004), 122.
[13]Ibid., 123.

Spirit's relation to the Father as monarchical principle. Even so, I will argue that Aquinas's position on the *filioque* not only is not rationalistic but in fact arises from a profound meditation on biblical revelation and on the councils of the church. If so, then perhaps the Holy Spirit is the "Love" and "Gift" of the Father and the Son after all.

A rule of Holy Scripture: the Son has all the Father has. Aquinas addresses the issue of the *filioque* in *Summa theologiae* 1, question 36, article 2, and this article will be the focus of our attention in the remainder of this essay.[14] It is necessary first to review the seven objections that Aquinas sets forth in this article, so as to see fully what he considers to be at stake here. As we will see, Aquinas considers that his task is not simply to show that without the *filioque* there would be no way of distinguishing between the Son and the Holy Spirit. More importantly, his task involves asking how Scripture and tradition are authoritative with respect to trinitarian doctrine. The central authority for Aquinas is neither the analogy of the mind nor philosophical doctrines such as substance and relation, but rather Scripture as interpreted in the tradition.

The first objection gets to the nub of the matter. Aquinas grants that the procession of the Holy Spirit from the Son is not explicitly taught in Scripture. He also accepts Pseudo-Dionysius's principle, articulated in *The Divine Names*, that one should say nothing about God except what divine revelation, given in Scripture, has expressed about God. In this light, it seems that to adopt the *filioque* would be rationalism. The objection quotes John 15:26 as evidence that the Spirit proceeds from the Father, since Jesus here says that "when the Counselor [*parakletos*] comes, whom I shall send to you from the Father, even the Spirit of truth, who proceeds from the Father, he will bear witness to me."[15] Aquinas does not here challenge the objector by appealing to Jesus' economic sending of the Spirit "from the Father"; instead Aquinas grants that this text says only that the Holy Spirit "proceeds from the Father." As he says in his response to the first objection, "We do not find it verbally [*per verba*] expressed in Holy Scripture that the Holy Spirit proceeds from the Son."

---

[14]Thomas Aquinas, *Summa Theologica*, trans. The Fathers of the English Dominican Province, 5 vols. (Westminster, MD: Christian Classics, 1981).

[15]All biblical quotations will be drawn from the Revised Standard Version unless otherwise noted.

What then is his avenue for defending the *filioque*, since he has admitted that it is not found verbally in Scripture and since (against rationalism) he affirms Pseudo-Dionysius's principle for a scriptural dogmatics? Aquinas's path is to argue that Pseudo-Dionysius's principle does not limit speech about God solely to what Scripture explicitly says. Rather, the principle also allows for what Scripture implicitly says. As Aquinas puts it, the *filioque* is present in Scripture not *per verba* but *per sensum*.

In defense of this view, Aquinas turns to John 16:14, where Jesus says of the Spirit, "He will glorify me, for he will take what is mine and declare it to you." (Aquinas's Latin text reads *Ille me clarificabit, quia de meo accipiet*, and the Greek word *lēmpsetai* can mean "take" or "receive.") What is included in Jesus' reference to "what is mine"? The answer, as Aquinas knows, comes in the very next verse, where Jesus adds, "All that the Father has is mine; therefore I said that he will take what is mine and declare it to you." In short, the Son has all that the Father has, with the obvious exception of the Father's paternity.

On this basis, Aquinas identifies as a "rule of Holy Scripture" the principle that the Son has all that the Father has. In support of this, he also quotes Matthew 11:27, "All things have been delivered to me by my Father; and no one knows the Son except the Father, and no one knows the Father except the Son and any one to whom the Son chooses to reveal him." Aquinas draws the conclusion that other than what is contained in the relational distinction (Father-Son, begetting-begotten), the Son fully has all the Father has, so that the Son knows and expresses the Father fully. The fullness of the Son's expression of the Father includes even the Father's spiration of the Holy Spirit, so that the Son shares in the Father's spiration of the Spirit. Given that the Son can truly affirm that "all that the Father has is mine," it follows for Aquinas that "when we say that the Holy Spirit proceeds from the Father, even though it be added that he proceeds from the Father alone, the Son would not thereby be at all excluded."

All of this is found in Aquinas's response to the crucial first objection, which makes clear that what is at stake is not a philosophical analogy or philosophical categories (such as opposed relations of origin), but a point of exegetical engagement with what the living God has revealed about himself and has communicated to us in Scripture.

In the same response to the first objection, Aquinas also employs the philosophical point about opposite relations (*oppositas relationes*) but in a way that makes clear that this philosophical apparatus, while helpful, is secondary. Specifically, in interpreting Jesus' claim that Jesus has all that the Father has, Aquinas draws on the doctrine of relations, since Jesus is describing the relation Father-Son. Aquinas states, "As regards being the principle of the Holy Spirit, the Father and the Son are not opposed to each other, but only as regards the fact that one is the Father, and the other is the Son." It should be clear that the Father and the Son are not one "principle" as an undifferentiated amalgam: the Father is principle as the begetter of the Son, and so the Son's sharing in the spiration does not impair the personal distinctiveness of the Father and Son.

Changing the creed: a theology of church councils. After this first objection pertaining to Scripture, the second objection pertains to the creed and to conciliar decrees. Although Aquinas is unaware of the Spirit-specific signification of *ekporeusis*, he certainly knows that the Latin church changed the creed of Constantinople. He observes in the second objection, therefore, that adding something to the creed—like inventing things about the Spirit with no scriptural basis—seems to be anathema. The question then is whether, and by whom, the creed can be changed, in response to new controversies that are continually arising.

How are we to interpret past councils, and who is to interpret them? What is the means of arriving at a definitive interpretation of a past council? For Aquinas, the answer is found in Constantinople itself, which provided a definitive interpretation of Nicaea. The means of interpreting past councils is inevitably, under the guidance of the Holy Spirit, by further councils. This is not a vicious circle. It simply shows that the church is alive; a living church cannot help but continually interpret its past, and the primary way of doing that is through councils. The East, of course, privileges the seven ecumenical councils, after which it does not recognize any further ecumenical councils, due not least to the separation of East and West. But the East continues to have local councils of various kinds at which important matters of interpretation are decided. And the West, for its part, does not fail to give a privileged position to the first seven councils; they remain at the heart of the most important elements of Christian faith, namely, the identity of Jesus Christ and of the triune God.

The key point for Aquinas is that since under the Spirit's guidance council interprets council, subsequent councils can and should interpret Constantinople and its creed. Indeed, subsequent councils have done so and have determined that the affirmation of the Spirit proceeding from the Father and the Son does not undermine what Constantinople was affirming regarding the person of the Spirit. The additions made by subsequent councils do not negate the original creed; instead, such additions develop the doctrine of the earlier creed in order to meet new challenges. The best example of this process, Aquinas suggests, is Constantinople itself. As he states in his reply to the second objection, "Hence in the decision of the council of Chalcedon it is declared that those who were congregated together in the council of Constantinople, handed down the doctrine about the Holy Spirit, not implying that there was anything wanting in the doctrine of their predecessors who had gathered together at Nicaea, but explaining what those fathers had understood of the matter."

We do not here have an instance of refusal to take Constantinople seriously as a historical phenomenon, nor do we have a rationalistic procedure whereby certain claims about relations and causality dictate the interpretation of Constantinople. On the contrary, Aquinas argues on the basis of the history of the councils, in which he finds Chalcedon commenting on Constantinople, and Constantinople commenting on and augmenting Nicaea. Assuming the operation of the Holy Spirit, then, we need not imagine the Nicene fathers themselves being able to spell out all that the later Council of Constantinople said; we need only to imagine the Nicene fathers as being able to arrive at these later conclusions (such as the divinity of the Holy Spirit) had the Nicene fathers been present at the Council of Constantinople.

Aquinas's claim that "in another council assembled in the west, the matter was explicitly defined by the authority of the Roman Pontiff" introduces another principle regarding the interpretation of past councils, namely, the role of the bishop of Rome. This papal role, however, does not take away from the fact that Aquinas's emphasis here remains focused on later councils authoritatively interpreting earlier councils. His interpretation of what later councils were doing, and of whether later councils (let alone popes) possessed authority to make decisions for the whole church, is obviously contestable. But far from following a rationalistic path, it is Scripture as interpreted by church councils that is determinative for Aquinas.

The perfection of the Holy Spirit's procession. Of the remaining objections in article 2 of question 36, the most significant are the fourth, sixth and seventh. Before turning my attention to these objections, however, let me briefly review the less valuable third and fifth objections. The third is a quotation from John of Damascus, in which Damascene affirms that the Holy Spirit is from the Father and denies that the Holy Spirit is from the Son. The authority of Damascene is obviously respected by Aquinas, but in this case Aquinas suggests that Damascene's opinion—if it is true (Aquinas adds) that Damascene was intending to deny the *filioque*—derives from a Nestorian creed that, among other things, denied the *filioque* and was condemned at the Council of Ephesus. Aquinas is working with faulty historical information here: Siecienski observes that "the council of Ephesus had approved certain portions of the Nestorian creed presented by the priest Charisius, including the statement that 'the Holy Spirit is not the Son, neither does he take his existence through the Son.'"[16] Aquinas may be right that Damascene's views flow from this creed, but the story is clearly more complicated than Aquinas supposes.

The fifth objection seems to have its origin, probably not known to Aquinas, in Gregory of Nyssa's theology. The objection states that "our breath [*spiritus*] does not seem to proceed in ourselves from our word," and so it would appear to follow that the Holy Spirit does not proceed from the Son/Word. Aquinas's answer here is to distinguish between an exterior word and an interior word; it is the latter that supports the procession of the Holy Spirit from the Father and his Word.

The fourth and sixth objections are significant because they help to illumine how the *filioque* influences our understanding of the Holy Spirit, beyond the mere affirmation that the Holy Spirit proceeds not only from the Father but also from the Son. In other words, why does the *filioque* matter? In the fourth objection, citing a formulation taken from the legend of St. Andrew, Aquinas affirms that the Holy Spirit "rests" (*quiescit*) in the Son. But how could the Holy Spirit "rest" or abide in the Son if the Holy Spirit proceeds from the Son? Answering the objection, Aquinas points out that the Son himself rests or abides (*manere*) in the Father (see Jn 1:18). Proceeding

---

[16]Siecienski, *The Filioque*, 159.

from the Father does not mean that the Son cannot rest in the Father; likewise proceeding from the Father and the Son does not mean that the Spirit cannot rest in the Son. The abiding of the Son "in the bosom of the Father," an image of supreme intimacy, fits with the abiding of the Spirit in the Son, an abiding that procession from the Father and Son supports.

The sixth objection is a marvelously simple one: "The Holy Spirit proceeds perfectly from the Father. Therefore it is superfluous to say that he proceeds from the Son." In other words, why complicate matters? What is gained by the affirmation "and the Son," even if it happened to be true?

In reply, Aquinas remarks that if one affirms that the Holy Spirit proceeds perfectly from the Father, one should equally insist that the Son proceeds perfectly from the Father. This means that the Son perfectly receives all that the Father is, except—of course—paternity. And if the Son perfectly receives *all* that the Father is, this can hardly exclude a share in the spiration of the Spirit, so long as the Father's monarchy is not threatened. The *filioque*, in other words, helps to emphasize that indeed the Father is able to communicate himself perfectly. His perfect communication of himself is what requires that the Holy Spirit, in proceeding perfectly from the Father, proceed also from the Son. At stake, then, is the *perfection* of the Holy Spirit's procession. In this reply, Aquinas again shows that the unity of the Father and Son as the principle of the Spirit follows precisely from the specific character of their personal differentiation: "Whatever is from the Father must be from the Son unless it be opposed to the property of filiation; for the Son is not from himself, although he is from the Father."

Relations of origin and trinitarian persons. Having emphasized, as fruits not least of the *filioque*, the intimacy of the Son and Spirit and the perfection of their procession, Aquinas in the seventh objection takes up Anselm's point that the difference between generation and procession, by itself, would suffice to differentiate the Son and Spirit, whether or not the Spirit is also differentiated by proceeding from the Father *and* the Son. Anselm's view mirrors that of the Greek fathers and the East in general, although Anselm of course accepts the *filioque*. The significance of this objection consists primarily in its leading Aquinas into the major themes of his *respondeo*. In his reply to the objection, Aquinas states that the personal distinction of the Son and Spirit requires a distinction of origin. If the Son and the Spirit both had the exact same origin, then they would not be distinct persons. This is the argument that so concerned Bulgakov (and that has been unpersuasive to generations of Orthodox theologians), on the grounds that it seems to know too much about the second procession and to view the Trinity too much in terms of philosophical categories such as causality, origin and relation.

To undermine the position of his adversaries, or at least to soften their opposition, Aquinas cites (or tries to cite) Athanasius in the pivotal *sed contra* of article two. The Athanasian Creed is now known, however, to have been composed in the Latin West around the year 500.[17] Its testimony in favor of the *filioque* is therefore not relevant to addressing the concerns of the East, other than perhaps exacerbating those concerns due to its history as a forged proof text. From this inauspicious beginning, Aquinas opens his *respondeo* with the claim that if the Holy Spirit were not from the Father and the Son, then the Holy Spirit could not be distinguished from the Son. The persons cannot be distinguished by substance, and so they must be distinguished by relations, since relation is the only accident that does not import finitude/materiality. The Father is one person despite having two relations: to the Son and to the Spirit. Why do these two relations not constitute two persons (two Fathers)? In order to be a distinct relation in God, the relation must be an opposed relation based on origin. For example, the Father is Father because he has a Son, since "Son" is opposed relationally to "Father." If the Holy Spirit were also opposed relationally to the Father in this way, the Holy Spirit would be simply another Son, indeed no different at all from the Son. It must be, therefore, that the Son and Holy Spirit are "related to each other by opposite relations" of origin. This can be the case only if the Holy Spirit is from the Son (and the Father). Earlier, Aquinas had noted that "spiration belongs to the person of the Father, and to the person of the Son,

---

[17]See Siecienski, *The Filioque*, 8, 68. Siecienski adds, "Most of the quotations used by Thomas Aquinas in the *Contra Errores Graecorum*, which had been taken from the *Libellus de fide ss. Trinitatis* of Nicholas of Cotrone, have since proven to be spurious, and the version of Basil's *Contra Eunomium* employed by the Latins at Florence is now known to include sections of Eunomius's own work, added later by an ancient editor" (8). Siecienski complains that "despite the hundreds of texts collected over the centuries either proving or disproving the orthodoxy of the *filioque*, there were few efforts made to understand the fathers or their writings on their own terms. . . . It would not be until the twentieth century, when Catholic and Orthodox scholars in Europe began to study the sources together, that serious dialogue on the meaning of these patristic texts finally started" (9).

forasmuch as it has no relative opposition either to paternity or to filiation."[18] Thus spiration does not constitute a new person, whereas procession constitutes the Holy Spirit.

Whatever else might be said of it, this portrait of the Holy Spirit does not shut down personal distinctiveness in the Trinity. Even the fact that the Father and the Son are one principle of the Holy Spirit stems from the personal distinctiveness of Father and Son, according to which the Son receives all that the Father is except paternity. Paternity and filiation are not opposed to each other in relation to spiration, and so the only person produced via spiration is the Holy Spirit, who proceeds. The monarchy of the Father remains firm, since the Son spirates precisely as the one begotten by the Father: the unity of one principle is not an impersonal amalgam. The Holy Spirit and the Son are distinguished by different relations of origin because the Son, with the Father, is the principle of the Holy Spirit. The model of the persons as subsisting relations based on order of origin helps to specify the distinctiveness of the persons in relation to each other; it sheds light on the threeness of the one God.

This model also fits with the analogy of the mind, which relies on knowing and loving—the very core of personal relationality. In his *respondeo* of article 2, Aquinas moves directly from his argument that only relations can truly distinguish persons without dividing the divine "substance" to an argument based on the analogy of the mind, rooted in John 1:1 and in the fact that the processions must be conceived as truly *interior* rather than as directed outward. He states that "the Son proceeds by way of the intellect as Word, and the Holy Spirit by way of the will as Love." Here he takes up Augustine's oft-repeated point that only if we know something in some way can we love it. Aquinas states, "Now love must proceed from a word. For we do not love anything unless we apprehend it by a mental conception." To this argument, Aquinas adds a third, based on the "order of nature." He observes that while one craftsman may make many knives without these knives having an order to each other, in things that differ on more than a material basis there is always an order. The Son and the Holy Spirit both proceed from the Father; for there to be a relational order between the Son

---

[18]Thomas Aquinas, *Summa Theologiae* 1, q. 30, a. 2.

and the Holy Spirit, one of them must be the principle of the other. Aquinas considers this argument to be the strongest one for persuading the East, since the Greek fathers also describe some order between the Son and the procession of the Holy Spirit. As Aquinas says, albeit without a full understanding of the theology of the East on this point, "They grant that the Holy Spirit is the Spirit *of the Son*; and that he is from the Father *through the Son*. Some of them are said also to concede that *he is from the Son*; or that he *flows from the Son*, but not that he proceeds."

All three of these arguments in Aquinas's *respondeo* should be seen in light of the scriptural and conciliar testimony that governs the first two objections and their replies. If we reach to the heart of these arguments, we can see that each of them promotes two aspects of the trinitarian mystery: the extraordinary intimacy between the Son and the Holy Spirit, and the personal distinction of the two. This is accomplished by the relational model through showing that the Son and Spirit must be related to each other in a way that distinguishes them. It is accomplished by the analogy from the mind through showing that loving arises from knowing, thus probing the revealed data via the wellsprings of interpersonal relationships. Last, it is accomplished by the "order of nature" through pointing out that when two things (differentiated by more than matter) proceed from the same source, they possess an order to each other. Both the kinship and the distinction of the Son and Spirit are thereby underscored. In each case, it can be seen how closely the argument follows the scriptural teachings, which certainly display, in the economy of salvation, both the inseparable intimacy and the relational differentiation of the Son and Holy Spirit.[19]

---

[19]Siecienski notes that "most biblical scholars today doubt that the New Testament authors even thought in trinitarian terms (i.e., with Father, Son, and Spirit each understood as distinct 'persons' within God). While post-Nicene writers would find the Scriptures littered with texts describing Jesus' divine origin, modern exegetes question whether the New Testament ever explicitly refers to Jesus as 'God' or whether Jesus thought of himself as such. There are many verses that might be references to the persons or activity of the Trinity (Luke 1:35, 3:22, 4:1-14; Matt 1:18-23, 3:16-17, 28:19; Acts 1:1-6, 2:33, 38-39), but one must be careful about imposing later categories upon the biblical witness. Even Paul's frequent allusions to the activity of Father, Son, and Spirit (Eph 4:4-6; Gal 4:4-6; Tit 3:4-6; 1 Cor 12:4-6) do not necessarily prove an explicit understanding of God's triune nature" (*The Filioque*, 17–18). It is clear that the New Testament authors did not teach Nicene-Constantinopolitan doctrine in the manner that the Council of Constantinople taught it, but it still seems to me that their formulations are intelligible, as a whole, only in light of the doctrine taught by the Council of Constantinople.

CONCLUSION

Marcus Plested observes that in modern Orthodox theology, "Aquinas, where he is mentioned at all, is still routinely treated as an archetype of the West against which East must set its face. Only rarely has the idea that he might have something to offer the Orthodox world been seriously entertained."[20] But in Plested's view, "The oppositional theologizing that has dominated Orthodox discourse in the twentieth century is . . . a sign of weakness rather than strength."[21] As Plested rightly emphasizes, a major step toward overcoming this "oppositional theologizing" would be to put to rest the notion that Thomas Aquinas embodies the movement of Latin theology into full-fledged rationalism. Although I am certainly not the first to defend Aquinas's theology of the procession of the Holy Spirit from the charge of rationalism—one thinks here of the notable recent work of Bruce Marshall and Gilles Emery[22]—I hope that the present essay makes a small contribution to the ongoing ecumenical rapprochement regarding the One whom Gregory Palamas calls "the Spirit of the most high Word," who "is like an ineffable love of the Father for this Word ineffably generated."

---

[20]Plested, *Orthodox Readings of Aquinas*, 219.

[21]Ibid., 226.

[22]See for example Bruce D. Marshall, "The Deep Things of God: Trinitarian Pneumatology," in *The Oxford Handbook of the Trinity*, ed. Gilles Emery and Matthew Levering (Oxford: Oxford University Press, 2011), 400–13; Marshall, "The Filioque as Theology and Doctrine," *Kerygma und Dogma* 50 (2004): 271–88; Marshall, "The Defense of the *Filioque* in Classical Lutheran Theology: An Ecumenical Appreciation," *Neue Zeitschrift für systematische Theologie und Religionsphilosophie* 44 (2002): 154–73; Marshall, "Action and Person: Do Palamas and Aquinas Agree About the Spirit?" *St. Vladimir's Theological Quarterly* 39 (1995): 379–408; Gilles Emery, "The Procession of the Holy Spirit *a Filio* According to St. Thomas Aquinas," in *Trinity in Aquinas* (Naples, FL: Sapientia Press, 2006), 209–69; Emery, "Trinity and Truth: The Son as Truth and the Spirit of Truth in St. Thomas Aquinas," trans. Mary Thomas Noble, in Emery, *Trinity, Church, and the Human Person: Thomistic Essays* (Naples, FL: Sapientia Press, 2007), 73–114.

5

Enthusiasts, Rationalists and Pentecost

The Holy Spirit in Eighteenth-Century Methodism

Jeffrey W. Barbeau

Is Christianity, scriptural Christianity, found here? Are we . . . so
"filled with the Holy Ghost" as to enjoy in our hearts, and show
forth in our lives, the genuine fruits of that Spirit?

JOHN WESLEY[1]

The legacy of John and Charles Wesley, those stalwart Methodists of eighteenth-century England, has inspired a wide array of theological and ecclesial traditions. Adam Clark, Richard Watson and William Burton Pope, among others, brought Wesleyan theology into systematic form in the second generation of Methodism. In time, the pneumatological dimension of Wesleyan theology gradually diminished. Richard Watson, for example, was "the most influential theologian within Methodism on both sides of the Atlantic during the second and third quarters of the nineteenth century."[2] Yet Watson's most famous work, his massive and widely used textbook, *Theological Institutes* (1823–1828), relied on a distinctly scholastic and apologetic methodology that muted the doc-

---

[1] John Wesley, Sermon 4, "Scriptural Christianity," 4.3, in *The Works of John Wesley, vol. 1, Sermons I,* ed. Albert C. Outler (Nashville: Abingdon, 1984), 174.
[2] Thomas A. Langford, *Practical Divinity: Theology in the Wesleyan Tradition,* rev. ed. (Nashville: Abingdon, 1998), 50.

trine of the Spirit.[3] Watson devoted only one chapter of his *Theological Institutes* to the Holy Spirit compared to seven on the existence and attributes of God, four on the Trinity, five on Christology and eleven others on sin and redemption.[4] Many other theologies followed not only in England but also in America and around the world. Methodists as diverse as William Arthur, Georgia Harkness, D. T. Niles, John Cobb Jr., James Cone, Mercy Amba Oduyoye and Geoffrey Wainwright all represent different facets of the Wesleyan theological inheritance.

Meanwhile, a separate stream of Wesleyan theology actively developed and spread rapidly through local revivals and missionary endeavors. In the eighteenth century many believed that John Wesley's mantle as leader of the movement would eventually be assumed by the preacher and theologian John Fletcher. Fletcher, who first came under the influence of Charles and John in the early 1750s, developed a doctrine of "baptism in the Spirit," a term that he used to capture John Wesley's proclamation of "entire sanctification." Fletcher's association of the Spirit with sanctification proved so influential that there is strong evidence that John Wesley even adjusted his language (if not his views) to reflect Fletcher's position.[5] While Fletcher's sudden death from epidemic fever in 1785 preempted his anticipated succession among the leaders of English Methodism, Fletcher's theology found new life overseas. His doctrine of baptism in the Spirit inspired American Holiness churches to elevate entire sanctification to a position of cardinal significance in the *ordo salutis*. Phoebe Palmer, more than any other American, became associated with the doctrine, and her mystical and evangelical theological vision still influences many to this day.[6] Fletcher's theology of entire sanctification and baptism in the Spirit also continued to shape churches around the world through the expansion of Pentecostalism. American Pentecostalism, as is well known, originated in the Holiness movement, and some explicitly

---

[3]Robert E. Chiles, *Theological Transition in American Methodism: 1790–1935* (New York: Abingdon, 1965), 49.

[4]Richard Watson, *The Works of Rev. Richard Watson*, vol. 10, *Theological Institutes*, ed. Thomas Jackson (London: John Mason, 1834–1837).

[5]Laurence W. Wood, *The Meaning of Pentecost in Early Methodism: Rediscovering John Fletcher as John Wesley's Vindicator and Designated Successor*, Pietist and Wesleyan Studies 15 (Lanham, MD: Scarecrow, 2002).

[6]On Fletcher's influence on Palmer, see Elaine A. Heath, *Naked Faith: The Mystical Theology of Phoebe Palmer* (Eugene, OR: Pickwick, 2009).

hybrid varieties of Pentecostal Methodism continue to flourish as well, including Latin American denominations such as the *Iglesia Metodista Pentecostal de Chile.*[7] If estimates for the growth of Pentecostal and charismatic
churches continue along current statistical trajectories, one can reasonably
maintain that in the coming years a majority of Christians around the world
will be able to trace at least part of their theological heritage back to the
Wesleys and eighteenth-century Methodism.[8]

    Even in such a simplistic account of the diverse Wesleyan theological
and ecclesial traditions, the challenges of speaking in any meaningful way
of a Wesleyan theology of the Spirit are readily apparent. At least part of
the theological diversity among the Wesleyan family of churches stems
from the earliest sources of Wesleyan and Methodist theological reflection.
Early Methodists were "downright *Bible Christians*—taking their Bible, as
interpreted by the primitive Church and our own, for their whole and sole
rule,"[9] to be sure, but hymnbooks and prayer books, conversion narratives
and deathbed narratives, liturgical guides, catechisms, and accounts of
frontier and field-preaching revivals provided the interpretive resources
for early theological reflection far more than did systematic expositions of
Christian belief. To this day, for all the limitations of denominational bu-
reaucracy, when Methodists want to discuss doctrine and practice in the
churches, their instinctual move is to gather together for holy confer-
encing in prayer, praise and discussion together. In this essay, I argue that
eighteenth-century Methodism emerged out of the tension between the
powerful overflow of emotions stirred up by the work of the Spirit and
efforts to moderate the excesses of perceived enthusiasm with an appeal
to rationality and self-control. In order to demonstrate this I will explore
two historical-theological narratives that illustrate the emerging practical
pneumatology of early Wesleyanism: Charles Wesley's conversion in 1738
and John Wesley's response to the Maxfield-Bell schism of 1762. Out of such

---

[7]Walter J. Hollenweger, foreword to Wood, *Meaning of Pentecost in Early Methodism*, x.
[8]Allan Anderson et al. note that Pentecostalism is "the most rapidly expanding religious movement in the world. Within the past thirty years there has been an estimated 700 percent increase
in the number of Pentecostals and two-thirds of all Protestants" ("Introduction," in *Studying
Global Pentecostalism: Theories and Methods*, ed. Allan Anderson, Michael Bergunder, André
Droogers and Cornelis van der Laan [Berkeley: University of California Press, 2010], 2).
[9]John Wesley, "A Short History of Methodism," in Works, vol. 9, *The Methodist Societies: History,
Nature, and Design*, ed. Rupert E. Davies (Nashville: Abingdon, 1989), 368.

competing narratives—between enthusiasm and rationalism—churches and theologians in the Wesleyan tradition inherited not a coherent theological system, but rather trinitarian (and necessarily pneumatological) narratives that illustrate the boundaries of a Christian way of life after Pentecost.

BEFORE ALDERSGATE

Methodism has a long tradition of celebrating the great "Wesleyan" event at Aldersgate Street. On May 24, 1738, John Wesley experienced a profound renewal of faith that seldom fails to remind Wesleyans of the centrality of divine assurance in the order of salvation. By the year 1738, John Wesley had already established himself as a fellow at Lincoln College, Oxford, where he led one of several small bands of students into deeper practices of spirituality and service. Those so-called Methodists devoted themselves to prayer, fasting and participation in the Lord's Supper as well as works of charity such as visiting the sick and those in prisons. John Wesley's zeal brimmed over. He even risked the dangers of traveling across the ocean to serve as a clergyman for the new colony named Georgia. The arduous journey challenged Wesley's faith far more than any event before: as storms rocked the ship, John Wesley's trust foundered. Ministry in the new settlement at Savannah, too, proved far less glamorous than the young man had imagined. His relationship with a young woman soured, and soon he found himself the victim of his own impetuous decisions: he barred his paramour from the Communion table, and her new husband and family brought an indictment against him. Wesley returned to England a broken man: "I went to America to convert the Indians; but Oh! who shall convert me? Who, what is he that will deliver me from this evil heart of unbelief? I have a fair summer religion."[10]

The backdrop of the eager first rise of Methodism at Oxford and the abortive second rise of Methodism in Georgia makes the legendary third rise of Methodism in London all the more powerful in Methodist lore. Under the influence of Moravian Christians such as Peter Boehler, John Wesley gradually became convinced that he required a deeper experience of faith. As he sat "unwillingly" at a society meeting at Aldersgate Street on May 24, 1738, and listened to a reading of Martin Luther's *Preface to the Epistle to the*

---

[10]John Wesley, January 24, 1738, in *Works*, vol. 18, *Journal and Diaries (1735–1738)*, ed. W. Reginald Ward and Richard P. Heitzenrater (Nashville: Abingdon, 1988), 211.

Romans, John Wesley experienced divine assurance—an experience of grace he had never known before: "About a quarter before nine, while he was describing the change which God works in the heart through faith in Christ, I felt my heart strangely warmed. I felt I did trust in Christ, Christ alone for salvation, and an assurance was given me that He had taken away *my* sins, even *mine,* and saved *me* from the law of sin and death."[11] With these words, John Wesley's Aldersgate experience—a powerful testimony to trust in God—ranks among the seminal moments in the history of Christianity.

Two features stand out that deserve mention. First, John Wesley's Aldersgate experience is intensely individualistic. While reading the Romantic poet and biographer Robert Southey's description of Wesley's experience some eighty years after the event, Samuel Taylor Coleridge noted the prevalent individualism of this and related Methodist stories. "The pervading I, I, I, I," Coleridge explains, "disturbs . . . me."[12] Second, Aldersgate is profoundly christological. The work of Christ permeates the entire scene, so much so that one can hardly imagine the scene in any other way: it is "faith in Christ," "trust in Christ" and "Christ alone" that saves from sin and death. The experience of assurance recalls the rise of the Reformation itself. Wesley's explicit emphasis on Luther's *Preface to the Epistle to the Romans* intimates the doctrine of justification and brings to mind the intense debates over the imputation of Christ's righteousness. Almost by definition, to know God in the Aldersgate experience requires the experience of Christ crucified. How could it be any other way? To have faith in God is to do so by faith in the work of Christ, trust in his sufficiency for our salvation and the knowledge that comes by Christ alone.

Yet fewer in the Wesleyan tradition tell the story of that other great Wesley: Charles. Charles, of course, was John's younger brother, and he has long been underestimated in the history of the movement. A good case can be made, for example, that it was Charles who first gathered the small group at Oxford for prayer, study and service, and that it was Charles who invited John to help guide the group and bring order to these Anglicans seeking spiritual renewal. Charles, it should be noted, traveled to America and served in Georgia too, but he was no better equipped for the task than his

---

[11]John Wesley, May 24, 1738, in *Journals and Diaries I,* 249-50.
[12]Samuel Taylor Coleridge, *The Collected Works of Samuel Taylor Coleridge,* vol. 15, *Marginalia,* ed. H. J. Jackson and George Whalley (Princeton, NJ: Princeton University Press, 2000), 15.5:133.

brother. Before the trip, John had convinced Charles to give up his plan to remain at Oxford, to seek ordination and to take up the missionary journey to the colony. Charles also recognized his need for a deeper experience of God's grace and assurance of salvation. Like his brother John, Charles encountered Moravian pietism, and he hungered for the certainty of forgiveness, the lifting of the burdens of sin and the freedom found in the fullness of divine love.

In fact, days before John Wesley's Aldersgate experience, Charles discovered the very same Christian assurance that each of the brothers had long desired. The event may well be one of the most profound examples of practical pneumatology in early Methodism. Charles's journal entries from May 1738 persuasively and evocatively describe the days leading up to his own "Aldersgate" experience. He writes, above all, of a continual striving after deeper faith: "I could pray for nothing else."[13] In christological language akin to his brother's incipient experience of faith, Charles explores his longing for complete renewal.

> *Saturday, May 6.* God still kept up the little spark of desire, which he himself had enkindled in me, and I seemed determined to speak of, and wish for, nothing but faith in Christ. Yet could not this preserve me from sin, which I this day ran into with my eyes open. So that after ten years' vain struggling, I own and feel it absolutely unconquerable.[14]

Charles continued in this state of openness and seeking, "hungry and thirsty after God" and desirous of the knowledge that "Christ loved me," throughout the month.[15] As with his brother, Charles found solace in Martin Luther. He read from Luther's *Commentary on the Epistle of St. Paul to the Galatians.* His friend William Holland was so overwhelmed by their reading together that Holland breathed "out sighs and groans unutterable."[16] For his part, Charles wondered how he had ever imagined the doctrine of justification by faith was a new doctrine and, henceforth, he "endeavoured to ground as many of our friends as came in this fundamental truth . . . not an idle, dead

---

[13]Charles Wesley, *The Manuscript Journal of the Reverend Charles Wesley, M.A.*, ed. S. T. Kimbrough Jr. and Kenneth G. C. Newport (Nashville: Kingswood, 2008), 1:101.

[14]Ibid., 1:101.

[15]Ibid., 1:102.

[16]Ibid., 1:103.

faith, but a faith which works by love, and is necessarily productive of all good works and all holiness."[17]

Throughout the month, Charles was troubled in mind and body. He describes a struggle with pleurisy, a condition of the lungs and abdomen, that left him weak and often bedridden. Though he tried leeches to bleed out the illness and called for the surgeon to bring him further relief, he found only temporary rest before his pains returned. Charles sought divine grace through the Eucharist, too. On May 19, Charles notes pathetically that he "Received the Sacrament, but not Christ."[18] He even conferred with other believers where he was staying, such as Mrs. Turner, who claimed such assurance of her peace with God that she declared herself willing "to die this moment. For I know all my sins are blotted out."[19]

Finally, on May 21, 1738, Charles experienced the release from sin and assurance of salvation that he so desperately sought. The events of the day cast a new light on the rise of Methodism in London. After waking with great expectation, Charles met with John and a few other friends. Together they sang a "Hymn to the Holy Ghost."

> Come holy Spirit, send down those Beams
> Which gently flow in silent Streams
>   From thy eternal Throne above:
> Come thou enricher of the Poor,
> Thou bounteous source of all our Store,
>   Fill us with Faith and Hope and Love.
>
> Come thou, our Soul's delightful Guest,
> The wearied Pilgrim's sweetest rest,
>   The fainting Sufferer's best relief:
> Come thou, our Passions cool allay:
> Thy Comfort wipes all Tears away,
>   And turns to Peace all Joy and Grief.

---

[17]Ibid., 1:104. A remarkable interest in the inward testimony marks Charles's journal and predates John Wesley's famous record at Aldersgate: "I spent some hours this evening in private with Martin Luther, who was greatly blessed to me, especially his conclusion of the second chapter. I laboured, waited, and prayed to see 'who loved *me*, and gave himself for *me*'" (ibid., 1:104).
[18]Ibid.
[19]Ibid., 1:105.

Lord, wash our sinful Stains away,
Water from Heaven our barren Clay,
  Our Sickness cure, our Bruises heal:
To thy sweet Yoke our stiff Necks bow,
Warm with thy Fire our Hearts of Snow,
  And there enthron'd for ever dwell.

All Glory to the sacred Three
One everlasting Deity,
  All Love and Power and Might and Praise;
As at the first, e'er time begun,
May the same Homage still be done
  When Earth and Heaven itself decays.[20]

Soon after, the assembled friends departed and Charles devoted himself to prayer, recalling the promise that the Comforter would draw near and, by the Spirit, the Father and Son would dwell with God's people. He laid down to rest, when suddenly Charles heard the voice of a woman say, "In the name of Jesus of Nazareth, arise and believe, and thou shalt be healed of all thy infirmities!"[21] Struck to the heart, Charles arose and inquired of Mrs. Turner, who was in the household with him, if she heard the voice of the woman who had spoken. She denied that anyone else was in the home. His heart sank, but he inquired again with "strange palpitation of heart" in hopes that the word was for him. Mrs. Turner finally confessed: "It was I, a weak sinful creature spoke, but the words were Christ's. He commanded me to say them and so constrained me that I could not forbear." Charles, distraught by these events, turned to both Scripture and a friend alike for comfort, until his struggle ceased: "The Spirit of God strove with my own and the evil spirit, till by degrees he chased away the darkness of my unbelief. I found myself convinced—I knew not how, nor when—and immediately fell to intercession."[22]

In several respects, Charles's experience closely corresponds to one of the most famous events in early Christian history: the conversion of Augustine in

---

[20]John Wesley, ed., *Collection of Psalms and Hymns* (Charlestown: Lewis Timothy, 1737), 22–23. Kimbrough and Newport note the hymn was drawn from George Hickes, *Devotions in the Ancient Way of Offices* (1700).
[21]Charles Wesley, *Manuscript Journal*, 1:106.
[22]Ibid., 1:107.

the Garden of Milan.[23] Just as Augustine heard the words of a child, *tolle lege, tolle lege* ("Pick it up, read it; pick it up, read it"), so too Charles heard the voice of the woman as he lay sleeping. In fact, even as Augustine immediately turned to Scripture for signs of the divine promise, so also Charles took up the good book and read words that brought release from the torments of doubt and despair: "The words that first presented were 'And now, Lord, what is my hope? Truly my hope is even in thee' [Ps 39:8, BCP]. . . . I now found myself at peace with God and rejoiced in the hope of loving Christ."[24]

Still, when Charles wrote in his journal of these profound events—events that preceded his brother John's Aldersgate experience by three days—he presented the whole under a single heading in large neat letters:

The Day of Pentecost

In the mind of Charles Wesley, May 21, 1738, was not merely a day of new birth. Rather, by divine providence, the day of his conversion fell on Whitsunday (Pentecost Sunday). The day signified his belief that true renewal in Christ is a necessarily pneumatological event. This explains the fourth stanza of Wesley's noted "Glory to God, and Praise and Love" (also known as "For the Anniversary Day of One's Conversion" or "O For a Thousand Tongues to Sing").

> Then with my heart I first believed,
> Believed with faith divine,
> Power with the Holy Ghost received
> to call the Savior mine.

The day of Charles's so-called conversion was a day of the Spirit. In one unpublished hymn, he describes the promised outpouring of the Spirit as "Your day of Pentecost . . . You shall the Holy Ghost receive."[25] It was also a day of Pentecost-like miracles. Charles was awakened by what he always regarded as nothing less than a divinely guided voice. Even after Mrs. Turner's confession, Charles continued to believe that the voice was identical to that of another woman.[26] Moreover, Charles's journal explains that Turner's act was not a matter of sudden, impulsive witness. Rather, as Charles notes in the

---

[23]The story is found in Augustine, *Confessions* 8.12.
[24]Charles Wesley, *Manuscript Journal*, 1:108.
[25]John R. Tyson, ed., *Charles Wesley: A Reader* (Oxford: Oxford University Press, 1989), 43–44.
[26]Charles explains, "The sound of her voice was entirely changed into that of Mrs. Musgrave (if I can be sure of anything sensible)" (*Manuscript Journal*, 1:108).

same extended journal entry, she believed that Christ himself had com-manded her to speak: "At night, and nearly the moment I was taken ill, she dreamed she heard one knock at the door. She went down and opened it; saw a person in white; caught hold of and asked him who he was; was answered, 'I am Jesus Christ' and cried out with great vehemence, 'Come in, come in!'"[27] The powerful dream left her "wavering and uneasy" for days, but also filled her with an enlarged "love and prayer" for all humanity.

The recovery of Charles's "Aldersgate" experience develops a pneumato-logical element otherwise absent from John's account. In the days after, Charles prayed that his brother would come to a similar knowledge and, at one point, "almost believed the Holy Ghost was coming upon him."[28] Perhaps most significantly, Charles's journal reveals that he expected to be filled with love as a direct result of his Pentecost-conversion experience. At one point, a vision of Christ's "broken, mangled body" left him speechless during the prayer of consecration. "Still," he claimed, "I could not observe the prayer, but only repeat with tears, 'O Love, Love!'"[29]

Tracing Charles's unique experience of assurance in the days preceding John Wesley's more famous Aldersgate conversion reveals a pivotal dimension of the Wesleyan theological heritage. The experience of assurance, so central to the Wesleyan *ordo salutis*,[30] is a fully trinitarian event. While the majority tradition of John Wesley's Aldersgate experience emphasizes the christological di-mension of acceptance by God, the minority tradition of Charles Wesley's "Day of Pentecost" underscores the pneumatological aspect of what the brothers discovered in the third rise of Methodism. While these stories may be dis-missed as isolated experiences of two individual Methodists (albeit the leaders of the movement), the controversy that raged in England around Methodist practices further reveals the vividly pneumatological core of Wesleyan theology.

Reasonable Enthusiasts

I have already mentioned Southey's nineteenth-century critical biography of John Wesley and Coleridge's corresponding marginalia. One other remark is

---

[27]Ibid., 1:107.

[28]Ibid., 1:109.

[29]Ibid., 1:111.

[30]On the Wesleyan *ordo salutis*, see Kenneth J. Collins, *The Scripture Way of Salvation: The Heart of John Wesley's Theology* (Nashville: Abingdon, 1997).

particularly relevant in recovering the theological coordinates of early Methodism. Commenting on the Aldersgate experience, a matter "considered by
[Wesley's] disciples as being of deep importance,"[31] Coleridge believed that
the recurrent doubts that flooded John Wesley's heart after Aldersgate could
easily be explained as signs of the aftermath of psychological coercion. Where
Southey criticized Wesley, stating, "Here was a plain contradiction in terms—
an assurance which had not assured him," Coleridge concludes: "the Life,
Sentiments and Writings of Wesley after this leads me to conclude, that this
Assurance amounted to little more than a strong *pulse* or throb of Sensibility
accompanying a vehement *Volition* of acquiescence—an ardent desire to *find*
the position true and a concurring determination to receive it as truth. That
the change took place in a society of persons all highly excited, aids in con-
firming me in this explanation."[32] Coleridge's statement, while inadequate to
explain Charles Wesley's experience, provides extraordinary insight into the
perception of eighteenth- and nineteenth-century critics. Both during Wesley's lifetime and immediately after, many English opponents of the movement
believed that the events and renewal associated with Methodism resulted not
from a divine work but from the excitability of human emotions. Talk of
throbbing sensibility, the strong pulse of emotions and an energized society
of believers all contributed to the Aldersgate experience. In short, Coleridge
concluded that Wesley and the Methodist movement resulted from little
more than *enthusiasm*.

   Labeling a Methodist an enthusiast was commonplace throughout the
eighteenth and early nineteenth centuries. The use of the insult in the English
language goes back to the early seventeenth century at least, when Samuel
Hieron labeled some early Christian "heretiques called Enthusiasts" who condemned the authority of the written word (1637) (*OED*). Joseph Glanvill's *The
Vanity of Dogmatizing; or, Confidence in Opinions* (1661) similarly disparages
"the Visions, Voyces, Revelations of the Enthusiast" (*OED*). By the eighteenth
century, the term was common enough that some sought to defend alleged
enthusiasts by demonstrating the commonplace nature of what many critics

[31]Robert Southey, *The Life of Wesley and Rise and Progress of Methodism*, new ed. (1820; London:
   Longman, Green, Longman, Roberts, & Green, 1864), 1:100.
[32]Coleridge, *Marginalia*, 15.5:126. On the relationship between romanticism and Methodism, see
   Jasper Cragwall, *Lake Methodism: Polite Literature and Popular Religion in England, 1780–1830*
   (Columbus: Ohio State University Press, 2013).

deemed distortions in Christian religious practice. John Byrom's *Enthusiasm* (1752), for example, attempted to reframe the use of the term.

> Fly from enthusiasm? Yes, fly from air,
> And breathe it more intensely for your care.
> Learn, that whatever phantoms you embrace,
> Your own essential property takes place.[33]

While Byrom could reimagine enthusiasm as in some sense necessary to the nature of all religion, other detractors found Methodist claims disturbing at best.

By 1760, Methodism had become a substantial movement in the Church of England. Many joined the societies and even claimed to have received "Christian perfection." Wesley defended his doctrine of perfect love by the power of the Holy Spirit on the grounds that perfection was no other than the union with God claimed by early Christians. In his *Christian Library*, John included the writings of Macarius and quietly substituted "perfection" for any reference to the doctrine of *theosis*.[34] But where John exercised caution in promoting the doctrine of perfection, not least because he himself never experienced such a remarkable work of the Spirit, others extended the claim to its furthest limits. In 1762, several events brought fresh scrutiny on the Methodist societies and John Wesley himself. In London, the movement had grown at a particularly rapid pace. According to John, "Many, who had hitherto cared for none of these things were deeply convinced of their lost estate. Many found redemption in the blood of Christ; not a few backsliders were healed. And a considerable number of persons believed that God had saved them from *all sin*."[35] Wesley claims that he recognized the potential dangers of the situation and took special measures to "apprize them" of the errors of "pride and enthusiasm." While he remained in the city, the society remained stable and sober-minded, but as soon as he left, "enthusiasm broke in. Two or three began to take their own imaginations for impressions from God, and thence to suppose that they should never die; and these, labouring

---

[33]John Byrom, *Enthusiasm, A Poetical Essay: In a Letter to a Friend in Town* (London: W. Owen, 1752), 19.

[34]Jeffrey W. Barbeau, "John Wesley and the Early Church: History, Antiquity, and the Spirit of God," in *Evangelicals and the Early Church: Recovery, Reform, and Renewal*, ed. George Kalantzis and Andrew Tooley (Eugene, OR: Cascade, 2012), 69.

[35]John Wesley, *A Plain Account of Christian Perfection* §20, in Works, vol. 13, *Doctrinal and Controversial Treatises II*, ed. Paul Wesley Chilcote and Kenneth J. Collins (Nashville: Abingdon, 2013), 179.

to bring others into the same opinion, occasioned much noise and confusion."
Soon after, other members claimed unique spiritual gifts as well: the end of
all sinful temptations, gifts of prophecy and discerning of spirits. Wesley refused to name the individuals publicly, but manuscript letters and journals
reveal that the Methodist enthusiasts were two of Wesley's preachers. Thomas
Maxfield had been especially close to John up until this point, as Henry Rack
explains: "He had indeed given him leave to preach, obtained ordination for
him, used him as an assistant and defended him when in trouble."[36] Maxfield
began to teach that those who had received the gift of Christian perfection
were superior to others in the society. George Bell, a former corporal in the
Life Guards who had converted in 1758, had claimed the gift of healing, began
holding raucous meetings and taught the rejection of the sacraments and the
restored purity of Adam and Eve among the perfected.[37] Wesley avoided a
heavy-handed response. He hardly wished to hinder a work of God. However,
the decisive break in what became known as the Maxfield-Bell schism occurred when Bell prophesied that the world would abruptly come to an end
on February 28, 1762. Wesley, who had previously attempted compromise
and urged moderation, now firmly rejected these teachers "both in public
and private. . . . I warned the society, again and again, and spoke severally to
as many as I could."[38] While John's labors meant that relatively few members
of the society followed Bell and Maxfield in their break with the Methodists,
still the damage was done: "They made abundance of noise, gave huge occasion of offence to those who took care to improve to the uttermost every
occasion against me, and greatly increased both the number and courage of
those who opposed Christian perfection."[39]

The Maxfield-Bell schism created space for opponents of Methodism to
attack the practical outcomes of Wesleyan pneumatology. William Warburton,
bishop of Gloucester, was one such opponent. Throughout much of the eighteenth century, Warburton pursued enemies of the faith with legal exactness
and righteous indignation. In 1762, stirred by controversy in London, Warburton published a scathing rebuke of John Wesley: *The Doctrine of Grace, or,*

---

[36]Henry D. Rack, *Reasonable Enthusiast: John Wesley and the Rise of Methodism* (London: Epworth,
    1992), 338.
[37]Ibid., 338–39.
[38]Ibid., 339; Wesley, *A Plain Account of Christian Perfection* §22.
[39]Wesley, *A Plain Account of Christian Perfection* §22.

The Office and Operations of the Holy Spirit Vindicated from the Insults of Infidelity, and the Abuses of Fanaticism (1762). Warburton believed that enthusiasm stemmed from the misuse of imagination and a tendency toward superstition "raised and inflamed by fanaticism."[40] Modern fanatics, he claimed, completely misunderstand the order of divine government and the economies of different dispensations in the history of Christianity: "FANATICS . . . pretend to as high a degree of divine communications as if no such *Rule of Faith* was in being; or at least, as if that Rule was so obscure as to need the further assistance of the Holy Spirit to explain his own meaning; or so imperfect as to need a new inspiration to supply its wants."[41] Enthusiasm, in Warburton's view, arises when Methodists claim divine assurance, the witness of the Spirit, and the miraculous reception of moral perfection. "They look with admiration on the privileges and powers conferred on those chosen Instruments," Warburton explains. "Their imagination grows heated: they forget the difference between the *present* and the *past* economy of things . . . and they assume the airs, and mimic the Authority of Prophets and Apostles."[42] The work of the Holy Spirit lies at the heart of *The Doctrine of Grace*—Warburton believes that Wesleyan enthusiasm is nothing short of a fundamental misunderstanding of pneumatology. Enthusiasts claim direct access to divine power, to healing and the working of miracles, to speaking with tongues and prophecy, to inspired knowledge and discerning of spirits. All such miraculous claims, however, undermine the infallible authority of Scripture, the unerring rule given by God to the church: "THE MIRACULOUS POWERS OF THE CHURCH WERE TO CEASE ON ITS PERFECT ESTABLISHMENT. . . . . SUPERSTITION and FANATICISM equally laboured under the wound inflicted on them by the hand of the Apostle, when he made this virtual Declaration of the total withdrawing of those *Powers*."[43]

There is little doubt that some aspects of the eighteenth-century Wesleyan revival were outside the norms of life in the Church of England. Field preaching itself was born of necessity because clergy deemed Methodist

---

[40]William Warburton, *The Doctrine of Grace, or, The Office and Operations of the Holy Spirit Vindicated from the Insults of Infidelity, and the Abuses of Fanaticism*, 3rd ed. (London: A. Miller and J. and R. Tonson, 1763), 11–12. Warburton's work attacked Conyers Middleton and George Whitefield along with John Wesley.

[41]Ibid., 82.

[42]Ibid., 82–83.

[43]Ibid., 79.

preaching on the inward witness of the Spirit outside the bounds of established religion. Undoubtedly, too, some aspects of the Wesleyan revival both in England and abroad were highly emotive affairs. Preaching and society meetings were often accompanied by reports of bodily gesticulations and auditory responses to the preaching of the gospel. John Wesley did entertain the notion that Montanus in the early church was unjustly condemned.[44] Against Conyers Middleton, John Wesley also defended the presence of miraculous gifts among early Christians until the time of Constantine, when the love of God had grown cold among erstwhile believers.[45] Yet elsewhere he explicitly distances himself from such controversies.

In his sermon "The Nature of Enthusiasm," first preached in May 1741, John Wesley warns against the errors of enthusiasm even as he challenges those who refuse to wholly yield themselves to the work of God's Spirit. Wesley refers to enthusiasm as "a religious madness arising from some falsely imagined influence or inspiration of God; at least from imputing something to God which ought not to be imputed to him, or expecting something from God which ought not to be expected from him."[46] Some imagine that they have a *grace* of God that they simply do not have. At both ends of the spectrum—both the religious zealot and the self-deceived Christian—one can find those who lack true grace. A second form of enthusiasm is found among those claiming *gifts* of God that they do not have. While Wesley notes that all ministry depends on "the real influence of the Spirit of God," some believe that every spoken word has been dictated by God or that they receive "particular directions" from God in even "the most trifling circumstances of life."[47] Yet the most dangerous form of enthusiasm arises among those who neglect the means of grace whereby God draws all people to a full and holy love of God. In this way, Wesley urges, "expect a daily growth in that pure and holy religion which the world always did, and always will, call enthusiasm; but which to all who are saved from real enthusiasm—from merely nominal Christianity—is the wisdom of God and the power of God . . . a fountain of living water, springing up into everlasting life!"[48]

---

[44]John Wesley, *The Works of John Wesley*, ed. Thomas Jackson, 4th ed. (London: John Mason, 1984), 11:465–66.

[45]On John Wesley and early Christianity, see Barbeau, "John Wesley and the Early Church," 52–76.

[46]Wesley, Sermon 37, "The Nature of Enthusiasm," §12, in *Works*, 2:50.

[47]Ibid., §19–20, in *Works*, 2:53–54.

[48]Ibid., §39, in *Works*, 2:60.

Similarly, in his sermon "Scriptural Christianity" (1744), opening with Acts 4:31 ("And they were all filled with the Holy Ghost"), John Wesley intentionally discourages Methodists from prioritizing the extraordinary gifts of the Spirit above the fruit of the Spirit:

> Whether these gifts of the Holy Ghost were designed to remain in the church throughout all ages, and whether or not they remain in the church throughout all ages, and whether or not they will be restored at the nearer approach of the "restitution of all things," are questions which *it is not needful to decide*. . . . "Were all" even then "prophets?" Were "all workers of miracles? Had all the gifts of healing? Did all speak with tongues?" No, in no wise. Perhaps not one in a thousand. Probably none but the teachers in the church, and only some of them. It was therefore for a more excellent purpose than this that "they were all filled with the Holy Ghost."[49]

Wesley maintains that far more important than the extraordinary gifts are the "*ordinary* fruits, which we are assured will remain throughout all ages."[50] Christianity could not be identified with a special gift ("a set of opinions") or a statement of beliefs ("a system of doctrines"), but must be always be associated with a way of life.[51] Above all, from the earliest days of Christianity, such a life meant love of God and love of neighbor.

The Maxfield-Bell schism of 1762 prompted John Wesley to deny the extraordinary gifts of the Spirit once again. The theological outcome can hardly be described as systematic. He only repeated the occasional claims he had previously made two decades earlier. He warned against enthusiasm, encouraged biblical and rational reflection and distanced himself from those who claimed spiritual knowledge for what amounted to vain imagination. Yet all the while Wesley surely spoke as much to himself as to others.[52]

LIFE IN THE SPIRIT

The recovery of two historical moments—each a narrative that reveals the centrality of the Holy Spirit in early Methodism—helps explain the prolifer-

---

[49]Wesley, Sermon 4, "Scriptural Christianity," §3, in *Works*, 1:160 (emphasis added).
[50]Ibid., in *Works*, 1:161.
[51]Ibid., in *Works*, 1:161.
[52]For example, when Wesley reminds others to avoid mistaking divine providence for a sign of divine favoritism (Wesley, Sermon 37, "The Nature of Enthusiasm," §29, in *Works*, 2:57).

ation of diverse beliefs about the Holy Spirit in the family of Wesleyan churches. While Charles Wesley typically represents a staunch commitment to the Church of England against John Wesley's nimble willingness to break from tradition, the conversion of Charles as well as John's response to the Maxfield-Bell schism embody astonishing pneumatological reversals in the standard narrative of early Methodism. Charles's conversion on Whitsunday, his personal "Day of Pentecost," represents enthusiastic openness to divine intervention and a heightened concern for assurance of salvation. His journal account of the day reveals profound inner anxieties, dream states, prophetic voices and miracles that drew him into a state of peace with God. John's battle against charges of enthusiasm, on the other hand, recall his continual rejection of enthusiasm and insistence that enthusiasm amounts to madness. John preached against individual claims to peculiar works of grace and special gifts of the Spirit in favor of the steady enlivening influence of the Spirit and the cultivation of fruit. Such competing narratives—though each supported by hymns, letters, sermons and journals—bequeathed to the family of Wesleyan churches a pneumatology riddled with tensions and ambiguities.

What might Charles and John tell Christians today? Several prominent themes come to mind. First, they would no doubt remind others that Christianity depends on the *practice* of faith. For the Wesleys, life in the Spirit cannot be subordinated to theological reflection. Indeed, even in the clearest explication of doctrine, the ongoing work of the Holy Spirit ought to be recognized and affirmed by our experiences of God. A truly practical divinity guards against a neglect of the Spirit in theological formulations.[53] Second, pneumatology provides the theological framework for the persistent Wesleyan appeal to *love*.[54] Again and again in the sermons and hymns, the Wesleys taught a gospel of love. Love of God and love of neighbor are the refrain of Wesleyan theology, and the experience of love by the work of the Spirit made such a

---

[53]In this regard, the Wesleys would certainly affirm Timothy Larsen's emphasis on the Spirit's work in the definition of an evangelical: An evangelical is one "who stresses the work of the Holy Spirit in the life of an individual to bring about conversion and an ongoing life of fellowship with God and service to God and others" ("Defining and Locating Evangelicalism," in *The Cambridge Companion to Evangelical Theology*, ed. Timothy Larsen and Daniel J. Treier [Cambridge: Cambridge University Press, 2007], 1).

[54]For one recent example of a Wesleyan theology of the Holy Spirit, see Beth Felker Jones, *God the Spirit: Introducing Pneumatology in Wesleyan and Ecumenical Perspective*, Wesleyan Doctrine Series (Eugene, OR: Cascade, 2014).

theological distinctive possible. Third, the Wesleys would encourage all of us to go on to *perfection*. No doubt John and Charles differed markedly in their beliefs on the nature of entire sanctification, the possibilities of such a work in this life and the momentary or gradual process of being filled with God's love. Yet despite such differences, the two wholeheartedly agreed that the Christian life—life after Pentecost—ought to reflect grace upon grace in the knowledge and love of God and neighbor: "Are we considered as a community . . . so 'filled with the Holy Ghost' as to enjoy in our hearts, and show forth in our lives, the genuine fruits of that Spirit?"[55] Fourth, the Wesleys believed that the Spirit had implications for the entire *community* of faith. Men and women, young and old, rich and poor, educated and uneducated alike were all deemed fitting recipients of the Spirit.[56] John Wesley's love feasts intentionally included space for all to testify with total liberty about the work of God in their lives. John's active admittance of women preachers among the ranks of the Methodists exemplified his belief that the Spirit brings liberty throughout the entire community. When Sara Crosby first reported that she had come "perilously close to preaching," she sought John's guidance. His reply, a break with cultural norms in England, stemmed directly from his belief that the Spirit liberates men and women alike: "I think you have not gone too far. You could not well do less."[57] Finally, the diverse experiences of the Spirit among members of the community continually call believers to gather together in holy *conference*. For the Wesleys, individual experiences of God matter immensely, but individual experience must be scrutinized by the authority of Scripture, the rule of right reason and the traditions and experiences of the wider body of believers from the primitive church to the present. The Wesleys earnestly sought the powerful work of the Spirit in their midst, but they also called others around them to holy conversations that they might be tempered in humility by mutual understanding as they gathered in prayer, praise and openness to wisdom from above.

---

[55]Wesley, Sermon 4, "Scriptural Christianity," §4.3, in *Works*, 1:174.

[56]Such a belief, grounded in pneumatology, also has profound implications for the intersection of disability, theology and church practice (e.g., Amos Yong, *The Bible, Disability, and the Church: A New Vision of the People of God* [Grand Rapids: Eerdmans, 2011]).

[57]Quoted in Jean Miller Schmidt, *Grace Sufficient: A History of Women in American Methodism, 1760–1939* (Nashville: Abingdon, 1999), 29. By the end of the eighteenth century, there were more than forty women preachers among the Methodists (32).

6

Uniting Us to God

Toward a Reformed Pneumatology

Oliver D. Crisp

This essay offers what might be called a dogmatic sketch of a doctrine of the Holy Spirit that draws on the Reformed tradition. It is offered as a step in the direction of a more comprehensive account of the redemptive work of God that I hope to provide in due course. It is also intended to be a modest contribution to a much larger theological discussion conducted by theologians of different Christian theological traditions from which the Reformed (including the author) have as much to learn as they have to contribute. When it comes to Christian dogmatics, and perhaps especially to the subject matter of pneumatology, humility is an important intellectual virtue that theologians ought to cultivate.

PNEUMATOLOGICAL PRELIMINARIES

Usually doctrinal discussion of the Holy Spirit divides the topic into two halves. There is discussion of the person of the Spirit as a member of the Holy Trinity; and an account is also usually given of the work of the Holy Spirit in the economy of creation and salvation. However, this division of pneumatology may also go some way to explaining why it is that the Reformed contribution to this dogma has often been regarded as rather thin. For, on the one hand, discussion of the person of the Holy Spirit properly belongs to the dogma of the Holy Trinity. On the other hand, discussion of the work of the Spirit is parceled out to several different doctrinal loci, including the doctrines of creation, providence and salvation (soteriology), as well as (in my view) an important role in Christology. In fact, if we were to look closely, we could find aspects of the work of the Spirit scattered across almost every topic in Reformed theology. The reason is not hard to find: the Spirit is that person of the Trinity whose work has to do with the execution of various divine functions in the economy of creation and salvation. But he does this without drawing attention to himself, so to speak. He is (as has often been observed) the quiet member of the Trinity, who goes about his work of creation, conservation, salvation and consummation without fanfare and without us sometimes even noticing his presence in the creation or life of the church.

So the first thing to say about a Reformed account of pneumatology is that we should not mistake the absence of an elaborate discussion of the person and work of the Spirit as a distinct theological topic in systematic theology with the absence of a serious theological engagement with pneumatology. This is not a new insight. In his Warfield Lectures on pneumatology in 1964, the Dutch Reformed theologian Hendrikus Berkhof noted that "the Spirit constantly leads our attention away from himself to Jesus Christ. So he hides himself, on the one hand, in Christ; and, on the other hand, he hides himself in his operations in the life of the church and the lives of individuals."[1] We shall see that this is certainly true of Reformed accounts of the work of the Spirit.

A second preliminary comment follows on the heels of the foregoing. Discussion of the person and work of the Spirit involves drawing out issues connected to other doctrines, locating his work within the larger context of other theological topics. So, discussion of the person of the Spirit must be drawn from the broader attempt to give account of the Holy Trinity as part of the doctrine of God. The work of the Spirit must be gleaned from his activity in creation, providence, soteriology and eschatology. The same is not true of, say, the person and work of Christ. Christology is a separate topic in systematic theology, and for good reason. The person of Christ is God the Son, and his work is the redemption of fallen humanity. We encounter the flesh-and-blood Jesus of Nazareth in the ca-

---

[1]Hendrikus Berkhof, *The Doctrine of the Holy Spirit*, The Annie Kinkead Warfield Lectures 1963–1964 (Richmond, VA: John Knox, 1964), 10.

nonical Gospels, and extrapolate from these accounts views about who Jesus is and what he was about. We do not have to look hard to find questions about who Jesus is and what it is that he accomplished; these are matters that lie, as it were, close to the surface of the text. We do have to look harder to find a developed pneumatology, just as we have to look harder to find a doctrine of the Trinity. At least part of the reason for this is that these two dogmas are not as immediately apparent to readers of the New Testament.

THE PERSON OF THE HOLY SPIRIT

Let us turn to consideration of the person of the Spirit. The catholic creeds provide us with the basic dogmatic framework. The Nicene-Constantinopolitan Creed says, "We believe in the Holy Ghost, the Lord and life-giver, Who proceeds from the Father *and the Son*, Who is worshipped and glorified together with the Father and Son, Who spoke through the prophets."[2] As is well known, the *filioque* clause, expressed in the words "who proceeds from the Father and the Son" (*ex patre et filioque procedit*), was added unilaterally to the Nicene symbol by the Western church and was a cause of the Great Schism in A.D. 1054. I do not intend to comment on this, except to say that what is dogmatically non-negotiable here—what the *filioque* was intended to underscore (whether rightly or wrongly)—is the full divinity of the third person of the Trinity. This is reinforced by the Second Council of Constantinople in A.D. 553, whose canons include the following solemn anathema:

> If anyone does not confess that the Father and the Son and the Holy Spirit are one nature or essence, one power or authority, worshipped as a Trinity of the same essence, one deity in three hypostases or persons, let him be anathema. For there is one God and Father, of whom are all things, and one Lord Jesus Christ, through whom are all things, and one Holy Spirit, in whom are all things.[3]

This statement of Nicene trinitarianism is reiterated by the Reformed confessions. Take, for instance, the Heidelberg Catechism (1563):

---

[2]This English translation of the creed (slightly adapted) is from John H. Leith, ed., *Creeds of the Churches: A Reader in Christian Doctrine from the Bible to the Present*, 3rd ed. (Louisville: John Knox, 1982 [1963]), 33.

[3]The text of this first canon can be found in ibid., 46.

Question 53. What do you believe concerning the "Holy Spirit"?

Answer: First, that, with the Father and the Son, he is equally eternal God; second, that God's Spirit is also given to me, preparing me through a true faith to share in Christ and all his benefits, that he comforts me and will abide with me forever.[4]

Similarly, article 11 of the Belgic Confession of 1561 states:

We believe and confess also that the Holy Spirit proceeds eternally from the Father and the Son—neither made, nor created, nor begotten, but only proceeding from the two of them. In regard to order, the Spirit is the third person of the Trinity—of one and the same essence, and majesty, and glory, with the Father and the Son, being true and eternal God, as the Holy Scriptures teach us.[5]

The Second Helvetic Confession (1566) provides a sophisticated account of the Trinity, including an endorsement of the *filioque* in the following terms:

Notwithstanding we believe and teach that the same immense, one and indivisible God is in person inseparably and without confusion distinguished as Father, Son and Holy Spirit so, as the Father has begotten the Son from eternity, the Son is begotten by an ineffable generation, and the Holy Spirit truly proceeds from them both, and the same from eternity and is to be worshipped with both.[6]

Similar words can be found in the second chapter of the Westminster Confession (1646).

In the unity of the Godhead there be three persons of one substance, power, and eternity: God the Father, God the Son, and God the Holy Ghost. The Father is of none, neither begotten nor proceeding; the Son is eternally begotten of the Father; the Holy Ghost eternally proceeding from the Father and the Son.[7]

The upshot of this sampling of symbolic material is clear enough: the Reformed confessions uphold and elaborate on a basically Western, catholic view of the Godhead in which the Holy Spirit is regarded as a constituent member

---

[4]The entire text of the Catechism can be found in *The Constitution of the Presbyterian Church (U.S.A.), Part I: The Book of Confessions* (Louisville: Office of the General Assembly, 2004), chap. 3, 5.016, p. 56.

[5]Translation by the Christian Reformed Church, "The Belgic Confession," 2011, www.crcna.org/sites/default/files/BelgicConfession_2.pdf.

[6]This translation of the text of the Second Helvetic Confession can be found in *Book of Confessions*, chap. 3, 5.016, p. 56.

[7]Ibid., 6.013, p. 124.

of the Godhead, fully divine, personal and proceeding from the Father and the Son. He is the Comforter and the divine agent that unites us to Christ.

For present purposes I have little to add to this dogmatic deposit about the person of the Holy Spirit. This is not because I think this unimportant, but because I think we are not in a position to say a great deal about the divine nature beyond what we find set forth for us in the Catholic creeds and Reformed confessions, as they reflect the teaching of Scripture. God's inner life is hidden from us (Ex 33:18-23; Deut 29:29; 1 Jn 4:12). We do not have access to it because God has revealed very little about himself (that is, about his divine nature) to us. This is true even if we take the incarnation into account, as any adequate Christian theology must (Jn 1:18). So what we can say with confidence about the divine life is rather slim. The psalmist says that

> He parted the heavens and came down;
> dark clouds were under his feet.

What is more,

> He made darkness his covering, his canopy around him—
> the dark rain clouds of the sky.
> Out of the brightness of his presence clouds advanced,
> with hailstones and bolts of lightning. (Ps 18:9, 11-12)

The correlation of God's activity with various meteorological phenomena is obvious. Yet surely there is something here suggestive of what Pseudo-Dionysius the Areopagite called "the brilliant darkness" of God.[8] We cannot penetrate the darkness of God's mysterious presence in order to ascertain the intricacies of his divine life. This is because we stand on the creaturely side of the great chasm that separates God from everything else; without divine revelation we can know little about our Creator, and almost nothing salvific. Nevertheless, God reveals himself to us in Scripture and in the economy of salvation. We can glean from these economic functions something of the life of God, that is, something of the immanent relations that exist among the divine persons. But our grasp of such things is piecemeal, fragmentary, partial and fallible, and is not something into which (as Calvin would put it) we should pry.

---

[8]Pseudo-Dionysius the Areopagite, *The Mystical Theology*, in *Pseudo-Dionysius: The Complete Works*, trans. Colm Luibheid, Classics of Western Spirituality (Mahwah, NJ: Paulist Press, 1987), 135.

A dim analogue: we cannot know the inner workings of the mind of anyone but ourselves. We can glean from what we are able to see of a person, in what they communicate to us of themselves, in their gestures and expressions, something of their inner life. Nevertheless, our understanding of such things is bound to be piecemeal, fragmentary, partial and fallible—even in the case of a person we know well. *Mutatis mutandis*, we have only our fallible and fallen experience, and the testimony of those who committed into words the revelation of Scripture, to guide us in our understanding of the divine nature.

Well, what can we say about the person of the Spirit then? That he is fully divine, being the third person of the Trinity; that he is to be worshiped together with the Father and the Son; that he is the Lord, the Giver of Life, the Comforter, the Paraclete—in short, that he has a special responsibility for the application of salvation to creatures.

Some modern Reformed thinkers have argued that the classical, orthodox dogma of the Holy Spirit is erroneous because he is not a distinct divine person in the Godhead. On this view, the ascription of personhood to the Spirit of God is a later dogmatic development that does not reflect the earliest apostolic witness. Biblical passages cited in support of this include the farewell discourse in the Fourth Gospel.

> And I will ask the Father, and he will give you another advocate to help you and be with you forever—the Spirit of truth. The world cannot accept him, because it neither sees him nor knows him. But you know him, for he lives with you and will be in you. *I will not leave you as orphans; I will come to you. Before long, the world will not see me anymore, but you will see me.* (Jn 14:16-19, emphasis added)

Similar ideas can be found in the theology of St. Paul. In 2 Corinthians 3:17-18 he writes, "Now *the Lord is the Spirit*, and where the Spirit of the Lord is, there is freedom. And we all, who with unveiled faces contemplate the Lord's glory, are being transformed into his image with ever-increasing glory, which comes from *the Lord, who is the Spirit*" (emphasis added). Passages like these are said to imply that Christ becomes the Spirit upon his ascension; or, alternatively, they are evidence that the Spirit is not a distinct divine person at all but merely a mode of the presence of God in the creation. A clear example of this view in modern Reformed theology is the aforementioned Hendrikus

Berkhof, who writes, "Christ and the Spirit are identical . . . the Spirit is Christ in action." He goes on to say, "The Spirit in Scripture is not an autonomous substance, but a predicate to the substance God and to the substance Christ. It describes the fact and the way of functioning of both."[9]

But this is hopeless. For one thing, it involves biblical cherry-picking. The beginning of the Johannine passage just quoted clearly states that God will give the disciples "another advocate" to help and be with them forever, which Christ calls "the Spirit of truth." Only by strangling the text could one make of this "other" a predicate of a divine person. But, second, in making this sort of appeal Berkhof sets himself against his own tradition. He becomes a latter-day disciple of the patristic *pneumatomachoi*, the "fighters against the Spirit," who denied the deity of the third person of the Trinity and subordinated, or even assimilated, the Holy Spirit to Christ. In his later work on the subject, Berkhof goes beyond this, claiming that there is one event in God that pertains to two persons, the divine Father and his human representative, the Son, between whom the Spirit acts as a bond. Yet not as divine person: he is God's action in history, who creates Jesus and is in turn sent by Jesus in order to bring about salvation.[10]

In repudiating the catholic doctrine of the person of the Spirit, Berkhof thinks he is able to appeal to both the New Testament authors and the early patristic witness, against which the later symbolic material is pitted. Traditions may be wrong, of course, but the claim to be a Reformed theologian surely implies a positive and constructive relationship to that theological tradition and its confessions, even if it is not a slavish one. (Reformed theology does pride itself on being Reformed and always reforming itself according to the Word of God, after all.) Yet in this fundamental dogmatic matter at least, Berkhof sets himself against both the Reformed confession-

---

[9]Berkhof, *Doctrine of the Holy Spirit*, 25–26 and 28, respectively.

[10]See Hendrikus Berkhof, *The Christian Faith: An Introduction to the Study of the Faith*, trans. Sierd Woudstra (Grand Rapids: Eerdmans, 1979), 326 and 331. In the latter passage he writes, "The Father is the divine partner, the Son the human representative, the Spirit the bond between them and therefore the bond between the Son and the sons whom he draws to the Father." He goes on to say, "May we then call the Spirit a person? No, if thereby we put him separately beside the person of God. Yes, if we understand that this name expresses the personhood of God in its outward action." As Moltmann observes, this is tantamount to Unitarianism (see Jürgen Moltmann, *The Spirit of Life: A Universal Affirmation*, trans. Margaret Kohl [Minneapolis: Fortress Press, 1993], 13).

alism of his forebears and the catholic faith more generally. For if the Spirit is a predicate of Christ or merely a mode of the presence of God in history and not a divine person at all, one is left without an orthodox doctrine of the Trinity.[11] That is an uncomfortable place in which to practice dogmatic theology. It is also, I think, an untenable position for someone who self-identifies with the Reformed tradition, given its essentially confessional nature. One cannot claim to stand within a particular theological tradition while repudiating fundamental tenets of the tradition.

THE WORK OF THE HOLY SPIRIT

With this in mind, we segue from the person of the Spirit to his work. Here two theological principles will guide us. The first of these is that "the external works of the Trinity are indivisible, the distinction and order of the persons being preserved" (*opera trinitatis ad extra sunt indivisa servato discrimine et ordine personarum*). The second is that "what is first in intention is last in application."[12]

As to the first of these, which we shall call the *Trinitarian Appropriation Principle* (TAP), it safeguards two important theological claims relevant to our discussion of pneumatology. The first is that the external works of God, that is, his works in creation and the economy of salvation, are all works of the Trinity. The twentieth-century Swiss Reformed divine Emil Brunner denies this. He claims that "there are works of the Father, which are most certainly not the works of the Son. For the Scriptures never speak of the 'works of wrath' of Christ, but only of the wrath of God."[13] For this reason, he says, caution should be exercised in using the TAP without what he calls

---

[11]At the beginning of his treatment of pneumatology, Moltmann says that the Holy Spirit "is not a characteristic of God's being. It is a *mode of his presence* in his creation and in human history" (*Spirit of Life*, 11 [emphasis original]). It is unfortunate that he chooses "mode" here, given its associations with less-than-personal views of the members of the Godhead. I take it that by "mode" he does not mean to connote the modality or manner of God's presence (as per Berkhof, whom he criticizes on this point), but rather his way of being as a third divine person. God has three "ways of being," three "modes" (to borrow the phrase used by Rahner and Barth, with which Moltmann is decidedly unhappy!), and these are to be identified with divine persons, not predicates.

[12]This can be found in St. Thomas, e.g., *Summa Theologiae*, 1–2, q. 1, a. 1, reply 1: "*Ad primum ergo dicendum quod finis, etsi sit postremus in executione, est tamen primus in intentione agentis. Et hoc modo habet rationem causae.*" Kathryn Tanner makes good use of the principle in her account of Barth's doctrine of creation (see Tanner, "Creation and Providence," in *The Cambridge Companion to Karl Barth*, ed. John Webster [Cambridge: Cambridge University Press, 2000], 114).

[13]Emil Brunner, Dogmatics, vol. 1, *The Christian Doctrine of God*, trans. Olive Wyon (London: Lutterworth, 1949), 234.

the "Augustinian Clause," namely, the latter part of the principle, which speaks of "the distinction and order of the persons being preserved."

There are divine works that are the preserve of particular divine persons—that much is surely right. The Father creates, the Son redeems, the Spirit regenerates. But if Brunner means to suggest that there are external works of the Trinity that belong to one, and only one, of the divine persons *all things considered*, then that seems to be mistaken. In fact, the TAP can only be construed along the lines he suggests if one misunderstands its import. For the TAP is actually a means by which we can hold on to the indivisibility of the Trinity while also making room, so to speak, for the particular works of the divine persons in the economy of creation and salvation. We can put it like this: all the external works of God are indivisible. All his external works are triune works involving all three divine persons. Yet for the most part these works devolve on a particular member of the Trinity (which is the second theological claim derived from the TAP that is relevant to pneumatology). Thus, for instance, creation is often thought of as the work of the Father. However, Genesis 1:2 has traditionally been thought to connote the Spirit's role in brooding over the deep,[14] and the prologue to the Fourth Gospel tells us that through the Word of God all things were made and that nothing was made without his agency (Jn 1:3). So it transpires that the work of creation is triune, even though it is traditionally thought to be God (the Father) who says in the beginning, "Let there be light!" The same goes for all other divine works in creation, the relevant changes having been made. Even the incarnation, which is the work of the Son, is commanded by the Father, and brought about by the agency of the Spirit in the virginal conception, and in his empowering of Christ in his ministry from his baptism onward.

Applied to pneumatology, we can say this: the Spirit is at work everywhere, at all times, in all places and in particular ways in the action of creation, conservation, redemption and the consummation of all things. He is at work in this way as a member of the Godhead because all the divine persons are at work in this manner, though their particular roles in any given work may differ. What is more, there are works that terminate on the

---

[14]Assuming one translates *rûaḥ* in Gen 1:2 as connoting a divine person, the Spirit, rather than as an impersonal breath or wind.

Spirit in particular, or are associated with him, such as the virginal conception of Christ and the application of redemption to the believer. However, one of the reasons why the universality of the Spirit's work is sometimes overlooked is that the TAP is not taken with sufficient metaphysical seriousness. He is not merely at work in certain divine actions and not others. Necessarily, he is involved in every divine action in creation.

What then of our second principle? Let us call it the *Intention Application Principle* (IAP). It is related to the TAP in the following way. What God ordains must surely come to pass according to his good pleasure and will, as the writer of Ephesians reminds us (Eph 1:5). Nevertheless, there is an order to what God ordains. Even if this is not a temporal ordering, it is a conceptual or logical ordering. I may make a to-do list and put down one thing after another, one thing at a time. We do not suppose God does that. He does not take time to ponder his options—at least, not according to the traditional, confessional Reformed theology that is our focus here. Instead, God eternally ordains all that takes place in the created order, from beginning to end. But what he first intends, what is logically or conceptually first in his ordered list, is what will obtain last in time. Suppose you go on a journey. Your ultimate goal (your final destination) is your first intention. But it is the last thing your action brings about because it can only be reached once the other components of the event have been successfully executed, such as the distance that must be traversed in order to reach the destination.

The IAP makes the claim that God intends his ultimate goal in creation first as well. This ultimate end is variously described depending on the theologian you are reading. However, in common with several Reformed theologians and with a number of theologians in other Christian traditions, I want to suggest that the ultimate end of God in creation is union with his creatures.[15] This is a peculiar work of the Holy Spirit. For it is the Spirit who is particularly responsible for the regeneration of fallen human beings, the union of believers to Christ and the transformation of creation at the end of the age (Rom 8:22-27), all of which are subordinate ends to the ultimate end of union with God. Al-

---

[15]This candidate for the ultimate end of God in creation does not necessarily instrumentalize creatures as, arguably, Jonathan Edwards does in his great work on the subject (*Concerning the End for Which God Created the World* in *The Works of Jonathan Edwards*, vol. 8, *Ethical Writings*, ed. Paul Ramsey [New Haven, CT: Yale University Press, 1989]).

though this IAP is a triune work, as TAP would lead us to expect, it is also a work that has an important, indeed fundamental, pneumatological dimension.

UNION WITH GOD IN CHRIST

It is to this fundamental pneumatological work of uniting creatures to God that I want to turn in the final constructive phase of this paper. In the course of this reasoning, I will offer a brief account of the union in question. There are two things to say about this union by way of preamble. The first is that there is a renewed interest among theologians, including Reformed theologians, in the notion of union with Christ. This is the recovery of a doctrine that had to some extent dropped out of discussion, and which I think is most welcome not least because of its ecumenical implications. What I say here builds on much of this recent work, although my particular account is slightly different from many others, for reasons I shall go into in a moment.[16] The second thing to say about this doctrine is that although it is only one of several important external works of the Trinity traditionally associated with the agency of the Spirit, this is, I think, the fundamental motif by means of which we can explain almost all the other activities particularly associated with him that fall under the topic of the economy of salvation. By this I mean that other aspects of the Spirit's work in the redemption and reconciliation of fallen creatures can be understood as in some way connected to or implied by this more fundamental theological motif. Although I will not be able to fully demonstrate my point in this short essay, I will offer some indication of what I mean by this at the conclusion of my argument. In par-

---

[16]Recent important treatments of union with Christ from Reformed theologians that are germane to my argument here include J. Todd Billings, *Calvin, Participation, and the Gift: The Activity of Believers in Union with Christ*, Changing Paradigms in Historical and Systematic Theology (Oxford: Oxford University Press, 2007); Billings, *Union with Christ: Reframing Theology and Ministry for the Church* (Grand Rapids: Baker Academic, 2011); Julie Canlis, *Calvin's Ladder: A Spiritual Theology of Ascent and Ascension* (Grand Rapids: Eerdmans, 2010); William B. Evans, *Imputation and Impartation: Union with Christ in American Reformed Theology*, Studies in Christian History and Thought (Milton Keynes, UK: Paternoster, 2007); Mark A. Garcia, *Life in Christ: Union with Christ and Twofold Grace in Calvin's Theology*, Studies in Christian History and Thought (Milton Keynes, UK: Paternoster, 2008); Michael S. Horton, *Covenant and Salvation: Union with Christ* (Louisville: Westminster John Knox, 2007); Marcus Peter Johnson, *One with Christ: An Evangelical Theology of Salvation* (Wheaton, IL: Crossway, 2013); Robert Letham, *Union with Christ: In Scripture, History, and Theology* (Phillipsburg, NJ: P & R, 2011); and Carl Mosser, "The Greatest Possible Blessing: Calvin on Deification," *Scottish Journal of Theology* 55, no. 1 (2002): 36–57. The wider literature on the topic is growing apace.

ticular, I will intimate how this notion of union makes sense of one of the practical, liturgical works of the Spirit, namely, his work in the sacraments.[17]

Union with Christ is an important doctrine in much historic Reformed theology. For instance, in his *Institutes of the Christian Religion* Calvin says, "First, we must understand that as long as Christ remains outside of us, and we are separated from him, all that he has suffered and done for the salvation of the human race remains useless and of no value for us." Moreover, "The Holy Spirit is the bond by which Christ effectually unites us to himself." He goes on to say, "By the grace and power of the same Spirit we are made his members"— that is, the members of Christ with whom we are mystically united.[18]

Yet union with Christ is also a very broad doctrine, one that bundles together a number of discrete components, including but not comprising the work of the Spirit. The Scottish Reformed divine John Murray in his classic treatment of the atonement writes:

> Union with Christ is really the central truth of the whole doctrine of salvation not only in its application but also in its once-for-all accomplishment in the finished work of Christ. Indeed the whole process of salvation has its origins in one phase of union with Christ[,] and salvation has in view the realization of other phases of union with Christ.[19]

Although the doctrine bears the name union with *Christ*, it should be tolerably clear that the agent who brings about this union is the third person of the Trinity. Thus, uniting us to Christ is part of the larger trinitarian work

---

[17]Of course this motif of union has implications for other doctrines, e.g., original sin and its transmission. But (1) there is not the space to enter into discussion of this and other wider implications of the doctrine here, and (2) these wider theological implications of the union motif are not necessarily tied up with doctrines that are particularly associated with the agency of the Spirit, so I have chosen not to discuss them here. However, I have given an account of the notion of union with regard to original sin and atonement in my essay "Original Sin and Atonement," in *The Oxford Handbook to Philosophical Theology*, ed. Thomas P. Flint and Michael C. Rea (Oxford: Oxford University Press, 2009), chap. 19. An argument that has interesting parallels can be found in Marcus Johnson, "The Highest Degree of Importance: Union with Christ and Soteriology in Evangelical Calvinism," in *Evangelical Calvinism: Essays Resourcing the Continuing Reformation of the Church*, ed. Myk Habets and Robert Grow, Princeton Theological Monographs Series (Eugene, OR: Pickwick, 2012).

[18]John Calvin, *Institutes of the Christian Religion*, ed. John T. McNeill, trans. Ford Lewis Battles (Philadelphia: Westminster, 1960 [1559]), 3.1.1 and 3.1.3, respectively. William B. Evans's very helpful study, *Imputation and Impartation*, traces the development of the theme of union with Christ in a number of major European and American Reformed theologians and repays careful reading.

[19]John Murray, *Redemption Accomplished and Applied* (Edinburgh: Banner of Truth, 1965), 161.

of union with God that terminates on the Holy Spirit.

Recall that what is first in divine intention is last in application—our second theological principle, the IAP. Suppose that God's first intention is union with his creatures. Not long ago this would have been thought an Orthodox, not a Reformed, doctrine. However, one of the most interesting developments in recent work on soteriology has been the recovery of "Western" forms of *theosis*,[20] including that of the great evangelical theologian Jonathan Edwards. He speaks of our union with God in Christ in the following terms: "If strictness of union to God be viewed as thus infinitely exalted, then the creature must be regarded as infinitely, nearly and closely united to God."[21] What is more:

> If by reason of the strictness of the union of a man and his family, their interest
> may be looked upon as one, how much more one is the interest of Christ and
> his church (whose first union in heaven is unspeakably more perfect and
> exalted, than that of an earthly father and his family), if they be considered
> with regard to their eternal and increasing union! Doubtless it may justly be
> esteemed as so much one that it may be supposed to be aimed at and sought,
> not with a distinct and separate, but an undivided respect.[22]

If the ultimate end of God's work in creation is an "infinitely strict" union with his creatures, as Edwards puts it, then this is a work that is everlasting. For, as he goes on to point out, there will never come a time either in this world or the next at which we can say that we have become completely united to God through Christ. No, this is a work that, like a mathematical asymptote, continues on into eternity. We are to be ever more closely united to God in Christ by the power of the Holy Spirit, yet without ever losing ourselves in God, without ever (as Edwards puts it) being "godded with God."[23] Thus our union

---

[20]For a helpful treatment of the convergence between Reformed and Orthodox accounts of *theosis*, see Michael Horton, *Covenant and Salvation: Union with Christ* (Louisville: Westminster John Knox, 2007), chap. 12.

[21]Edwards, *The End of God in Creation*, 535. Edwards is not the only Reformed theologian who held to a version of *theosis*, but his doctrine is one of the more pronounced versions of it in the Reformed tradition. This is true although he never uses the term *theosis* in his writings (see, e.g., Oliver D. Crisp, *Jonathan Edwards on God and Creation* [New York: Oxford University Press, 2012], chap. 8; Kyle Strobel, "Jonathan Edwards and the Polemics of *Theosis*," *Harvard Theological Review* 105, no. 3 [2012]: 259–79; and Michael McClymond, "Salvation as Divinization: Jonathan Edwards, Gregory Palamas, and the Theological Uses of Neoplatonism," in *Jonathan Edwards: Philosophical Theologian*, ed. Paul Helm and Oliver D. Crisp [Aldershot: Ashgate, 2003], 139–60).

[22]Edwards, *The End of God in Creation*, 535.

[23]Jonathan Edwards, *The Works of Jonathan Edwards, vol. 2, Religious Affections*, ed. Paul Ramsey

with God in Christ that the Spirit brings about is a journey into God that has no end; it is an ever-closer participation in the divine life.[24] The Spirit unites us to God in Christ in "infinite strictness" yet not so that we lose our identity, becoming "part" of God as a drop of water becomes part of the ocean into which it is poured. To use a distinction Edwards does not (but that is consistent with what he does say), in *theosis* we creatures are invited to participate in the divine life but not the divine essence. Union does not imply fusion.

Now, God ordains this world. He ordains a world where human beings fall into sin and Christ is required to bring about human reconciliation with an estranged God. Does God ordain union with himself as the destiny of his creatures logically prior to his decision to create this world? That is, is the work of the Spirit in uniting us to Christ contingent on his decision to create a world where human beings rebel against God and need to be reunited to him by means of the work of Christ? In short, does the Spirit's work depend on the need for an incarnation? My own view is that even if God had created a world where sin never occurred, the unfallen creatures that inhabited it would still need the work of the Spirit to unite them to God. Such a union is not natural to us; it requires a special divine action. The nearest analog in the New Testament is that of marriage. But even when discussing the sexual union of a man and woman as a correlate to the union between Christ and the church, St. Paul has to admit that the comparison is inadequate. The union between us and Christ, brought about by the agency of the Spirit, is deeper and closer than even the most intimate physical union here on earth, though we know not how to express it (Eph 5:25-32). I also think that our union with God would require an incarnation independent of any fall of human beings. Christ, the God-Man, is the image of the invisible God, and the one in whose image we are formed as image-bearers. We image God as we image Christ. And we image Christ as we are conformed to his image by the work of the Holy Spirit uniting us to him.

How then does the Spirit unite believers to Christ? This is where things get

---

(New Haven, CT: Yale University Press, 1959 [1754]), 203.

[24]Marcus Peter Johnson claims that deification has unhelpful connotations of losing oneself in the divine that *theosis* does not (*One with Christ*, 50–51). However, I am not so sure that this is a sustainable distinction. In their helpful work on the topic Stephen Finlan and Vladimir Kharlamov argue that the terms deification, divinization and *theosis* are synonyms and should be treated accordingly (see Stephen Finlan and Vladimir Kharlamov, introduction to *Theosis: Deification in Christian Theology* [Eugene, OR: Pickwick, 2006]).

interesting. Often at this juncture Reformed theologians gesture toward the mystical union between Christ and the believer. This is a real union, perhaps, but not one that we can really fathom—rather like the doctrine of a real but noncorporeal presence of Christ in the Eucharist proposed by Calvin, who frankly admits that he has no notion of exactly how the Spirit unites the believer to Christ in partaking of the elements.[25] The English Puritan John Owen is a good example of a defender of this mystical union with Christ. He writes, "Although they [Christ and his church] are not one in respect of personal unity, they are, however, one—that is, one body in mystical union, yea, one mystical Christ—namely, the surety is the head, those represented by him the members."[26]

However, what if we take the notion of a real union between Christ and the church brought about by the work of the Spirit with full metaphysical seriousness? That is, what if the Spirit really and truly unites us to Christ so that we are, in some carefully circumscribed sense, one entity with him? Other Reformed thinkers have wondered the same thing in the past. Take the Mercersburg divine John Williamson Nevin. At one point in his work *The Mystical Presence*, he writes, "Strange, that any who hold to the Augustinian view of Adam's organic union with his posterity, as the only basis that can properly support the doctrine of original sin, should not feel the necessity of a like organic union with Christ, as the indispensable condition of an interest in his salvation."[27] Perhaps we can sketch an answer to Nevin's suggestive question.

Suppose we think of the church on analogy with an organism—say, a great oak tree. It is a living, growing thing that can be damaged and stunted and that can flourish and develop. The church grows from a seed, namely, Christ. He is that principle without which the church would not exist. The church is an outgrowth of the work of Christ; it is the product of Christ's redemptive

---

[25]"Now, should any one ask me as to the mode, I will not be ashamed to confess that it is too high a mystery either for my mind to comprehend or my words to express; and to speak more plainly, I rather feel than understand it. The truth of God, therefore, in which I can safely rest, I here embrace without controversy. He declares that his flesh is the meat, his blood the drink, of my soul; I give my soul to him to be fed with such food. In his sacred Supper he bids me take, eat, and drink his body and blood under the symbols of bread and wine. I have no doubt that he will truly give and I receive. Only, I reject the absurdities which appear to be unworthy of the heavenly majesty of Christ, and are inconsistent with the reality of his human nature" (Calvin, *Institutes* 4.17.31).

[26]John Owen, *The Works of John Owen, vol. 10, A Dissertation on Divine Justice*, ed. William H. Goold (Edinburgh: Banner of Truth, 1967 [1850–1853]), 598.

[27]John Williamson Nevin, *The Mystical Presence, A Vindication of the Reformed or Calvinistic Doctrine of the Holy Eucharist* (Philadelphia: J. B. Lippincott, 1846), 212.

action. As more are added to the church, so the organism that Christ has founded enlarges. Some parts of the organism may be in better shape than others. And at some points in the life of the organism, it may have suffered setbacks, periods of slow or no growth, even events that led to the withering or removal of certain branches. But it continues to grow nonetheless, under the watchful eye of the gardener. To be a member of this organism or body is to be joined to it, to be a part of it, a constituent. Just as a tree has a lifespan, different phases to that life, different stages of growth and development, so does the church. But unlike the organism, our union with Christ does not mean that the redeemed are numerically identical with Christ.

Again, Edwards comes to our aid. He conceives of the union between Christ and his elect as the union between the parts of a whole.[28] We are parts of Christ rather like the stages in the life of the tree are parts of the one whole lifespan across time from its planting to its withering. As the tree has different physical parts (trunk, branches, leaves and so on), and different phases to its life (shoot, sapling, mature tree), so also we are "parts" of Christ scattered across space and time—one four-dimensional entity with Christ as its head. The Spirit's work on this way of thinking is vital. It is as if the Spirit acts as a kind of adhesive, preparing and enabling the human subject to be joined to the body of Christ. Like the glue that holds together a composite object that is made up of different parts, such as a piece of furniture, or some other artifact, so the Spirit "glues" us to Christ. We become part of his body really and truly—as really and truly as the foam, wood, tacks, fabric and glue form the one composite object that is an armchair.[29] But, of course, the union he brings

---

[28]Here I am thinking of his famous discussion of four-dimensionalism in *The Works of Jonathan Edwards*, vol. 3, *Original Sin*, ed. Clyde A. Holbrook (New Haven, CT: Yale University Press, 1970), 4.3. For a fascinating discussion of this in relation to his doctrine of atonement, see S. Mark Hamilton, "Jonathan Edwards on the Atonement," *International Journal of Systematic Theology* 15, no. 4 (2013): 394–415. For discussion of the metaphysics of Edwards's position, see Oliver D. Crisp, *Jonathan Edwards and the Metaphysics of Sin* (Aldershot: Ashgate, 2005); and Michael C. Rea, "The Metaphysics of Original Sin," in *Persons: Divine and Human*, ed. Peter van Inwagen and Dean Zimmerman (Oxford: Oxford University Press, 2007), 319–56.

[29]Compare to the great Puritan divine William Ames, who writes, "The relationship is so intimate that not only is Christ the church's and the church Christ's, Song of Sol. 2:16, but Christ is *in* the church and the church *in* him, John 15:4; 1 John 3:24. Therefore, the church is *mystically* called Christ, 1 Cor. 12:12, and the Fullness of Christ, Eph. 1:23. The church is metaphorically called the bride and Christ the bridegroom; the church a city and Christ the king; the church a house and Christ the householder; the church the branches and Christ the vine; and finally the church a body and Christ the head. But these comparisons signify not only the union and communion between Christ and the

about is much more than the gluing together of disparate parts into a composite whole. His work is personal, intimate, the real union of one organism
with another, the bringing about of a new whole that is the body of Christ.
We might say that just as the Holy Spirit generates and prepares Christ's
human body at the incarnation, so he generates and prepares Christ's bride,
his ecclesiastical body, which in one sense will be complete at the inaugu-
ration of the eschaton, when God's ultimate end in creation will be accomplished, and creaturely participation in the divine life begins in earnest.

I said I would indicate at the end of my argument how this fundamental
soteriological work of union with God with which the Spirit is particularly
associated has implications for other areas of doctrine that depend on it in
some sense. Let me close the constructive section of this paper by doing that.
A leitmotif in Calvin's theology is the distinction between what is offered and
what is received.[30] The Spirit is offered to us in salvation. By his agency we may
be united to God through Christ. But much depends on whether we receive
that which is offered. Something similar obtains in the eucharistic teaching of
those Reformed theologians who look to Geneva rather than to Zurich for
their sacramental theology. The Spirit unites us to Christ so that in the Lord's
Supper we may be nourished by the real presence of Christ in the bread and
wine. On this way of thinking eucharistic presence is not a corporeal presence.
It is a real, mystical presence nonetheless. Not only does the Spirit act in this
manner in the Eucharist, thereby ensuring that believers commune with
Christ, but also his sacramental action divides those who truly receive that
which is offered in the eucharistic elements from those who do not. In other
words, we understand what goes on in the Eucharist, that central liturgical
Christian mystery, by reference to the more fundamental work of union that
the Spirit brings about, not vice versa. When we understand something of the
Spirit's action in uniting us to God in Christ and when we see its eschatological

---

church but also the relation showing Christ to be the beginning of all honor, life, power, and perfection in the church. *This church is mystically one*, not in a generic sense, but *as a unique species or individual*—for it has no species in the true sense" (*The Marrow of Theology*, trans. John Dykstra Eusden
[Grand Rapids: Baker, 1968], 176–77). I am grateful to Mark Hamilton for this reference.

[30]See, e.g., David Steinmetz, "Calvin and the Natural Knowledge of God," in *Calvin in Context*
(New York: Oxford University Press, 1995), 32. There he writes, "In short, Calvin draws a distinction between what is offered and received that becomes a guiding principle of his thought,
even outside the context of natural theology." In particular, Steinmetz notes the application of
this principle to his eucharistic theology.

import (being the firstfruits, as it were, of that final union of "infinite strictness" with Christ), then the Eucharist makes sense. It is a means by which the believer who is already united to Christ by the Spirit is inwardly nourished in her faith by the same Spirit, in anticipation of the stricter union between believer and Christ that will be obtained at the end of the age. Here too participation in the divine life is what is in view. The Eucharist becomes a sort of foretaste and reminder of the union that awaits us in Christ, a union that is generated, fostered and sustained by the agency of the Holy Spirit.

THE CONTRIBUTION OF REFORMED PNEUMATOLOGY

This completes my constructive pneumatological argument. Some might think that what I have done here only underlines the limitations of a Reformed pneumatology. It only goes to show that the Spirit does no significant work independent of the other two divine persons. Rather than drawing attention to neglected aspects of the person and work of the Spirit, I have only demonstrated how few resources Reformed theology possesses for providing an adequate testimony to his work. After all, no mention has been made of important contemporary matters like the charismata, physical healing, speaking in tongues and other unusual manifestations of his presence in the life of the church.

This is to mistake the nature of my argument. First, I have shown that by adopting two widely accepted theological principles we see that (1) the external work of the Spirit is always in concert with the other members of the Godhead, and that (2) his peculiar work is bound up with God's first intention to be united to his creatures. The charisms of the Spirit (including the so-called charismata, which are not the only charisms known in Scripture or tradition) are, it seems to me, yet another indication of this work of the Spirit. We might say that they are visible indications of his secret work in the hearts of fallen humans, as he reconciles them to God through Christ. But, as Jonathan Edwards has pointed out at length and in detail, these and other extraordinary physical manifestations in liturgical contexts are no reliable indication of a true work of the Spirit of God.[31] That must be sought elsewhere. Indeed, that must be sought in the place we have located them: namely, in the heart, where a person is united by the Spirit to God through Christ.

---

[31]Jonathan Edwards, *Religious Affections*.

7

The Dynamics of Global Pentecostalism

Origins, Motivations and Future

Allan Heaton Anderson

THE GROWTH OF GLOBAL PENTECOSTALISM

At the beginning of an essay like this it is important to define what is meant by "Pentecostalism." There is a plethora of movements accepted by scholars as "Pentecostal," but there is absolutely no theological uniformity among them. There is no single form of Pentecostalism, nor any clear-cut theological criteria by which it can be defined.[1] The various movements can be divided historically into four very broad, often overlapping groups. First, there are the so-called classical Pentecostals with origins at the start of the twentieth century. Second, there are the independent churches from the same era, especially those in Africa, India and China. But in the statistics so frequently quoted the term also includes our third group: "charismatics" in older churches from the 1960s onward, in which Roman Catholic charismatics are as numerous as classical Pentecostals. Fourth, Pentecostalism also includes what is probably the fastest-growing sector: independent megachurches and neocharismatics that emerged in the mid-1970s, often promoting the prosperity gospel; these are the most controversial globally. Some prominent megachurches have been hit by financial and sexual scandals. In this paper, "Pentecostalism" and "Pentecostal" will refer to all these different types. Facts and figures on the growth

---

[1] Allan Anderson, "Varieties, Taxonomies, and Definitions," in *Studying Global Pentecostalism: Theories and Methods*, ed. Allan Anderson, Michael Bergunder, André Droogers and Cornelis van der Laan (Berkeley: University of California Press, 2010), 13–29.

of any global religious movement are notoriously difficult to come by. The most frequently quoted are those of Todd Johnson and his team, who estimate that Pentecostalism has some 631 million adherents in 2014, about a quarter of the world's Christians, a figure predicted to rise to almost 800 million by 2025. This number was placed at only 63 million in 1970.[2] North America made steady progress in the course of the twentieth century, but classical Pentecostalism there, while influential, is not as significant as is sometimes claimed—about 4 percent of the population (compared to 24 percent Catholic, 18 percent mainline Protestant and 11 percent Baptist).[3] Europe is very different. It retains significant remnants of former state churches: Catholic, Orthodox, Protestant and Anglican. Although classical Pentecostals have made modest increases, they remain a very small minority—less than 2 percent of the overall population in all European countries except Portugal, where Pentecostalism has been influenced by the vibrant Brazilian variety. They are more significant as a proportion of the European churchgoing population. Pentecostalism does not do as well where there is a strong national church—unless there is more religious plurality with a significant minority of free churches, as is the case in Romania and Ukraine, where the numbers of classical Pentecostals are greater than in any other European nation.

But it is in Africa, Asia and Latin America that Pentecostalism has grown most remarkably. Taken as a whole, it was the fastest growing section of Christianity in the twentieth century and one of the most remarkable occurrences in church history. Its expansion in recent years is so significant that Harvey Cox reversed his well-rehearsed position on inevitable secularization and wrote of Pentecostalism as a manifestation of the "unanticipated reappearance of primal spirituality in our time."[4] Although American Pentecostal denominations have been aggressive in their missionary and evangelistic efforts, at least two-thirds of Pentecostalism is now in the majority world and less than a quarter of its membership is of European descent. In recent years the greatest increase has been in sub-Saharan Africa, Indonesia,

---

[2]Todd M. Johnson and Peter F. Crossing, "Christianity 2014: Independent Christianity and Slum Dwellers," *International Bulletin of Missionary Research* 38, no. 1 (2014): 29.

[3]Pew Research, Religion and Public Life Project, "Religious Landscape Survey," 2013, http://religions.pewforum.org/affiliations.

[4]Harvey Cox, *Fire from Heaven: The Rise of Pentecostal Spirituality and the Reshaping of Religion in the Twenty-First Century* (London: Cassell, 1996), 83.

the Philippines, South Korea and throughout Latin America. The rapidly growing house-church movement in China is mostly of an autochthonous Pentecostal type, even though it may not recognize itself as "Pentecostal." Enormous buildings holding thousands of worshipers in many parts of the world reflect the emerging Pentecostal middle class. Pentecostals in the majority world, however, are usually and predominantly a grassroots movement appealing especially to the disadvantaged and underprivileged. Many, if not most, of the rapidly growing Christian churches are Pentecostal but operate independently of western Pentecostalism. American-founded classical Pentecostal denominations are rapidly growing in many parts of the world, but the vast majority of their international membership is from Latin America, Africa and Asia. Nevertheless, as Robert Wuthnow reminds us, stating this is not enough unless one gives sufficient attention to global networks and links, particularly those originating in the United States.[5] This essay looks at the origins of global Pentecostalism, its driving motivations and its future. The Global South has indeed seen a remarkable expansion of Pentecostalism in the last century, an expansion that has altered global religious demographics considerably.

ORIGINS AND PROLIFERATION

Pentecostalism was probably the most rapidly expanding religious movement in the twentieth century. But where did it come from? In answering this question, I hold dear the following three historical truths. First, there was much *continuity* with evangelical, Holiness and healing movements that preceded early Pentecostalism in the nineteenth century.[6] It did not suddenly appear from heaven. Even speaking in tongues, one of the most divisive aspects of the early movement, did not suddenly appear at the beginning of the century, and early Pentecostals themselves (then as now) were by no means united in their theology of tongues. Second, there was *no one place of origin*, despite the fairly widespread claims that it all began at Azusa Street in

---

[5]Robert Wuthnow, *Boundless Faith: The Global Outreach of American Churches* (Berkeley: University of California Press, 2009), 38–39.

[6]Anderson, *An Introduction to Pentecostalism*, 2nd ed. (Cambridge: Cambridge University Press, 2014), 19–39; Anderson, *To the Ends of the Earth: Pentecostalism and the Transformation of World Christianity* (New York: Oxford University Press, 2013), 11–43.

downtown Los Angeles in 1906.[7] Contemporary Pentecostalism is the product of a long process of development with precedents going back to a much earlier time. Its history was in continuity with the revivalist movements out of which it emerged. Azusa Street was indeed an important center for the early internationalizing of the movement, but it remains one center among several in North America, some of which preceded it, and there were other significant networks and centers of influence worldwide. Pentecostalism as we know it today has had many beginnings, sometimes connected, but sometimes isolated. Classical Pentecostal denominations were in a process of formation at least until the 1920s, and one might postulate that it has never ceased being in a process of formation. Third, there have been many *waves* of Pentecostalism, and it is as incorrect to speak of three "waves" of Pentecostalism in North America as it is anywhere else in the world. Besides Peter Wagner's threefold typology of classical Pentecostalism, the charismatic movement and the so-called third wave, there were other significant movements in North America that do not easily fit into this schema, such as the Latter Rain movement beginning in the late 1940s and the Jesus People in the late 1960s.

The internationalizing of the charismatic movement from the 1960s onward eroded the isolation of independent Pentecostal churches in the Global South, but these changes had already been brewing for decades. With new nation-states created out of former colonies came resistance to foreign cultural symbols, including Western hegemony in ecclesiastical affairs. Nowhere was this more apparent than in China after 1949, but the entire majority world was affected. China had been Christianity's largest mission field, but it developed its own forms of Christianity without recourse to the outside world. Although we may describe much of this as affected by Pentecostalism, applying this term to Chinese churches indiscriminately is as inappropriate as it is in the cases of independent churches in sub-Saharan Africa. India, with its closer ties to the West, has more claim on the title "Pentecostal" for many of its independent churches, but even this must be qualified. Latin America, with more than a century of independence, had its own momentum, and there Pentecostalism took a different turn, although not unaffected by what was happening in the North. Nevertheless, large denominations

---

[7]Cecil M. Robeck Jr., *The Azusa Street Mission and Revival: The Birth of the Global Pentecostal Movement* (Nashville: Thomas Nelson, 2006).

founded by Latin Americans emerged from the mid-1950s onward, sometimes referred to as the second phase of Pentecostalism in Latin America,
following the first denominations founded largely by foreigners. The Philippines, with its centuries of majority Catholicism, presented a somewhat
similar pattern, and Filipino leaders emerged to form new movements,
making a considerable impact on the religious and political scene.

Independent Pentecostal churches have proliferated worldwide. Those
formed in the first half of the twentieth century and birthed in revival movements were the thin end of the wedge. They expanded rapidly and formed
their own traditions, remaining isolated from mainstream Christianity for
decades. For the most part, classical Pentecostalism distanced itself from them.
In some parts of the world, Western Pentecostal missionaries saw them as a
threat or nuisance at best, or as heretics at worst—especially in the case of
more heterodox movements like the True Jesus Church in China and the Zion
Christian Church in southern Africa. Complex networks of new independent
churches have mushroomed in recent years, making them possibly the largest
grouping within Pentecostalism as a whole. The recent history of Pentecostalism is littered with "revival" movements causing schisms that have become
its defining feature. The rise of the charismatic movement in the Western
world certainly made Pentecostal ideas and practices more acceptable to traditional forms of Christianity. But this might also be seen as one result of the
privatization of religion beginning in the 1960s, when the established churches
no longer had a monopoly on all things sacred. It could be argued that charismatic Christianity provided a panacea for the spiritual deficit in organized
religion and in Western society as a whole. Or as Harvey Cox has put it, in the
1960s people were not only disillusioned with traditional religions but were
also disappointed by "the bright promises of science and progress." Cox remarks that the "kernel of truth" in the "overblown claims" of the "death of God"
theologians was that "the abstract deity of western theologies and philosophical systems had come to the end of its run." For Cox, the dramatic growth
of Pentecostalism seemed to confirm rather than contradict what he had
written about the "death of God" in *The Secular City* three decades earlier, but
it had provided an unanticipated and unwanted solution.[8]

---

[8]Cox, *Fire from Heaven*, xvi, 83, 104.

After the 1980s, the "Pentecostalization" of older churches outside the Western world, especially in Africa and Asia, accelerated as these churches adjusted to the rapid growth of new Pentecostal churches in their midst. They began to adopt their methods, particularly appealing to the young and urbanized. Simultaneously, the new form of Pentecostalism exhibited a fierce independence that eschewed denominations and preferred associations in loose "fellowships." The Pentecostal megachurches operate in cities like Lagos, Rio de Janeiro, Seoul and Singapore, but also in unexpected European places like Kiev (a Ukrainian church with a Nigerian leader), Budapest and Uppsala. Each of these European cases is the largest congregation in its respective country, and the largest congregation in London is predominantly Nigerian. The megachurches form networks of similar churches across the world, and these transnational associations are not only north-south, but also south-south and east-south. In most cases, the transnational churches in the North have been unable to break free from their ethnic minority character.

DRIVING MOTIVATIONS

There are many reasons for the emergence and growth of Pentecostalism in the majority world, and any attempt to enumerate these runs the risk of reductionism, but in what follows I will highlight what I think are four of the most significant motivational factors—factors that often overlap.

1. *Missiological factors.* First, Pentecostalism is an "ends of the earth" form of Christian mission. As I have written elsewhere, Pentecostalism is fundamentally a missionary movement. Early Pentecostals made a theological link between the experience of baptism in the Spirit and mission. Just as Spirit baptism is classical Pentecostalism's central, most distinctive doctrine, so mission is its central, most important activity.[9] Pentecostals' primary purpose is to evangelize and spread their influence worldwide. The constant efforts to expand are underpinned by a firm evangelical belief in the Bible as an independent source of authority—one that resonates with local customs and relates better to a spiritual and holistic worldview—and by theological convictions based on the common experience of the Spirit who empowers believers' mission to the world. The personal conversion of individuals is the

---

[9]Allan H. Anderson, *Spreading Fires: The Missionary Nature of Early Pentecostalism* (Maryknoll, NY: Orbis, 2007), 65.

primary goal of these evangelistic efforts. Pentecostalism's incessant evangelism, offering healing from sickness and deliverance from evil spirits, draws large crowds, and its organized system of following up contacts means that more "unchurched" people are reached with this message and joined to Pentecostal communities. Its cultural flexibility in its experiential and participatory liturgy—offering a place to feel at home, a measure of religious continuity with the past spirit world and (at least to some observers) the appearance of an egalitarian community meeting the "felt needs" of ordinary people—all combine to provide an overarching explanation for the appeal of Pentecostalism and the transformation of Christianity in the majority world. This brings us to the aspect of indigenization that occurs in Pentecostalism, which is probably more accurately a form of contextualization. Pentecostalism, with its flexibility (or "freedom") in the Spirit, has an innate ability to make itself at home in almost any context. To their credit, early Pentecostal missionaries, largely untrained themselves, practiced "indigenous church" principles. They quickly found thousands of local leaders, who took their message much further than they were able to do. This swift transfer to local leadership was unprecedented in the history of Christianity, and many Pentecostal churches became indigenous and "three-self" (self-governing, self-supporting and self-propagating) churches before the older missions had even begun the process. But these churches are also often self-contextualizing. The reason for the very existence of Pentecostals is their belief in the power of the Spirit working in the church. They consider the church primarily a gathering of local believers rather than an institution, and they place great stress on "church planting" in their mission. The downside is that this view has often created rampant individualism, causing a proliferation of new denominations, some of which may be no more than a handful of people. But the more Pentecostals have divided, the more they have multiplied.

2. Theological factors. Credit is given to the Holy Spirit for almost everything that takes place in Pentecostal activities, whether large or small, weird or sensible. An emphasis on receiving a conscious experience of the Spirit is a common characteristic of different kinds of Pentecostalism. The spiritual world of most societies is a personal, interrelated and interdependent universe. The power of the Spirit, a power greater than any other power threatening survival in this world, is good news. Early Pentecostals discovered that the biblical doctrine of the Spirit was not as detached and uninvolved as theologians had often projected it to be, and that the human need for divine involvement was met there. The pervading Spirit portrayed by Pentecostal preachers gave Christianity a new vibrancy and relevance: the experience of divine involvement in human affairs was possible, and this absorbed the whole life, not just the "spiritual" part of it. This often resulted in a release of emotion, a catharsis that had a cleansing effect. Criticisms of a perceived overemphasis on the Spirit and emotionalism in some Pentecostal churches may miss the point. These churches, like many older ones, are limited by their humanness and often need correction, but their innovative Christianity takes seriously the popular religious world with its existential needs. Their ability to adapt to and fulfill people's religious aspirations continues to be their strength: a divine encounter through the Holy Spirit and the involvement or breaking through of the sacred into the mundane in miraculous answers to prayer, including healing from sickness and deliverance from hostile evil forces. Perhaps above all, there is a heady and spontaneous spirituality that refuses to separate "spiritual" from "physical" or "sacred" from "secular"—these are all important factors in Pentecostalism's growth.

Social-scientific observations about the growth and future of religion are often generalizations based on observable phenomena only. But in the growth of Pentecostalism theological factors must be considered. The emphasis on a personal, heartfelt experience of God through the Spirit is offered to all people without preconditions, enabling them to be "powerful" and assertive in societies where they have been marginalized. They are offered solutions to their felt needs in all their varieties. This will continue to draw people in the majority world to Pentecostal churches. When yours is an all-encompassing, omnipotent and personal God who enters into a personal relationship with you as an individual believer, everything becomes a matter for potential prayer. The "born-again" experience, focusing on a radical break with the past, attracts young people disenchanted with the ways of their parents. Harvey Cox writes that our age suffers from an "ecstasy deficit" and that the restoration of the spiritual gifts enables people to become aware of "deeper insights and exultant feelings."[10] There is now

---

[10]Cox, *Fire from Heaven*, 83, 86.

a greater awareness that the work of the Spirit extends beyond personal piety and private experience of charismatic gifts. The Spirit is the Creator Spirit, who renews the earth and is concerned about all of this world's needs. A holistic approach to the role of the Spirit will remove the suspicion that Pentecostalism is a privatized and individualized religion unconcerned with the wider needs of society and those environmental needs of the whole creation.

Over forty years ago Anglican Bishop John V. Taylor wrote:

> I believe the time has arrived when we must take into account all that is positive in the Pentecostal movement if we hope to press further forward along any of the various roads of liturgical renewal, inter-faith dialogue, the indigenization of Christianity, experiments in Christian community and group experience, the ministry of healing, especially towards psychotics and addicts, and new approaches to church union.[11]

To these might be added the relationship between theology and spirituality and the ministry of prayer. All these elements are important in considering the value of charismatic experience for the church today, but (to highlight the first two) renewal in church life has always brought new vigor and vitality that has especially appealed to younger people, and this is usually first expressed in liturgical changes. The charismatic movement spearheaded a return to "Scripture in song" and a new psalmody that has refreshed many older churches. Interfaith dialogue is a more controversial aspect to consider, but because Pentecostals are so often at the forefront of the encounter with other faiths (to be sure, sometimes antagonistically so), it has lessons for the entire Christian community that are learned in real-life contact rather than in academic ivory towers of pluralistic Western theologians and philosophers of religion. Although often unconscious of this fact, Pentecostals have absorbed so much of the religious and cultural context into their Christian faith that they have much in common with other faiths. Amos Yong writes of "discerning the Spirit" in other faiths and calls for a theology of religions from the perspective of pneumatology.[12]

---

[11]John V. Taylor, *The Go-Between God: The Holy Spirit and Christian Mission* (London: SCM, 1972), 201.
[12]Amos Yong, *Discerning the Spirit(s): A Pentecostal/Charismatic Contribution to Christian Theology of Religions* (Sheffield: Sheffield Academic, 2000); Yong, *Beyond the Impasse: Toward a Pneumatological Theology of Religions* (Grand Rapids: Baker Academic, 2003).

3. *Cultural and social factors.* Although historical and political factors undoubtedly played some role in the spread of Pentecostal Christianity, these were probably not as significant as religio-cultural and social factors were. Pentecostalism has succeeded in tapping into ancient religious beliefs with one eye on the changing world of modernity. This combination of the old with the new has enabled it to attract people who relate to both of these worlds. With its offer of the power of the Spirit to all regardless of education, language, race, class or gender, Pentecostalism has been a movement on a mission to subvert convention. Unlike older forms of Christian mission, its methods were not as dependent on Western specialists and trained clergy and the transmission of Western forms of Christian liturgy and leadership. In fact, Pentecostalism in its earliest forms broke down the dichotomy between clergy and laity that was the legacy of older churches. Revival movements challenged Western dominance and created a multitude of new indigenous churches—a type of Christianity in local idiom that was both a cultural protest movement and a movement emphasizing power to overcome an evil spirit world and promoting the miraculous. Pentecostalism addressed allegations of both the foreignness and the irrelevance of Christianity in pluralistic societies. With its emphasis on the priesthood of all true believers, it broke down barriers of race, gender and class, and challenged the exclusive preserves of ordained male, foreign clergy. Included in Pentecostalism's mission, although not always overt or effective, was the liberation of ordinary people from colonial and ecclesiastical hegemony and the liberation of women from male patriarchy. It encouraged free enterprise in a global religious market. Of course, these developments included multiple schisms that, while increasing division, also proliferated local leadership and encouraged religious competition.

What is often not appreciated is the extent to which Pentecostalism takes on distinctive forms in different social contexts. A major reason for the growth of Pentecostalism has been its ability to adapt itself to different cultures and societies. These new, contextualized forms of Christianity are expressed in energetic and energizing worship and liturgies, in music and dance, in prayer with the free use of the emotions and in communities of concerned and committed believers. Pentecostals are becoming more socially aware and active in efforts to relieve poverty and disease. Of all Christian expressions, Pentecostalism has an ability to transpose itself into local cultures and religions effortlessly because of its primary emphases on the experience of the Spirit and the spiritual calling of leaders who do not have to be formally educated in church dogma. In particular, the ministry of healing and the claims of the miraculous have assisted Pentecostalism in its appeal to a world where supernatural events are taken for granted. Sometimes contemporary forms of Pentecostalism have become "popular religion" in that they present only that which the masses want to hear and omit important fundamentals of the Christian message. The reasons for crowds of people flocking to the new churches may have to do with more than the power of the Spirit, although we should not disregard this important factor. The offer of a better and more prosperous life often gives hope to people struggling in poverty and despair. Cox suggests that the rapid spread of Pentecostalism is because of its heady and spontaneous spirituality, "like the spread of a salubrious contagion."[13] The emphasis on experience touched people emotionally and was spread through testimony and personal contact. But there is more than "spirituality" to Pentecostalism; there are real, this-worldly concerns that it seeks to address, and these concerns have had at least as much impact as the otherworldly ones. In some forms of Pentecostalism, oracular prophecy fulfills many pastoral and therapeutic functions. Pentecostals believe in the primary function of spoken prophecy as being for "edification, and exhortation, and comfort," as an older English rendering of 1 Corinthians 14:3 (KJV) puts it. In some parts of the world this threefold function goes a step further and "prophets" become counselors, pastors and healers at the same time, treating human needs in ways consistent with the integrated beliefs of those who consult them.

4. *Transnational and globalizing factors.* Pentecostalism has a transnational orientation based on personal enterprise, the ubiquitous voluntarism of its membership and the constant multiplication of multicentered, variegated organizations whose driving ambition is to expand. Pentecostalism developed its own characteristics and identities in different parts of the world without losing its transnational connections. Besides its local context, it also exhibits a transnational metaculture. The widespread use of mass media, the setting up of new networks that often incorporate the word "international" in their titles, the frequency of conferences with international

---

[13]Cox, *Fire from Heaven*, 61, 71.

speakers that reinforce transnationalism and the growth of churches that provide total environments for members—these are all features of a multi-dimensional Pentecostalism that promotes a global metaculture constantly. The subject of globalization has attracted widespread and multidisciplinary attention. The opening up of what was formerly a closed world after the fall of the Iron Curtain and the post-1980 reforms in China rapidly accelerated the globalization process and the expansion of transnational movements like Pentecostalism. Robert Wuthnow's book on the globalization of American Christianity considers that this results from international communication, partnerships with foreign congregations, the considerable financial resources of American churches, the growth and influence of megachurches and the "saturation effect" by which American churches seek opportunities elsewhere.[14]

Globalization has affected the spread of Pentecostalism immensely. The phenomenon of globalization is usually seen as a radical departure from the modernizing paradigm and it is assumed that through globalization, the developing world will eventually resemble the developed Western world. In contrast, however, globalization implies fragmentation and disjuncture, diversity and multiple identities, a tension between the "global" and the "local." Pentecostalism provides a splendid example of a globalized religion, in particular the megachurches that have proliferated in many parts of the world with their common practices, use of mass media and patterns of activity. Birgit Meyer writes of Pentecostalism as "a distinctly global religion, with its own imaginary of the world as a whole that transcends more limited, local worldviews and promises to involve believers in a global born-again community."[15] Simon Coleman's study of a church in Sweden demonstrates this globalization by reference to three characteristic dimensions of Pentecostalism: (1) the use of the mass-communications media to disseminate its ideas; (2) a social organization that promotes internationalism through global travel and networking, conferences, and megachurches that function like international corporations; and (3) a "global orientation" or global charismatic "metaculture" that transcends locality and denominational loyalty and displays striking similarities in dif-

---

[14]Wuthnow, *Boundless Faith*, 3–6.
[15]Birgit Meyer, "Globalisation," in Anderson et al., *Studying Global Pentecostalism*, 121.

ferent parts of the world.[16] Contemporary Pentecostalism is very much the result of the process of globalization, and "health and wealth" advocates are as much at home in Lagos and Rio as they are in Tulsa or Fort Worth. In many cases, the only ones who get rich in poverty-ravaged countries are the prosperity preachers. The mass media (beginning with the use of periodicals and newsletters), followed by a ready acceptance of new technologies (first radio and then television and the Internet), tourism and pilgrimages to megachurches, ubiquitous voluntarism and an international economy combined to create conditions conducive to the spread of a globally friendly religion like Pentecostalism. This manifests itself in many different ways. Some of the networks formed have begun to take on the appearance of new denominations. Some passed to a second generation of leadership whose organizational ideas were quite different from those of their founders. Some of the new churches leave much to be desired, especially those with wealthy leaders whose questionable and exploitative practices continue to be exposed in public media. Globalization is a significant factor in analyzing Pentecostal expansion.

FUTURE PROSPECTS

Pentecostalism has continued to expand worldwide in many different forms. It is neither wise nor possible to predict its future, but a sense of where Pentecostalism has been in the past century will give an inkling of where it might go in the present one. It is no accident that the southward shift in Christianity's center of gravity over the twentieth century has coincided with the emergence and expansion of Pentecostalism. The number of Christians worldwide doubled in forty years: from 1.1 billion in 1970 to 2.2 billion in 2010.[17] In Africa, it was estimated that Christians exceeded Muslims for the first time in 1985, and African Christians are now the majority—a phenomenon so epoch-making that Lamin Sanneh describes it as "a continental shift of historic proportions."[18] There are now well over four times as many Christians in Africa as there were in 1970, and almost the same is true of

---

[16]Simon Coleman, *The Globalisation of Charismatic Christianity: Spreading the Gospel of Prosperity* (Cambridge: Cambridge University Press, 2000), 66–69.

[17]Todd M. Johnson, David B. Barrett and Peter F. Crossing, "Christianity 2010: A View from the New Atlas of Global Christianity," *International Bulletin of Missionary Research* 34, no. 1 (2010): 36.

[18]Lamin Sanneh, *Disciples of All Nations: Pillars of World Christianity* (Oxford: Oxford University Press, 2008), 274–75.

Asia. The Christian population of Latin America over this period has almost doubled. Of course, some of this has to do with differentials in population growth; but it remains true that much of the global growth of Christianity has occurred through conversion in the Global South, where the influence of Pentecostalism is strongest.

In contrast, the Christian population of Europe during the same period has increased only by about a quarter, and that of North America by about a third. The decrease in the percentage of world Christianity in the Global North is likely to continue. But even if statistics are wildly speculative, the fact that Pentecostalism had only a handful of adherents at the beginning of the twentieth century makes its obvious and incontrovertible growth an astounding development. Although in some developed countries like South Korea and among white North Americans, this growth has reversed, there is no sign that the rate worldwide has slowed down. In regions like sub-Saharan Africa, China, Latin America and India it may still be increasing. But even where it is decreasing, many Pentecostals have not left the faith altogether, but have simply transferred to other Christian groups. A 2006 Pew Forum report (admittedly focused on urban populations) estimated that classical Pentecostals formed 20 percent of the population in Guatemala, 15 percent in Brazil (the largest population of Pentecostals in any country) and 9 percent in Chile. Impressive also are the figures in the African countries of Kenya (33 percent), Nigeria (18 percent) and South Africa (10 percent). With charismatics and independent churches added in, the figures increase considerably, and what they term "Renewalists" approximate half the national populations in Guatemala (60 percent), Brazil (49 percent), Kenya (56 percent) and the Philippines (44 percent). In these countries Pentecostalism in all its various forms is not only a significant proportion of Christianity but also a sizeable chunk of the entire population, with enormous social influence and increasing political clout. Its adherents are often on the cutting edge of the encounter with people of other faiths, albeit often confrontationally so. These confrontations play out in places like Nigeria and India, where other religions form majorities, and this conflict, which has already claimed many lives, is in danger of escalating. Because of its tendency to proselytize, Pentecostalism also finds itself in conflict with other Christians in their traditional strongholds, such as with Orthodoxy in

Eastern Europe, Roman Catholicism in Latin America and the Philippines, and the (Coptic) Orthodox in Ethiopia and Eritrea.[19]

How has the growth of Pentecostalism affected theories of secularization? Émile Durkheim shared Max Weber's "disenchantment" view that modern society is one in which traditional forms of religion are in terminal decline. Weber saw modernity in terms of the rise of secular, rationalized and bureaucratic social systems. Durkheim described it as an age in which the influence of the old gods of traditional religion was being replaced by new, more scientific ways of understanding the world. Weber and Durkheim's firm belief in the secularization of society proved deeply influential, not only on later sociological theory, but also for subsequent generations of scholars and public thinkers who assumed that religion was an increasingly marginal force in modern social life. Because far fewer people in Western countries identify with traditional religious beliefs and institutions (particularly with the European state churches), issues of the appropriate role and influence of religion in public life have moved from being unthinkingly assumed to a matter of considerable contention. But at the same time, Weber and Durkheim failed to perceive the extent to which modern societies would function as part of a globalized system of markets, media and migration. The secular ethos of Western Europe they described in their work is now increasingly challenged by flows of people, money and ideas from other, more religiously vitalized parts of the world, and nowhere is this more apparent than in Pentecostalism, where many traditional religious ideas and values are embraced. The influence of traditional religion thus persists more than either of them could have imagined. Proponents of inevitable secularization have to reckon with the fact that the future of global Christianity is affected by this seismic change in its character. David Martin makes the point that secularization is a process that is neither inevitable nor undisputed and is subject to differentiation within different social spheres. This social differentiation, where religious and other cultural monopolies are broken, is determined by historical contexts and actually promotes religious competition and plurality in certain societies while favoring secularization in others. Martin considers that the

---

[19]Pew Research, Religion and Public Life Project, "Spirit and Power: A 10-Country Survey of Pentecostals," October 5, 2006, http://pewforum.org/Christian/Evangelical-Protestant-Churches/Spirit-and-Power.aspx.

grand metanarrative of secularization might be "an ideological and philosophical imposition *on* history rather than an inference *from* history."[20] The growth of Pentecostalism in Latin America is an example of the effects of social differentiation, where the dominant Catholic Church is no longer seen as the binding glue of society, especially among the poorer classes. Its monopoly was broken, and Latin American societies consequently became more pluralistic. The same is true among Buddhists in Korea and China, Hinduism among India's oppressed classes and tribals, and Orthodoxy in Ukraine. As one consequence, Pentecostalism has thrived in these contexts.

Some of its flamboyant representatives have been guilty of the grossest forms of corruption and exploitation, and some of its ambassadors jet around the world with their message of success and prosperity for all who will believe and support their organizations. But this seamy side is not a new phenomenon in the history of Christianity as a whole. Despite their many faults, Pentecostals are among the most enterprising entrepreneurs of the religious world, creatively adapting to changing contexts and making use of the most recent electronic media and advertising techniques. There seems to be no stopping the relentless advance of Pentecostalism, in contrast to some other contemporary expressions of Christianity. Anyone wishing to measure the religious temperature of our world must take a hard look at Pentecostalism. The future of Christianity itself and the encounter between Christianity and other faiths is deeply affected by it. Pentecostals may sometimes offer a pie-in-the-sky-when-we-die Christianity, but this is only one side of their message. There are real dangers, however, in the promises of instant healing, wholeness and prosperity for all. The preoccupation with these earthly concerns often comes at the expense of Christian virtues like humility, patience and peace. The freedom of the Spirit recognized by all Pentecostals renders them vulnerable to authoritarian leaders who may exploit their members and cause further division. The jet-setting, lavish and sometimes morally lax lifestyles of some of Pentecostalism's most notorious representatives, and the wiles of those religious charlatans who present themselves as specialists with miraculous powers, claim fake healings, and

---

[20]David Martin, *On Secularization: Towards a Revised General Theory* (Aldershot: Ashgate, 2005), 19, 58–59; Philip Jenkins, *New Faces of Christianity: Believing the Bible in the Global South* (New York: Oxford University Press, 2006), 187–89.

prey on the weaknesses of unsuspecting and credulous followers betrays the ethos of Christ and his most effective first-century disciples.

It would be premature to suggest, as some have done, that these movements have run their course and that we are now in a "postcharismatic" stage of Christian history. There are still many vital, flourishing renewal movements all over the world, including renewal within classical Pentecostal churches themselves. There are many reasons for the increasing disillusionment with the charismatic movement, among which might be the televangelist scandals in the United States, the appropriation of the term *charismatic* by prosperity preachers and the rise of "charismatic" independent churches with highly questionable practices that seem to be accountable to no one. But there is no escaping the fact that Pentecostalism and its various phenomena are now well and truly at home within the mainstream churches of the Catholic and Protestant world. As a result, there is significant potential for ecumenical cooperation.

If Pentecostalism is still the fastest-growing religious movement of our time, then what about its long-term future? Here, it is risky making predictions. Social scientists generally claim that when any religious movement leaves the "charismatic" phase and becomes institutionalized, its rate of growth slows markedly. Some have suggested that Pentecostalism has now entered this phase and will eventually be overcome by modernity and secularization. But other recent studies show that the opposite is the case. If the annual figures of 631 million "Pentecostals/charismatics/neocharismatics" in the world in 2014 are a reasonable estimate, projected to reach 796 million—about 29 percent of the world's Christians—by 2025,[21] then there are no signs yet that the growth of Pentecostalism is abating. Time will tell, but there can be no doubt that this has been one of the most significant expressions of Christianity in the past century, flexible and resilient enough to adapt to and be at home with both modernity and its elusive successor, postmodernity. In countries where its most remarkable growth has occurred, there are signs that as Pentecostalism has become more of a preferred option for the middle class than for the poor, so the numbers of new members have declined. South Korea is one example of this, as Pentecostal

---

[21]Johnson and Crossing, "Christianity 2014," 29.

decline began in the 1990s, together with that of other Protestant churches, aided by divisions and scandals. But Pentecostalism's ecclesiology is such that there is always the possibility of renewal and transformation under the working of the Spirit. Their theological emphases render most Pentecostals "conservative," as do their confessions of biblical literalism. But despite the similarities, this does not amount to a form of fundamentalism because Pentecostalism emphasizes the intuitive and emotional through the revelations and freedom of the Spirit rather than following a slavish biblical literalism. There is potential within Pentecostalism for ecumenical cooperation and social transformation. The experience of the Spirit can become the unifying factor that transcends petty differences and brings people together.

Within a century of its commencement, charismatic forms of Christianity existed in most countries and affected all forms of Christianity in our contemporary world—however we regard or manipulate the statistics on affiliation. As the subtitle of Cox's *Fire from Heaven* declares, religion itself in the twenty-first century has been "reshaped" through the "rise of Pentecostal spirituality." Whatever our opinion or personal experience of Pentecostalism might be, it is a movement of such magnitude that Christianity itself has been irrevocably changed. The mushrooming growth of Pentecostal and charismatic churches and the "Pentecostalization" of older, both Protestant and Catholic, churches—especially in the majority world—is a fact of our time. With all its warts and wounds, this composite movement continues to expand and increase across the globe. The enormous growth of charismatic Christianity in Asia, Africa and Latin America also means that it may continue to expand and influence all types of Christianity there. In creative ways Pentecostalism has promoted a globalized Christianity that has not lost touch with its local context. As Simon Coleman observes, ideas originating in the United States have been "subject to constant forms of cultural appropriation, repackaging, and redissemination into the transnational realm."[22] This preserves both global and local characteristics, making it possible to speak at the same time of "Pentecostalism" and "Pentecostalisms." So, at least for the foreseeable future, the continued vitality of charismatic Christianity is probably assured.

---

[22]Coleman, *Globalisation of Charismatic Christianity*, 36.

8

The Spirit of God

Christian Renewal in
African American Pentecostalism

Estrelda Y. Alexander

In late 1906, Charles Fox Parham—the white Holiness Bible teacher who formalized the doctrine that the "initial" biblical evidence of Holy Spirit baptism is glossolalia, or speaking in an unknown tongue—visited the revival led by his former student William Seymour. On entering the hall, he was disturbed to see what he referred to as "crude negroisms."[1] The exuberant worship of black and white believers embracing each other, fervidly singing and dancing together and laying hands on each other to pray for salvation, healing and Holy Spirit baptism, reminded him of primitive "heathen" rituals. Parham left that revival declaring what he saw as a work of Satan rather than a movement of God.

With the invitation to Parham, Seymour had expected his mentor to "come and see what the Lord is doing." He anticipated that Parham would be thrilled that God was marvelously using his former student in unfolding a vision of a body of believers fully embracing Parham's understanding of Holy Spirit baptism and that he would put his approval on the revival. Seymour sensed that the revival's validation of Parham's formulation would allow his mentor to assert that it was a fulfillment of God's promise to "pour out [his] Spirit on all people" (Acts 2:17).

Instead, Parham considered the unrestrained "Africanisms" displayed by "frenzied" whites, blacks and Latinos as scandalous, and he proclaimed, on

---

[1]Charles F. Parham, "New Year's Greetings," *The Apostolic Faith* (January 1912): 6.

leaving the revival, that "a full two-thirds of those who claimed to have been baptized in the Spirit . . . were . . . subject to nothing more than animal spiritism."[2] He called the famous "heavenly choir"—the singing in tongues about which many who visited the revival raved—"Negro chanting," declaring it had nothing to do with "the Pentecostal baptism."[3] His challenge was echoed by other detractors who were concerned about what they considered the "primitive" nature of the worship led by a one-eyed, "disheveled" son of Africa. For many outside the tradition, the mental portrait suggested by these depictions has come to negatively characterize the Pentecostal movement, particularly among African Americans. Yet, for more than a century, similar scenes have been repeated and celebrated, not only in small and large African American Pentecostal congregations, but also throughout the global Pentecostal community.

For many outsiders Pentecostals, particularly African American Pentecostals, have been considered as largely "disinherited," marginalized individuals who resort to religious fervor to mask social dislocation and lack of access to political and economic privilege. Such assessments place Pentecostal adherents in the "otherworldly" category of those who pay little attention to the social realities surrounding them in this world, routinely using worship as a means of escape into a better one. These assessments have led to a situation in which the broader Christian tradition has often denied, denigrated (as primitive or entirely pagan) or dismissed such worship, as if African American spirituality is unimportant and has little to contribute to the broader Christian tradition (especially since it was seen as lacking a codified theological framework). Since Pentecostalism generally, and African American Pentecostalism in particular, are largely oral traditions, there is no systematic tome laying out its theological self-understanding. And while immediate engagement of the Holy Spirit is a central theme of Pentecostal spirituality, there have been few attempts by African American Pentecostals to develop any theological explanation of what this engagement has meant.

Instead, these understandings may best be discerned through the lens of phenomenology—interrogation of the self-conscious awareness of what the practicing African American Pentecostal community is doing in their understanding of and engagement with the Holy Spirit. This approach affirms the

---

[2]Ibid.
[3]Ibid.

claim that how we act, and what we do within the faith community (in personal relationships and engagement with the world around us) reflects our belief system—our theology. As Christians, everything we do reflects our understanding of ourselves and our relationship with God. Using the lens of phenomenology, we recognize that African American Pentecostal theology is a lived theology, and therefore African American Pentecostal pneumatology is a lived pneumatology. Beginning our investigation here provides rich soil from which to unearth the contribution of African American Pentecostalism to the growing dialogue regarding the Holy Spirit in the contemporary Christian community.

ASSESSING AFRICAN AMERICAN PENTECOSTALISM

For the last quarter century, Pentecostal-Charismatic Christianity has been the fastest-growing segment of the African American church. Moreover, black Christians have been integrally involved in every aspect of the Pentecostal movement from its founding at the early twentieth-century Azusa Street Revival, through the launching of arguably the largest Pentecostal denominational in the world (the Church of God in Christ [COGIC]), to the dynamic global spread of the movement at the end of the twentieth century. The influence of African American Pentecostals has helped to shape every aspect of the ongoing evolution of Pentecostal styles of worship, preaching, music and engagement with social issues relevant to the various communities in which they live. Yet, again, until recent decades little attention has been given to their important contributions to an understanding of the person and work of the Holy Spirit.

Appreciating the breadth of black Pentecostal pneumatology—the understanding, of the work and role of the Holy Spirit in the African American Pentecostal community—requires a variety of angles from which to reflect for several reasons. For within the multifaceted reality that has historically come to be known as African American Pentecostalism are really *Pentecostalisms* involving distinctive yet integrally related expressions of Pentecostal spirituality. Indeed, what is perhaps most distinctive about African American Pentecostalism is its various modes of expression. These expressions can be found within storefront edifices on major boulevards and side streets of metropolitan areas, expansive megachurches of suburban communities and moderate structures in rural enclaves that stretch across the country. The character of worship within these structures ranges from forms that include high-church liturgical elements such as a trained clergy, Hammond organs, robed choirs, printed orders of worship and precision processionals to seemingly primal forms that depend heavily on spontaneity and individual charismatic gifting and show minimal or no appreciation for common liturgical aesthetics.

These congregations are no longer solely relegated to the poor and dispossessed, though they have a higher representation among these groups than among more advantaged communities. Unlike the first generation, however, later generations of African American Pentecostals represent the full range of socioeconomic and educational attainment. Their leaders range from high-school-educated pastors who, convinced of their call, assert that they need nothing more than the Scripture and the anointing of the Holy Spirit, to male or female graduates of some of the most prestigious seminaries in the country. Yet what these individuals and groups commonly share is an understanding that the Holy Spirit is personally accessible to the individual believer and that that brings a measure of empowerment and heightened spirituality as well as an openness to the Spirit's expressed presence and manifestation in the community's life and worship. However, while it may be easier to lump African American Pentecostals into a generic subculture within the broader movement, such a classification would be an oversimplification.

INFLUENCES ON AFRICAN AMERICAN PENTECOSTAL SPIRITUALITY

African traditional spirituality. The unfortunate characterization of early black Pentecostals as primitive by Parham and other detractors should not obscure the importance of one of the major roots feeding the worship of black Pentecostals: their African heritage and the experience of oppression through the American slave system. The men and women who came to the New World in bonds did not entirely fit the usual definition of "heathen"— people totally uncivilized, un-Christian or irreligious. Rather, their spiritual heritage incorporated facets that would resonate with Christian faith. Moreover, particular elements of that earlier spirituality are significant influences in African American Pentecostals' understanding of the person and work of the Holy Spirit and the outworking of that understanding in their lives and worship. Universal belief in a Supreme Being, a profound sense of the pervasive reality of the spirit world, creative use of rhythm, singing and dance in celebration of life and worship, the blurring of the line between the sacred and profane, practical use of religion in every aspect of life, the orality of African culture and the surrender of excessive individualism for community solidarity all play a role in the development of the theology and practice of the tradition as it relates to the Holy Spirit.[4]

Influences of traditional African religiosity figured prominently within the religious expression of newly freed persons and informed their very being. With the rise of Pentecostalism some forty years after emancipation, this spirituality remained embedded in the souls and psyches of persons whose recent ancestors had been slaves. The stamp of this spirituality is found throughout the African American Pentecostal tradition and, through it, the entirety of American Pentecostalism. Of course, iterations of this spirituality have been reframed and reinterpreted to fit each new context. Yet, beneath the surface, common elements are recognizable.

The most relevant element of African spirituality that resonates with both Christian slaves and African American Pentecostals was the universality of belief in a Supreme Being—the Great Spirit or Holy God. This God was not one among many or chief among equals, but rather the eternal creator of every other being, including lesser gods created to do God's bidding, other spirits, the universe, humanity and every animate being or inanimate object that exists. As in the Judeo-Christian tradition, this transcendent creator deity is believed to be the sustainer and controller of the universe. This God—just like the Christian God—is conceived as omnipotent, omnipresent, omniscient, sovereign and due singular reverence.

But this God is not the only spirited being. African spirituality incorporates a profound sense of the pervasive reality of the spirit world through openness to possession by the plethora of spirits that permeate created reality. Iain MacRobert contends that spirit possession in West African primal folk religion to some extent paralleled the experience of possession in Pentecostalism and made the experience a familiar one.[5] Such openness within Pentecostalism, however, becomes openness to possession by the Holy Spirit, who brings divine presence and power into the concrete realities of everyday life. The saints see themselves as having been delivered from former pre-

---

[4]See, e.g., John S. Mbiti, *African Religions and Philosophy* (Oxford: Heinemann, 1990).
[5]Iain MacRobert, *The Black Roots and White Racism of Early Pentecostalism in the USA* (Eugene, OR: Wipf & Stock, 2003), 90.

occupation with the variety of spiritual entities that inhabit and wreak havoc with the cosmos and make the individual fit for the divine. Indeed, they see themselves as having been delivered from a variety of possessions—or spirits, including fear, timidity, poverty and infirmity—or recurring illnesses. They also see themselves as delivered from a variety of "besetting sins," which are thought to include sexual immorality of various sorts, drunkenness, substance abuse and marital infidelity. All these are seen as emanating from spirits that hold the human spirit/psyche captive. Deliverance can only come by totally yielding oneself to another spirit: the Holy Spirit.

This radical openness to the Holy Spirit in all of life blurs the distinction between sacred and profane and promotes the practical use of religion in every aspect of life, as well. For the African American Pentecostal believer, worship occurs more often than on Sunday morning in the sanctuary, at a Wednesday night Bible study or in a Friday night prayer meeting. Indeed, worship—acknowledging and engaging the presence of the Holy Spirit—is an integral part of Pentecostal living. The most mundane situations become ripe territory for the Holy Spirit's intervention. Language that might seem like taking the Lord's name in vain actually expresses a complete dependency on God for one's very existence. The invoking of the name of the Lord, of Jesus or of the Holy Ghost is more than just a verbal gesture or a slip of the tongue. It is a confession that God's very presence and strength is required to get one through the struggle of the moment, from one day to the next day, or through the next hour or the next minute. Sometimes loudly, sometimes almost imperceptibly, the name Jesus is invoked to bring aid and comfort in a circumstance that appears hostile to one's very existence. A whispered or shouted prayer occurs spontaneously, and singing and holy dancing may break out as often at home as in the church.

Creative use of rhythm, singing and dance in celebration of life has always been an integral part of African culture. In Africa music was used to celebrate everything, but perhaps its highest use was in the worship of the Creator. The high regard for music was pervasively evident in the chants, spirituals and ring shout of the slaves. Many of those blacks at Azusa Street were born during or just after slavery. While the revival occurred in Los Angeles, many had migrated from Southern communities where they were part of, witnessed or were told of this musical heritage.

Music is a corporate endeavor; everyone in the community participates in some way. In its rawest, most spirited form, there are no professional musicians, no hymnals and no overhead screens. Songs are metered out one line at a time, similar to slave chants, and formal instruments with "trained" musicians on the organ, piano, guitar or drums are accompanied by informal instruments—washboard, improvised rattle or percussion sticks. Yet the most prized instrument is the human body: clapping time to the beat, stomping out the meter or swaying in time with the tempo.

Everyone dances: young and old, men and women, new convert and seasoned believer, high class and lowbrow, leader and congregant. Sometimes individually, sometimes collectively. Most often to the beat of an uptempo selection or the sound of a specific chord, but sometimes when there is no music at all. The dance may be a short, intense interlude or a protracted segment.

The holy dance is distinctive from all other dancing. The uninitiated who visits an African Pentecostal worship service may be moved by the emotion of the moment to attempt offerings of artistic or impromptu gesturing. The true believer can discern when the individual is dancing "in the Spirit," that is, under the Spirit's influence or in direct response to some spiritual prompting. The true believer can also discern when the dance is "in the flesh"—to show off one's own prowess and agility. More importantly, one can discern if another spirit or force prompts the display. As Charles Harrison Mason, founder of the Church of God in Christ, contended, "People may . . . dance with the wrong purpose or object in view."[6] Further, he was insistent that

> The people of God do not dance as the world dances, but . . . by the Spirit of God. So you can see it is all in the Spirit of God and to the glory of God. It is not to satisfy the lust of the flesh, or the carnal appetite, as the world's dance, but only to glorify God and satisfy the soul. The world dances of the world, about the world and to the world. The children of God dance of God, for God and to the praise and glory of his name. They have the joy of the Spirit of the Lord in them. They are joyful in their King—the Christ. . . . How sweet it is to dance in him and about him, for he that dances in the Spirit of the Lord expresses joy and victory.[7]

---

[6]Charles Harrison Mason, "Is It Right for the Saints of God to Dance?" in *History and Formative Years of the Church of God in Christ with Excerpts from the Life and Works of Its Founder—Bishop C. H. Mason*, ed. James Oglethorpe Patterson, German R. Ross and Julia Mason (Memphis: Church of God in Christ, 1969); and Estrelda Y. Alexander, ed., *Black Fire Reader: A Documentary Resource on African-American Pentecostalism* (Eugene, OR: Wipf & Stock, 2013), 9.
[7]Mason, "Is It Right for the Saints of God to Dance?" 9–10.

MacRobert sums up the importance of dance and other forms of musical performance in African American Pentecostal worship and clearly links these to their African predecessors: "The black Pentecostal, like the African, used music and rhythm as a means of attuning himself to the Spirit—as a vehicle for the power of God. Thus possessed by the Spirit, the Pentecostal sang and danced in celebration of life in the same way as his parents and grandparents had done during slavery, and in ways his ancestors would have recognized in Africa."[8]

Among the saints, the orality of African spirituality becomes "call and response" through the preached sermon, the prophetic word and the narrative of individual testimony. Because the Spirit speaks to the congregation, they speak back to the Spirit and to each other. Throughout the worship service, congregants converse with the preacher and one another by encouraging, admonishing and bringing comfort. To listen in silence and not respond with a hearty "amen," "hallelujah" or "thank you, Jesus," or to clap acknowledgment of a particularly good point at the appropriate moment is problematic. It indicates to discerning saints that one is a stranger and is possibly a candidate for either conversion or Holy Spirit baptism.

The communal nature of African traditional spirituality is displayed in African American Pentecostalism through such elements as collectively invoking the Spirit through song, through dance, through prophetic pronouncement to the gathered community and through response to the preached word. Further, discernment of the Spirit's presence is almost always communal discernment. Nowhere, however, is the communal nature of African American Pentecostalism more evident than in the enterprise of prayer within the congregation. Whether in the small urban storefront where, literally, "two or three are gathered in [God's] name" (Mt 18:20) or in a suburban megachurch, prayer is a corporate endeavor. No one prays alone in the African American Pentecostal context. Corporate prayers are never prescribed, and most often there is no single leader. Prayers are not spoken in unison but are (what seems to an outsider) a cacophony of voices, each calling out to God on behalf of themselves and of the other. When a single leader offers an invocation, pastoral prayer or benediction, these are peppered with the amens, hallelujahs or affirming groans of the saints and are often accompanied by singing or instrumental music.

---

[8]MacRobert, *The Black Roots and White Racism of Early Pentecostalism*, 91.

Though instigated by the pastor or preacher, the almost indispensable altar call is also a group endeavor. Several persons gather to lay hands on the individual; a single person strategically lays hands on another and leads out in supplication. Yet those who gather also pray silently or orally in English or in tongues. Someone takes the rear guard to "catch" individuals when the Spirit falls on and "slays" them, causing them to collapse prostrate. Those who remain seated are directed to join in interceding for such individuals, and many voices are heard invoking the assistance of the Spirit on their behalf.

Each of these elements—universal belief in God, the sense of the reality of the spirit world, the blurring of the sacred and profane, the practical use of religion in life, the use of rhythm in life and worship, orality and communal solidarity—may be, singly, found in other expressions of African American religion or of white Pentecostalism. Their collective presence in African American Pentecostalism, however, strongly ties that spirituality and mode of engaging the Spirit to its African roots. That tie makes this context different in degree, if not in kind, from white Pentecostal expressions and other African American traditions. At the same time these collective elements inform broader Pentecostalism through a common root in the Azusa Street Revival and have found their way into the worship of other contemporary African American Christian traditions in ways that sometimes make their worship hardly distinguishable from that of their Pentecostal brothers and sisters.

Wesleyan Holiness roots. The nineteenth-century Holiness movement swept through North America, bringing with it a renewed emphasis on personal and social holiness, an appreciation for the sanctifying work of the Holy Spirit in the life of the believer, a fervent camp-meeting revivalism and a measure of racial and gender egalitarianism that countered prevailing social mores. The movement attracted large numbers of African Americans for several reasons. The revivalist fervor of worship services resonated more closely with African spirituality than the staid worship of the slave-owning community. Radical egalitarianism, coupled with a strong abolitionist bent, resonated with their desire to achieve the physical liberation and freedom that the gospel represented. The message of the sanctifying work of the Holy Spirit offered freedom from spiritual bondage and an intimate personal relationship with the Creator: God loved them and was concerned with both their physical and spiritual well being.

The significant number of blacks who were drawn into the Holiness movement were exposed to a Wesleyan understanding of three distinctive works of grace in the salvation experience: regeneration, sanctification and Holy Spirit baptism. Like all evangelical believers, it is understood that regeneration brings the person into a living relationship with God and gives a measure of the Holy Spirit. Yet for the Holiness believer regeneration does not constitute the full measure of the Holy Spirit available to the individual. In short suit, a second impartation of grace follows regeneration through the experience of sanctification.

Sanctification is not a feat the individual accomplishes. Rather, it is a process accomplished in the believer by the Holy Spirit as the sole initiator. The believer simply cooperates through the disciplines of prayer, fasting and aligning one's thoughts and actions with spiritual and ethical principles of Scripture. It is not, then, that the believer has accomplished some significant spiritual feat or has reached a state of sinless perfection by their own merit. Rather, by virtue of the sanctification that has been accomplished by the Spirit one is designated a "saint." This sanctification is understood to be followed by the next work of grace, in which the believer is filled with the Spirit or has the Spirit poured out into one's heart. Within the Holiness tradition, this Holy Spirit baptism endows the believer with power to maintain the spiritual piety that sanctification made possible.

More than the measure of the Holy Spirit that all believers are understood to receive at regeneration, for Pentecostals the biblical question, "Did you receive the Holy Spirit when you believed?" (Acts 19:2), is to be answered by opening oneself up to the full measure of the Holy Spirit received through Holy Spirit baptism. Pentecostals contend that only the fully empowered believer can operate in the full measure of power that the Spirit makes available. It is understood that through the fullness of the Spirit, believers are enabled to accomplish those "greater [supernatural] works": to minister divine healing, to exorcise (or cast out) demons from individuals, to minister deliverance to those who are oppressed by evil spirits and to have supernatural faith to believe for other divine interventions.

Pentecostal believers insist that this full measure of power allows the individual to live a life that is aligned with the biblical mandate for holiness, for it is only through the fullness of the Spirit that he or she can sustain the holy lifestyle brought about through sanctification. It is not that the believer is no longer tempted to sin. Rather, through the fullness of the Spirit brought about by Holy Spirit baptism, he or she is supernaturally empowered to more forcefully resist and have victory over such temptation. Holiness believers hold that this Spirit baptism has an undeniable inner witness that expresses itself in deep peace and euphoric joy and is evident outwardly in love of one's fellow person and a strong bent toward social justice. Classical Pentecostal spirituality added an additional evidence of Holy Spirit baptism: the initial physical sign of speaking in tongues.

A further carryover from the Holiness tradition is the strong personal and social ethical dimension. The Pentecostal believer does not seek after Holy Spirit baptism simply for the sake of an experience or as an indication of spiritual superiority over other Christians. The expectation is that the impartation of the Holy Spirit in one's life will bring about an ethical change. Indeed, one will be able to "live right" because, according to the saints, "you can't live right without the [the baptism of the] Holy Ghost." They insist this baptism brings the supernatural ability to resist sin. An individual on whom the Holy Spirit has been poured out is expected to live and act in a way that is perceivably different. As the lyrics of the popular chorus suggest, "I looked at my hands, my hands looked new; I looked at my feet and they did too." In other words, there is expected to be a change in one's character and behavior.

MODES OF HOLY SPIRIT BAPTISM

In most African American Pentecostal churches, Holy Spirit baptism is not divorced from regeneration but is part of a continuum in the process of salvation. Once saved, the individual will seek and receive the baptism of the Holy Spirit, which generally will be accompanied with the initial evidence of speaking in tongues. It is this contention that separates classical Pentecostalism from its Holiness, charismatic and neo-Pentecostal siblings. While many within those traditions may experience the phenomenon, it is usually not considered an essential element in the salvation process.

Tarrying for the Holy Ghost. In a scene from James Baldwin's early novel *Go Tell It on the Mountain*, John, a young Pentecostal believer and the son of a pastor of a storefront congregation, is vividly depicted as participating in "praying through" to the baptism of the Holy Ghost.[9] In this scene, we are introduced to the ritual of tarrying, a prayer form that is a significant, central element of African American Pentecostal spirituality. David Daniels, the noted African American Pentecostal historian, highlights the significant role that tarrying has played in the spirituality of the Church of God in Christ. He contends that for COGIC, as with many other African American Pentecostal bodies, "tarrying was [a] key symbol or root metaphor, undergirding the . . . experience of conversion, sanctification, and baptism in the Holy Spirit."[10] Daniels underscores the communal nature of the ritual, in which seekers are surrounded by initiates exhorting them to yield to the Holy Spirit—to let go and "let God have God's way in them."[11] Simultaneously, seekers are instructed to persevere, to "hold on" and pray through. In both instances emphasis is on the necessity of denying one's own spiritual agency, submitting to the agency of the Holy Spirit and emptying oneself of all other spiritual influences, including those that have come down through a heritage of African spirituality.

Tarrying has its own language, which provides an illustration of the orality of African American Pentecostal spirituality. No one tarries in silence (though individual supplication is understood as a legitimate means of accessing Holy Spirit baptism). Key words or phrases such as "Yes, Lord" and "Thank you, Jesus," "Hallelujah" or "Glory," are repeated, each time in more rapid succession, and are understood to lead to a profound God-encounter that brings about that fuller measure of the Spirit.

The tarrying ritual also allows a significant role for women (most often the "mothers"). Older, seasoned women often lead this event and are essential in discerning whether the Spirit that gives utterance is the Spirit of God, some useless, feigned babble or another spiritual force. For despite what might appear to the eyes of the uninitiated as a cacophony of disjointed, unintelligible jabber, tarrying expressly opens the seeker to indwelling by the living God. It is neither an attempt to induce a self-provoked trance or to invoke possession by any of a plethora of lesser spirits.

Mothers discern when God's presence is most evident and admonish the

---

[9]James Baldwin, *Go Tell It on the Mountain* (New York: Knopf, 1953).

[10]David D. Daniels III, "'Live So Can Use Me Anytime, Lord, Anywhere' [sic]: Theological Education in the Church of God in Christ, 1970 to 1997," *Asian Journal of Pentecostal Studies* 3, no. 2 (2000): 299.

[11]Ibid.

congregation to reach out through praise to encounter God more fully. The ecstatic worship of the moment is highly charged with spiritual intensity. Daniels posits that through the experience of tarrying, "God offered the seeker salvation, deliverance, purging, cleansing, [and] the baptism [of the Holy Spirit]. Through a dramatic experience with God, the seeker's life is transformed."[12] The physical, immediately observable evidence of that impartation is ecstatic experiences ranging "from dreams and visions to overwhelming sensations to glossolalia."[13]

The tarrying ritual might occur as a segment at the beginning or end of a regular worship service. Or, more commonly, a separate tarrying service might precede or follow regular worship. For early classical Pentecostals, tarrying became a unifying experience. Before the charismatic movement introduced new forms of accessing the Spirit, nearly all in early generations could testify to having tarried at some time.[14] This remembrance differentiated Pentecostals from other evangelicals, who emphasized accepting Christ, or confessional Protestants, who emphasized baptism as a means of grace.[15]

Varieties of Spirit baptism. The ritual of tarrying does not stand apart from a central theme of Pentecostal spirituality: the experience of Holy Spirit baptism with initial evidence of speaking in tongues. While seekers may tarry for a number of reasons, including a deeper sanctification or deliverance from besetting sins, most often the goal is this signal experience. Yet the varied definitions, modes, qualities and views on the necessity of the experience of having spoken in tongues are examples of the diversity within African American Pentecostal self-understanding. Bodies first differ regarding whether Holy Spirit baptism is an essential element of salvation or a voluntary grace poured out on willing believers. They also differ on whether glossolalia is the essential initial evidence of Holy Spirit baptism or simply one of several spiritual evidences that the Spirit might bestow. Developing an understanding of the place of the Holy Spirit within African American Pentecostalism requires giving some attention to this variety.

Without insisting that Holy Spirit baptism or speaking in tongues is essential for salvation, the Church of God in Christ, the largest predominantly

---

[12]Ibid., 300.
[13]Ibid.
[14]Ibid.
[15]Ibid.

African American Pentecostal body, emphasizes the spiritual benefit of the experience for the believer, declaring that "the Baptism of the Holy Ghost is an experience subsequent to conversion and sanctification and . . . tongue-speaking is the consequence of [that] baptism . . . with the manifestations of the fruit of the [S]pirit."[16] The COGIC opposes the essentialism of Holy Spirit baptism, noting that "we are not baptized with the Holy Ghost in order to be saved." Yet the COGIC is as adamant as many classical Pentecostal bodies regarding tongues, insisting that when a believer is baptized in the Holy Spirit, "one will speak with a tongue unknown to oneself according to the sovereign will of Christ." More importantly, the COGIC contends that the experience is essential for effective ministry: "Since the charismatic demonstrations were necessary to help the early church to be successful in implementing the command of Christ," it is "mandatory for all men today."[17]

By comparison, the Fire Baptized Holiness Church of America (FBH) labels Holy Spirit baptism "the Pentecostal baptism of the Holy Ghost and Fire."[18] They insist that Spirit baptism is received by a "definite act of appropriating faith on the part of the wholly sanctified believer."[19] Further, as with the COGIC, the FBH asserts definitively that "the initial evidence of . . . this experience is speaking with other tongues as the Spirit gives utterance."[20]

The United Holy Church of America (UHCA), and the Mount Calvary Holy Churches of America (MCHCA), which descended directly from the UHCA, make no such assertion about either the necessity of Holy Spirit baptism or of speaking in tongues. Instead, the UHCA has never adopted Pentecostal language regarding Holy Spirit baptism or initial evidence, insisting instead that there are different valid understandings of the experience. Further, the faith statement of the MCHCA simply says that the Holy Spirit is "ever present and active in the church; convicting . . . and regenerating those who believe in Jesus Christ; dwelling in, sanctifying and comforting believers . . . and guiding them into all truths as in Christ Jesus."[21]

---

[16]The Church of God in Christ, "What We Believe," 2014, www.cogic.org/our-foundation/what-we-believe/.

[17]Ibid.

[18]Patrick L. Frazier Jr., *Introducing the Fire Baptized Holiness Church of God of the Americas: A Study Manual* (Wilmington, NC: Greater Eastern North Carolina District, 1990), 22.

[19]Ibid.

[20]Ibid., 81.

[21]See United Holy Church of America, Mount Calvary Holy Church of America, "What we Be-

Among Oneness Pentecostal church bodies, there is a similar variety of understanding. Along with the typical insistence of Oneness bodies that "water baptism (by immersion) in the Name of the Lord Jesus Christ for the remission of sins is an essential element of salvation, the Pentecostal Assemblies of the World (PAW), the multi-racial parent of all oneness bodies asserts that baptism of the Holy Ghost with speaking in other tongues as the Spirit gives utterance . . . [is also essential to what] constitutes the new birth."[22] The Church of Our Lord Jesus Christ of the Apostolic Faith (COOLJC), one of several bodies descended from PAW, is even more insistent that "rebirth by the Holy Spirit is absolutely essential today," even "as it was in the days of the Apostles."[23] The Church of Our Lord Jesus Christ, a splinter group from COOLJC, goes further. It adds to other Oneness essentials that "if you have not been baptized in water in Jesus Christ's name and filled with the Holy Ghost speaking with other tongues as the spirit gives you utterance . . . you are not saved; you do not have the New Birth Jesus spoke of. Therefore, you will not enter into the kingdom of God."[24]

Still, while many denominations or even congregations vary in following an essentialist paradigm, historically it has been expected that every member of a Pentecostal community will seek Holy Spirit baptism. Within those communities that maintain that there is no full salvation without this subsequent spiritual baptism, full participation and assumption of any leadership position is conditional on having had this experience. It is understood that only the Spirit-filled believer has the fullness of Pentecostal spirituality and that Holy Spirit baptism is the initiation rite into that spirituality.

THE SPIRIT IN THE LIFE OF THE COMMUNITY

The discernible presence of the Holy Spirit is expected, invoked and welcomed in all facets of the Pentecostal believer's life and the congregation's corporate worship. The Spirit is invoked through tarrying and welcomed

---

lieve," www.mchca.org/believe (accessed January 4, 2014).

[22]For more information, see "Creed, Discipline, and Doctrine," *Minute Book of the Pentecostal Assemblies of the World* (Indianapolis: Pentecostal Assemblies of the World, 1972); and the Pentecostal Assemblies of the World website, www.pawinc.org; cf. Alexander, *Black Fire Reader*, 286–87.

[23]Church of Our Lord Jesus Christ of the Apostolic Faith, "About Us: Statement of Faith," www.cooljc .org/?page_id=61 (accessed January 4, 2014).

[24]Sherrod C. Johnson, *The New Birth* (Philadelphia: Church of the Lord Jesus Christ of the Apostolic Faith, 2012), www.apostolic-faith.org/newbirth.asp.

through praise. The Spirit is imparted through laying on of hands to minister spiritual, emotional or physical healing, to consecrate leaders for stages of ministry or to minister deliverance from a variety of bondages. The Spirit speaks through testimony and the preached word, through spoken or sung messages in tongues that are interpreted and answered by the Spirit, and through prophetic pronouncement. She expresses joy through holy dancing and grief through travailing and tears.

The congregation gauges the Spirit's presence through both noise and silence. The indwelling Spirit tries the corporate spirit, not through human but through spiritual senses, bearing witness to whether it is of God, is a fleshly display or is demonic activity. There are times when only a few will make such a distinction. At other times the entire congregation is sensitive to whether there has been a visitation by the Spirit of God or what is before them is an imposter. When God's presence is discerned the atmosphere changes; there is heightened expectation that, through the Spirit, God will accomplish spiritual, emotional or physical healing—or that order might come out of personal, relational or community chaos.

Discernment of whether activity is the power of the Spirit or is "in the flesh" (that is, out of human ability) is a corporate responsibility. No matter how gifted, educated or articulate the minister, he or she must acknowledge and display dependence on the Spirit in carrying out ministry. The congregation waits for the moment when the self recedes and the Spirit "takes over" the sermon, prayer or song. There is a shared expectation that when the Spirit arrives and is given full liberty, there will be a demonstration of the power of God. Liberation or deliverance will be imparted through a word, touch, motion or prayer. But this only comes about through yielding oneself to the Spirit so that "the Holy Ghost can do what she wills." Declarations from the pulpit or the congregation that "the Spirit of the Lord is in this place" summon shouts of joy, thunderous applause or silent reverence. Where a strange spirit is discerned, the spiritually mature in the congregation go into action asserting spiritual authority to dispel that spirit and bring order to the situation.

Symbols for the Spirit in African American Pentecostalism include oil, wind and fire. Though each is significant for the saints, the most prominent symbol is fire. To invoke the Spirit is to invoke the life-giving, sanctifying fire of God. Pentecostal hymns and testimonies reference the connection between the Spirit and fire, referring back to the biblical Day of Pentecost, when the outpouring of the Spirit in the Upper Room was accompanied by "cloven tongues like as of fire" (Acts 2:3 KJV) or even back to the image of fire in Jeremiah's bones (Jer 20:9). The special significance of that symbol is outlined by the Fire Baptized Holiness Church of America.

> We believe that it is just [as] important to have Fire as the Holy Ghost. Hebrews 12:29 says, "For our God is a consuming fire." Fire is un-compromising. Fire Baptized Saints will not compromise with the wrong in themselves. Fire will do four things: First, light up; Second, warm up; Third, purge; and Fourth, purify. Fire Baptized folk are lit up, warmed up, purged, and purified. When we use "Fire" in our name we use it as a symbol of the uncompromising God.[25]

There is no fear of this fire; indeed, it is invited. Fire represents both cleansing and empowerment; it is expected to burn up traces of sin or uncleanness in believers. It brings power and creates life-giving energy. As with the prophet, it will not allow the believer to be still or quiet. Through sensing the presence of fire—burning in the depths of one's soul, as much as through evidence of tongues—the believer is assured of baptism in the Holy Spirit and can be heard testifying that "I'm saved, sanctified, and filled with the Holy Ghost, and that with a mighty burning fire."

The emphasis on other spiritual gifts in the contemporary charismatic movement was not present historically in early African American Pentecostalism. Neither was great attention given to any particular spiritual offices. Yet spiritual gifts have always been recognized among congregations. Prophecy was not understood as foretelling. Rather the prophetic gift indwells the congregation and rests on individuals as a vehicle for forth-telling God's word. This word comes from within the sermon or exhortation, by a leader or member of the congregation, as part of a testimony, or as an extemporaneous address prompted directly by the Holy Spirit.[26] The Spirit rests on and speaks through the prophet(s), giving potency and efficacy for healing, empowerment and correction of the community.

African American Pentecostalism holds a collective rather than personal understanding of the operation of spiritual gifts. The gifts rest in the com-

---

[25]Frazier, *Introducing the Fire Baptized Holiness Church of God of the Americas*, 8.
[26]See Gerald T. Sheppard, "Prophecy: From Ancient Israel to Pentecostals at the End of the Modern Age," *The Spirit and Church* 3, no. 1 (2001): 47–70.

munity, not on any isolated individual. Further, any person—a spiritually precocious child, an exuberant adolescent, a seasoned elder—might be prompted by the Spirit with a prophetic word. Such a word might be one of exhortation, comfort, admonition or correction. Likewise, the gift of healing does not necessarily rest in a single individual. Though at times the elders are called to anoint and lay hands on severely afflicted individuals, every Pentecostal believer fervently prays for and expects to effectuate healing. Testimonies abound of incidences where God has been "a doctor in the sickroom" for physical healing, and where he has been a "mind regulator," bringing psychic healing from emotional distress.[27]

Nevertheless, there is also a parallel concept of the particular anointing that rests on an individual's life and ministry. Persons in a congregation or community are recognized as being "anointed" or carrying a "heavier anointing." In some instances, the anointing is provisional, for specific acts of service such as preaching, teaching or laying on of hands for healing. Anointing is invoked by prayer directly preceding the action and is understood to be lifted at its conclusion. In other instances, the anointing remains with an individual. When these individuals are present, whatever they do is perceived as carrying an abundance of God's Spirit and presence. In some cases, certain ecclesial offices (e.g., bishop or overseer) are understood to carry an unction; but even this is intended to serve the community and must always be respected. These persons are identified as vessels set apart by the Holy Spirit for special use and are revered for the role they play in the community's life. Still, the movement's communal nature promotes a holistic, inclusive understanding that any gift that resides within an individual or congregation must benefit the entire congregation. The liberative motif of Jesus' assertion that "the Spirit of the Lord is on me" resonates with African American Pentecostal believers who see Holy Spirit empowerment as the source for their urgency to bring good news to the poor and who work to set free those who are captive (Lk 4:18).

While some observers, such as J. Deotis Roberts, contend that the Pentecostal movement is "notoriously short on social conscience and social justice"

---

[27]On healing and Black Pentecostalism, see MacRobert, *The Black Roots and White Racism of Early Pentecostalism*, passim.

with "little concern for social transformation,"[28] many African American Pentecostals would insist that personal Pentecostal piety will be played out in just communal relationships among themselves as well as with others in the faith and broader community. As MacRobert asserts, the distinction between personal and social ethics disappears in both African traditional spirituality and African American Pentecostal self-understanding.

> The sacred and profane [are] totally integrated in the holistic world view . . . of black Pentecostalism. God [was] experienced in all of life, bringing power, liberty, joy, and solace. Black people . . . believed that the same Spirit which had been in Christ and in the Apostles [was] in them as they carried salvation and healing to the urban ghettoes of America. Not only did the Spirit equip them to transform society—to obliterate the colour line through the power of love—She also liberated them spiritually, psychologically and socially, transforming poor, dispossessed, disenfranchised, ill-educated, powerless black people who were despised and constantly being told they were inferior by white society. Their self-concept was changed, for now they were the children of [G]od—the saints of the Most High! Their pneumatic experience affirmed black dignity and lifted the believer out of the mundane into "ecstatic" consciousness of God's presence, power and love.[29]

Such observations, as surveyed and recounted in this essay, reveal that African American Pentecostal theology is truly a lived theology springing from a rich heritage of lived pneumatology.

---

[28]J. Deotis Roberts, *Black Theology in Dialogue* (Philadelphia: Westminster, 1987), 59.
[29]MacRobert, *The Black Roots and White Racism of Early Pentecostalism*, 90–1.

PART TWO

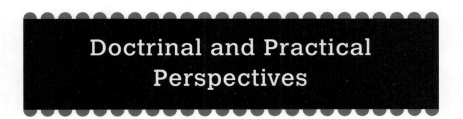

Doctrinal and Practical
Perspectives

9

The Spirit of Light After the Age of Enlightenment

Reforming/Renewing Pneumatic Hermeneutics via the Economy of Illumination

Kevin J. Vanhoozer

INTRODUCTION: DO OUR FIFTEEN STEPS TO BIBLICAL EXEGESIS SKIP OVER THE SPIRIT?

What is the role of the Holy Spirit in biblical interpretation? How should we understand the relationship between the Spirit of God, the written Word of God and the people of God? These two questions stand at the crossroads of pneumatology and hermeneutics, and therefore mark the spot the present essay sets out to address.

My outline resembles a three-way light bulb. I begin by rehearsing some of the issues raised over the past few years by examining conversations that, taken together, yield about 50 watts of light (much more in heat). Next, I'll mine some older sources to recover light from the past—100 watts. Then I'll attempt a 150-watt dogmatic account of my own that turns on both filaments and views the Spirit of understanding in the broader context of what I call the "economy of illumination." I shall conclude with some implications for the church today as a Spirited community of biblical improvisers.

We begin with my undergraduate course in Greek exegesis taught by Moisés Silva. He had presented a fifteen-step approach to biblical interpretation, similar to what one typically finds in hermeneutics textbooks: establish the historical context; analyze the sentence structure, grammar, and significant words; identify the literary form; look for allusions to other texts; formulate a hypothesis; rinse and repeat, and so on.[1] The particulars vary from author to author, and to be honest I can't recall all fifteen steps. What I do recall is uncharacteristically raising my hand and asking: "Where are you locating the work of the Holy Spirit?" You could have cut the ensuing silence with a knife. Then, just before the awkwardness became unbearable, he smiled broadly and said: "Everywhere." To this day I'm conflicted: was this a superficial brush-off, a gesture of pietistic legerdemain or a profound insight into what must ultimately remain a mystery?

Equally mysterious is why so few textbooks on hermeneutics make any mention of the Holy Spirit. Take, for example, W. Randolph Tate's *Biblical Interpretation*. Tate divides his book into three parts: the world behind the text, where grammatical-historical concerns dominate; the world of the text, where narrative and literary approaches rule; and the world in front of the text, where the focus is on the reader and where we find an entire chapter devoted to the question "What happens when we read?"[2] He discusses Umberto Eco, considers reader-response criticism and notes that some readers are more competent than others, but at no point acknowledges the Holy Spirit's activity in the world of the reader. However, he does offer this succinct, if skewed, definition of illumination in a handbook of hermeneutical terms: "In some evangelical circles, the term refers to the work of the Holy Spirit in elucidating some passage of the Bible to a person while studying."[3] He also includes the briefest of entries under "Spirit, Holy": "In Christianity, the Third Person of the Trinity,"[4] and this, believe it or not, after three pages (five columns) on speech-act theory!

---

[1] See, for example, Appendix B, "Practical Guidelines for Writing a Research Exegesis Paper," in Michael J. Gorman, *Elements of Biblical Exegesis: A Basic Guide for Students and Ministers*, rev. ed. (Grand Rapids: Baker Academic, 2009), 241–46; Gordon D. Fee, *New Testament Exegesis: A Handbook for Students and Pastors*, 3rd ed. (Louisville, KY: Westminster John Knox, 2002), xxi–xxiii; Henry A. Virkler and Karelynne Gerber Ayayo, *Hermeneutics: Principles and Processes of Biblical Interpretation*, 2nd ed. (Grand Rapids: Baker Academic, 2007), 225–28.

[2] W. Randolph Tate, *Biblical Interpretation: An Integrated Approach*, rev. ed. (Peabody, MA: Hendrickson, 1997), 157–86.

[3] W. Randolph Tate, *Interpreting the Bible: A Handbook of Terms and Methods* (Peabody, MA: Hendrickson, 2006), 175.

[4] Ibid., 351.

THE STATE OF THE QUESTION: ILLUMINATING (AND RENEWING) THE ISSUE

Biblical exegetes versus systematic theologians. How, then, should we understand the Holy Spirit's work in biblical interpretation? What is the nature of the Spirit's interventions in the world of the reader? Interestingly, the answer may depend on whether you are an exegete or theologian.

1970s: Daniel Fuller versus Millard Erickson. Daniel Fuller, an exegete, is fully aware of past and present Christians who believe "that the proper understanding of a passage in the Bible is gained only by those who go beyond the wording of the text and seek the illumination that the Holy Spirit provides."[5] Going "beyond the wording" is biblical-studies code for allegorizing or other exegetical misdemeanors. Fuller protests when readers appeal to illumination as an excuse for sidestepping the grammatical-historical method.

What, then, does he make of Paul's claim in 1 Corinthians 2:11, that only the Spirit of God comprehends the thoughts of God, and 1 Corinthians 2:14, that the natural person is not able to accept or understand the things of the Spirit of God "because they are spiritually discerned"? Is this the proof text that sunk a thousand grammatical-historical ships? May it never be! To "accept" (*dechomai*) the things of the Spirit means to receive them with gladness. It is not that the unregenerate cannot make sense of what Paul is saying, only that they fail to welcome it. Therefore, "the Holy Spirit's role in interpretation does not consist in giving the interpreter cognition of what the Bible is saying, which would involve dispensing additional information, beyond the historical-grammatical data.... Rather, the Holy Spirit's role is to change the heart of the interpreter, so that he loves the message that is conveyed by the historical-grammatical data."[6]

Millard Erickson, a systematic theologian, takes exception to Fuller's exegesis—and theology. Fuller reads too much out of (or into?) the definition of *dechomai* when he draws "the unwarranted conclusion that sin has seriously affected human will, but not human reason."[7] In response, Erickson affirms the noetic effects of sin, and cites a number of biblical texts that emphasize the blindness or deafness of unbelievers. The Spirit therefore

---

[5]Daniel P. Fuller, "The Holy Spirit's Role in Biblical Interpretation," in *Scripture, Tradition, and Interpretation*, ed. W. Ward Gasque and William S. LaSor (Grand Rapids: Eerdmans, 1978), 189.
[6]Ibid., 192.
[7]Millard Erickson, *Christian Theology*, 2nd ed. (Grand Rapids: Baker, 1998), 281.

opens up both hearts and minds of biblical interpreters. Natural persons do not accept the things of the Spirit because they do not fully understand.[8]

1980s: Roy B. Zuck versus Fred Klooster. Round 2 of this discussion begins in 1984, when Roy Zuck, professor of Bible exposition at Dallas Theological Seminary, sets out fourteen theses in an attempt to clarify the relationship between hermeneutics and the Holy Spirit.[9] Here are a few of his claims:

- The Spirit does not give new revelation, disclose hidden meaning, or make one's interpretations infallible.

- The Spirit's role is no substitute for diligent study, common sense, or logic. (Many of Zuck's theses focus on what the Spirit does *not* do.)

- The Spirit does not bestow the ability to understand the words but rather to receive, rejoice in, and apply them.

Fred Klooster, professor of systematic theology at Calvin Theological Seminary, counters with sixteen theses.[10] He introduces the term "heart-understanding" to make the point that understanding is not merely theoretical, but involves the whole person—mind, will, and emotions alike. He also insists that what we're trying to understand is not simply what the original human authors meant but rather "the pneumatically Christological theocentric message of Scripture." This message is rightly heard only in faith, and faithful exegesis "requires the preunderstanding that Scripture itself demands."[11] It follows that the unbeliever's preunderstanding "must be fundamentally re-directed by the regenerating power of the Holy Spirit."[12]

We can sum up the debate by contrasting "thin" with "thick" understanding. To understand a text "thinly" is to grasp its sense, that is, the semantic content of its expressions: *what* is said. We do not need the Spirit's help for that, just linguistic competence. In contrast, "thick" understanding includes grasping a text's reference: what it is said *about*. Erickson and Klooster, the two theologians, think we need the Spirit's illumination to grasp

---

[8]Ibid., 274. For more on the Erickson-Fuller debate, see David J. McKinley, "John Owen's View of Illumination: An Alternative to the Fuller-Erickson Dialogue," *Bibliotheca Sacra* 154 (1997): 93–96.

[9]Roy B. Zuck, "The Role of the Holy Spirit in Hermeneutics," *Bibliotheca Sacra* 141 (1984): 120–30.

[10]Fred Klooster, "The Role of the Holy Spirit in the Hermeneutic Process: The Relationship of the Spirit's Illumination to Biblical Interpretation," in *Hermeneutics, Inerrancy, and the Bible*, ed. Earl D. Radmacher and Robert D. Preus (Grand Rapids: Zondervan, 1984), 451–72.

[11]Ibid., 470.

[12]Ibid., 464.

the christological message—to see the face of Christ in Scripture, one might say—especially if we're reading Deuteronomy, Amos or the Song of Songs.[13]

1990s: Robert Stein versus Moisés Silva. Returning to 1 Corinthians 2:14, Robert Stein asks what Paul means by saying that apart from the Spirit the things of which he speaks are "folly." In context, "folly" probably does not mean "unintelligible" but "not worth affirming or accepting." It has this sense in 1 Corinthians 3:19, where God considers the wisdom of the world as "folly." God understands the world's wisdom but judges it negatively. So do the unregenerate as concerns Scripture. Stein considers two groups of college students, Christians and non-Christians, and asks whether their grades would be significantly different if they were assigned the task of saying what Paul meant by Romans 3:20-21. He suspects the grade curve for both groups, all other things being equal, would be quite similar, because unbelievers too can correctly grasp the human author's intent: "Even without the Spirit, they are able to describe accurately and well what the authors of Scripture meant in their texts."[14] Stein avoids any distinction between "thin" and "thick" understanding, probably because he equates sense and reference, and reduces the divine authorial meaning to the human without remainder.

In the epilogue to his book *Interpreting Galatians*, Silva poses the very question I had directed to him years earlier: "And where is the Holy Spirit in all this?"[15] His mature answer merits our attention. He acknowledges the exegetical brilliance of many biblical scholars who do not accept the lordship of Christ. As we have seen, evangelicals typically explain this by drawing a distinction between understanding and application and then limiting the Spirit's role to the latter. Silva is unwilling to draw a hard-and-fast distinction between the intellect and heart when it comes to understanding. The real issue is not the distinction between exegesis and application but between human and divine authorship. Much of what falls under the rubric of exe-

---

[13]I. Howard Marshall, like Zuck, thinks that the Spirit's work is especially necessary at the level of application, though, unlike Zuck, Marshall includes "pointing to Jesus" under application (i.e., the NT use of the OT): "It is the Spirit, then, who supplies the key to the understanding of the Old Testament" ("The Holy Spirit and the Interpretation of Scripture," in *Rightly Divided: Readings in Biblical Hermeneutics*, ed. Roy B. Zuck [Grand Rapids: Kregel, 1996], 70).

[14]Robert H. Stein, *A Basic Guide to Interpreting the Bible: Playing by the Rules*, 2nd ed. (Grand Rapids: Baker Academic, 2011), 64.

[15]Moisés Silva, *Interpreting Galatians: Explorations in Exegetical Method*, 2nd ed. (Grand Rapids: Baker Academic, 2001), 210.

gesis has to do with the human features of Scripture only—the ways we read the Bible "like any other book." Other things—reading the Law and the Prophets and the Writings as testimony to Christ; reading each part in canonical context—fit better under the rubric of divine authorship. I agree. We achieve what I have called "thick" (i.e., properly theological) understanding only when we read the Bible as divine testimony to Jesus Christ.

People of power (Pentecostals) versus people of paper (evangelicals): the twenty-first century. We now turn to consider the Pentecostal contribution. Obviously I cannot do justice to the whole of Pentecostal hermeneutics. Yet not to say something would be irresponsible, for members of "renewal traditions" have been steadily producing important texts on biblical hermeneutics.[16]

Pentecostal hermeneutics. What is Pentecostal hermeneutics? According to one influential way of telling the story, early Pentecostals avoided the fundamentalist-modernist controversy raging in the academy by staying on the more popular Wesleyan-Holiness level, where what mattered most was faithful living, not defending the Bible's historicity or articulating a system of doctrine.[17] A modern critic might accuse Pentecostals of fusing the Bible's two horizons—the perspectives of text and reader—to the point of blurring the boundary between their twentieth-century world and that of the first-century early church. Yet Francis Martin argues that precisely this experience of charismatic renewal is the missing hermeneutical link, the "essential principle of continuity" that allows interpreters to bridge historical distance.[18] The living experience of the Spirit in the believing community is a Pentecostal prerequisite to right preunderstanding.

Whatever unique countercultural contribution early Pentecostals had to give the broader church was significantly dampened, however, when in the 1940s Pentecostals began to conform to the prevailing norms of evangelical scholarship in order to get a hearing. At this point (so the story goes), a majority of Pentecostal scholars replaced their primitive "Bible Reading Method" with academically acceptable exegetical methods, a modified historical-

---

[16]See especially Kenneth J. Archer, *A Pentecostal Hermeneutic: Spirit, Scripture, and Community* (Cleveland, TN: CPT, 2009).

[17]Ibid., chaps. 2–3. See also the more systematic account of L. William Oliverio Jr., *Theological Hermeneutics in the Classical Pentecostal Tradition: A Typological Account* (Leiden: Brill, 2012).

[18]Francis Martin, "The Charismatic Renewal and Biblical Hermeneutics," in *Theological Reflections on the Charismatic Renewal* (Ann Arbor: Servant, 1979), 4.

critical approach.[19] A dissenting remnant remains, however, and according to this minority, what gets lost in the Reformed Protestant methodology that has come to dominate evangelicalism is precisely "the importance of the Pentecostal community's role in the hermeneutical process."[20] To speak of renewing hermeneutics, in this context, is to call for the recovery of the distinctly *paramodern* character of early Pentecostal biblical interpretation.

Paramodern or postmodern hermeneutics? Is it paramodern or postmodern?[21] Three points, in response:

First, whichever it is, the spirit of Pentecostalism does appear to be radically at odds with the spirit of modernity. Evangelical biblical scholars, insofar as they adopt modern methods, are people of paper, intent on recovering the original author's intention with objective critical procedures without considering "how the Spirit is involved in the mediation of meaning."[22] While evangelicals try to preserve the original textual meaning, Pentecostals want to preserve the original experience of the Spirit.

Second, the Pentecostal focus on the Spirit's role in the community offers biblical hermeneutics something beyond Enlightenment rationality, hence the perceived commonality with certain postmodern concerns: for community experience as a criterion of truth rather than universal reason, for stories that give shape to community identity and for seeing meaning as a joint production of text and reader rather than the product of a single author's intention.[23]

This overlap of Pentecostal and postmodern concerns leads to my third point: how pneumatological is it? Is there a distinct role for the Holy Spirit, or does everything reduce to community experience? Mark Cartledge anticipates this objection: what stops the community from becoming the norm rather than Scripture? His answer: "What a renewal hermeneutic does is to highlight the Holy Spirit as a distinct influence within the community in the appropriation of the text and thus reintegrates spirituality into academic scholarship."[24]

---

[19]Archer, *A Pentecostal Hermeneutic*, 209.

[20]Ibid.

[21]See Bradley Truman Noel, *Pentecostal and Postmodern Hermeneutics: Comparisons and Contemporary Impact* (Eugene, OR: Wipf & Stock, 2010).

[22]Mark J. Cartledge, "Text-Community-Spirit: The Challenges Posed by Pentecostal Theological Method to Evangelical Theology," in *Spirit and Scripture: Exploring a Pneumatic Hermeneutic*, ed. Kevin L. Spawn and Archie T. Wright (London: T & T Clark, 2012), 130.

[23]See Noel, *Pentecostal and Postmodern*, esp. chap. 3.

[24]Cartledge, "Text-Community-Spirit," 142.

Pneumatic hermeneutics. A recent collection of essays on "pneumatic hermeneutics" attempts to do just that.[25] The collection is important, first, because it contains essays by those in the renewal tradition and by three scholars who are not (Craig Bartholomew, James Dunn and Walter Moberly), and second, because the renewal authors seem to agree that a pneumatic hermeneutic ought to include three components: the biblical text, the believing community and the Holy Spirit.

Not surprisingly, the Jerusalem Council of Acts 15 features prominently as a case study in pneumatic hermeneutics. It begins with the community testifying to its present experience of the Spirit (he converts the Gentiles too!) and only then engaging Scripture to validate the experience.[26] In modern grammatical-historical exegesis, by way of contrast, one moves from text to context. Yet it was precisely the community's experience of the Spirit that "helped the church make its way through this hermeneutical maze."[27] John Christopher Thomas insists that the Spirit does more than merely "illumine" the community.[28] What is this "more"?

A number of renewal scholars speak of a "hermeneutic trialectic" consisting of Word, Spirit and community.[29] The goal is to hear what the Spirit is saying to the church through Scripture today, not simply to recover what the human author meant yesterday. A pneumatic hermeneutic makes the contemporary reading community essential to the interpretive process. One contributor boldly asserts, "The Holy Spirit inspires the contemporary reading of the text, just as he inspired the original authors."[30] Therefore,

---

[25]Kevin L. Spawn and Archie T. Wright, introduction to Spawn and Wright, *Spirit and Scripture*, xvii. This is not to be confused with what G. C. Berkouwer calls "pneumatic exegesis," the view that understanding Scripture comes more from praying for the Spirit's aid than consulting lexical aids (*Holy Scripture* [Grand Rapids: Eerdmans, 1975], 111).

[26]John Christopher Thomas, "Reading the Bible from Within Our Traditions: A Pentecostal Hermeneutic as Test Case," in *Between Two Horizons: Spanning New Testament Studies and Systematic Theology*, ed. Joel Green and Max Turner (Grand Rapids: Eerdmans, 2000), 108–22. Luke Timothy Johnson uses much the same approach, based on Acts 15, to justify same-sex relationships, in his *Scripture and Discernment: Decision Making in the Church* (Nashville: Abingdon, 1996). Dunn specifically mentions this issue in his response ("The Role of the Spirit in Biblical Hermeneutics," in Spawn and Wright, *Spirit and Scripture*, 155).

[27]Thomas, "Reading the Bible," 118.

[28]Ibid., 119.

[29]See Amos Yong, *Spirit-Word-Community: Theological Hermeneutics in Trinitarian Perspective* (Burlington, VT: Ashgate, 2002).

[30]Cartledge, "Text-Community-Spirit," 134.

"pneumatology provides the link between text and community."[31]

We have to ask: In *which* communities is the Spirit actively involved? And the equally obvious answer (especially to Pentecostals) is, those in renewal traditions. After all, the essence of Pentecostalism is the belief that the spiritual experiences of biblical characters, including speaking in tongues, are possible for contemporary believers too. Members of renewal traditions therefore enjoy what we could call a "pneumatic edge"[32]—namely, the advantage of being formed by a narrative tradition that predisposes members to view themselves as participants in the new outpouring of God's Spirit (i.e., the "latter rain").

But what precisely does the Spirit contribute to hermeneutics? Moberly's response to the essays is surprising, and not a little bit ironic, for he says that the key concern of the volume—how the Spirit mediates a contemporary meaning from the ancient biblical text—is left hanging.[33] We get something of a more definite answer from Kenneth Archer in his constructive final chapter, where he devotes seven pages to "Word," five and a half pages to "Spirit" and twenty-three pages to "Community." However, most of the material on the Spirit deals with his speaking in and through the community; there is only one page devoted to the Spirit speaking in and through Scripture. That's because Archer refuses to reduce the Spirit's voice to the words of the biblical text: "The community, the Scripture, and the Spirit must negotiate the meaning in the context of faithful praxis."[34]

There is something deeply right and important in the renewal tradition's desire to get beyond exegetical excavation. The positive point I take from the Pentecostal challenge concerns the importance of a renewing herme-neutic, a way of interpreting that enlists readers as active participants in the Spirit's ministry of Scripture's subject matter: the new order in Jesus Christ, who lives and reigns today.

I also have three concerns. In their zeal for community, their insistence that meaning is produced rather than consumed in community and their will-ingness to employ various kinds of reader-response theories that privilege interpretive communities, I wonder, in the first place, whether some renewal

---

[31]Ibid., 140.

[32]See Noel, who speaks of a "Pentecostal edge" (*Pentecostal and Postmodern Hermeneutics*, 164).

[33]Walter Moberly, "Pneumatic Biblical Hermeneutics: A Response," in Spawn and Wright, *Spirit and Scripture*, 165.

[34]Archer, *A Pentecostal Hermeneutic*, 260.

scholars may have inadvertently sold their spiritual birthright for a mess of postmodern pottage.[35] Second, when it comes to giving a nitty-gritty account of the Spirit's role in hermeneutics, there is less a mighty rushing wind than a whispering shrug of the shoulders. And third, I am struck by the way in which some of the more zealous voices privilege the renewal tradition in relation to other interpretive traditions. In particular, I am disturbed by Archer's identification of Reformed biblical interpretation with modern rationalist exegesis.[36] Walter Moberly's response to the essays in *Spirit and Scripture* echoes my own: "As I read, I was . . . struck by how many of the essayists' concerns are well represented within other Christian traditions, both present and past."[37] Is Reformed theology the problem? On the contrary, I believe it offers *premodern* resources for understanding the Spirit's role in hermeneutics. I therefore turn, at least momentarily, from renewing to reforming by means of a Johannine trio.

"JOHANNINE" RESOURCES: LIGHT (FOR REFORMING) FROM PAST AND PRESENT

My Johannine resources include John Calvin, John Owen, John Webster and of course John the disciple that Jesus loved. It's in the Gospel of John that Jesus tells his disciples that his going away is the condition for the coming of the Spirit of truth, who will dwell in them (Jn 14:17), teach them all things (Jn 14:26) and guide them into all truth (Jn 16:13).

John Calvin. Calvin takes his cue from John 16:13: "He [the Spirit] will not speak on his own; he will speak only what he hears." The Spirit instills in our minds what he has handed on through the Word. The Spirit's speaking is not a new revelation but a sealing of what has already been revealed in Christ through the Scriptures on our minds: "He is the Author of the Scriptures: he cannot vary and differ from himself."[38] Calvin's signature move is

---

[35]For example, Wolfgang Vondey is willing to employ Gadamer's notion of play as a heuristic to explain the Spirit-word-community dynamic: "The contribution of global Pentecostalism lies in the . . . dynamic concept of revelation as the interplay of Spirit, Word, and community" (*Beyond Pentecostalism: The Crisis of Global Christianity and the Renewal of the Theological Agenda* [Grand Rapids: Eerdmans, 2010], 71).

[36]Archer, *A Pentecostal Hermeneutic*, 192, 209.

[37]Moberly, "Pneumatic Biblical Hermeneutics," 161.

[38]John Calvin, *Institutes of the Christian Religion*, ed. John T. McNeill, trans. Ford Lewis Battles (Philadelphia: Westminster, 1960), 1.9.2.

to ensure, at every theological point, that Word and Spirit work together. The Word, living and written, is the objective aspect of revelation; the Spirit is the subjective aspect, the writing of that revelation on our hearts, the power behind our perception of the truth.[39] God sends the Spirit, says Calvin, "to complete his work by the efficacious confirmation of the Word."[40]

John Owen. I cannot hope to do justice to John Owen's *Pneumatologia*, perhaps the greatest corpus of works on the Spirit ever penned. I shall confine myself to summarizing one treatise only: "The Causes, Ways, and Means of Understanding the Mind of God as Revealed in His Word" (1678). Owen is relevant because, like us, he is keenly aware that many Christians lack what we could call the "assurance of interpretation," because "all sorts of persons are divided about their sense and meaning."[41] Owen had to confront rationalists (i.e., early modernists), who thought they could understand Scripture by reason alone; enthusiasts (Quakers), who believed they could do so by the Spirit alone; and Roman Catholics, who looked to magisterial church tradition to arbitrate interpretive disputes.

Causes: the Spirit as principal efficient cause. Owen defines the aim of biblical interpretation as understanding the mind of God revealed in Scripture. Scripture is "a light shining in a dark place" (2 Pet 1:19), the radiation of God's majesty, holiness and truth. It is no criticism of the light that the blind cannot see it. The principal efficient cause of our understanding of God's Word is the Holy Spirit, the one who makes the blind see. Owen is no enthusiast, however: the Spirit does not teach by prophetic inspiration. Whatever we know about God's mind, we know by our own understanding, but never in an unaided, merely natural manner.

The Spirit is the one who enlightens the "eyes of your heart" (Eph 1:18). In opening the eyes of the understanding, the Spirit does not reveal something new but, like a telescope, enables us to discern the things that are already objectively there, in Scripture. The grammatical sense informs the mind, but does not illumine it: "Men may have a knowledge of *words*, and the *meaning* of propositions in the Scripture, who have no knowledge of the *things them-*

---

[39]"We are to expect nothing more from his Spirit than that he will illumine our minds to perceive the truth of his teaching" (Calvin, *Institutes* 4.8.13).

[40]Calvin, *Institutes* 1.9.3.

[41]John Owen, "Causes, Ways, and Means of Understanding the Mind of God," in *The Works of John Owen*, ed. Thomas Russell (London: Richard Baynes, 1826), 3:372.

selves designed in them."[42] The Spirit leads us unto all truth by giving us understanding of these things of God revealed in Scripture.

Ways: the Spirit's communicative work on minds and hearts. By "ways" of understanding, Owen refers to the Spirit's renewing of our hearts and minds, not least by regenerating our natures, delivering us from the domain of darkness (Col 1:13). The Spirit's illumination is his restoring right functioning to our cognitive and affective capacities, our intellect and volition. The Spirit's work does not replace our minds but establishes them: "The mind in its exercise is our understanding."[43] The Spirit does not merely propose things to be understood but graciously and efficaciously *communicates* them, making sure they reach their destination. Whereas human teachers can only try to make themselves understood, the Spirit is, as it were, the "Lord of the hearing."

Means: spiritual, disciplinary and ecclesial. The "means" of understanding include all the creaturely instruments the Spirit employs to accomplish his work.[44] Owen's real emphasis, however, is on what human interpreters do, for interpreters must avail themselves of these means of hermeneutical grace. Prayer, for example, is a spiritual means that helps to mortify sinful presuppositions and prejudices that blind us to the mind of God. Obeying the truth is another spiritual means that increases real rather than notional understanding, where "real" understanding means learning not the mere notions of things like godliness, but rather having the form and power of godliness implanted in our souls. For Owen, the end of interpretation is not theoretical understanding of God's mind, something merely informational, but a real participation in God's holiness, a transformation of the interpreter into the image of the things known.[45] True knowledge "gives the mind an experience of the power and efficacy of the truth known . . . so as to transform the soul."[46] This is the end that justifies the disciplinary means.

John Webster. John Webster takes John Owen as his muse in a recent essay on illumination, on "the ways in which the operation of creaturely intelligence is caused, preserved, and directed by divine light, whose ra-

---

[42]Ibid., 3:418 (emphasis original).
[43]Ibid., 3:428.
[44]Cf. J. I. Packer: "The Spirit is not given to make Bible study needless, but to make it effective" (*Fundamentalism and the Word of God* [Grand Rapids: Eerdmans, 1958], 112).
[45]Owen, "Causes, Ways, and Means," 3:507.
[46]Ibid., 3:417.

diance makes creatures to know."[47] Webster acknowledges the perennial challenge of describing the Spirit's work in biblical interpretation, but says it is especially difficult to do so in age when the study of Scripture has been "uncoupled" from divine activity and ecclesial life. Whereas many adopt a god-of-the-hermeneutical-gaps approach, Webster opts for the longer route—an Owenesque description of the entire work of theology and interpretation, including a dogmatic account of readers and the activity of reading. Rather than trying to find a place in our hermeneutic schemes wherein to slot the Spirit, Webster proposes instead to fit biblical interpretation in the broader triune economy of revelation and redemption. In doing so he works not a Copernican but a Johannine or dogmatic revolution.

An account of illumination is "a theological meditation on the economy of the Spirit."[48] The Spirit is the giver of life, and his work is not to work violence on nature but to restore creatures to their proper natures and right functioning. The Spirit is also the giver of light: divine illumination restores us to our senses, setting our intellects in motion as they were created to move, namely, toward the light of truth. We see by God's light, but it is we who see. So far, so Owen. God works in ways that do not destroy but rather establish creaturely means, including "scientific" exegesis. However, unillumined, naturalistic interpretations of Scripture fall short of a "thick" understanding of the gospel of Jesus Christ. Webster's insistence that we interpret the event of reading with theological categories works a "Johannine revolution" in biblical interpretation. For Webster, exegesis produces understanding only when created reason works within the economy of the Spirit: "Illumination is subjective revelation in its reconciling and regenerative effectiveness."[49]

Concluding undogmatic, quasi-Johannine postscript. On the strength of my middle name (Jon), I'd like to add my own two cents to the Johannine project of reforming hermeneutics. Twenty years ago I explained the Spirit's role with a little help from speech-act theory. God's authorship of Scripture is a triune communicative act. The Father initiates and the Son executes communicative action, and I discerned a connection to locuting (producing

---

[47]John Webster, "Illumination," in *The Domain of the Word: Scripture and Theological Reason* (London: T & T Clark, 2012), 50.
[48]Ibid., 53.
[49]Ibid., 62.

speech) and illocuting (what we do in speaking), respectively.[50] The Spirit's
task is to complete and perfect the triune work. In Calvin's words: "To the
Spirit is assigned the power and efficacy of that activity."[51] Translated into
speech-act terms, this makes the Spirit's illumination a matter of perlocutionary prowess, where perlocutions are the effects in a hearer or reader
brought about by speech acts. The Spirit is the empowering perlocutionary
presence who renders the biblical word efficacious by eliciting the desired
response in interpreters, thereby enabling God's communicative action to
accomplish the purpose for which it was sent (Is 55:11).[52] In terms of 1 Corinthians 2:14, the natural man does not understand because he neither accepts nor feels the perlocutionary force of what is said.[53]

I can't help it. I still find the anatomy of a speech act to be an illuminating
analogy as concerns the inspiration and interpretation of the triune discourse that is Scripture.[54] The good news is that I'm a recovering "actaholic,"
for I have come to see the importance of placing the whole discussion of the
Spirit's role in hermeneutics in a properly dogmatic framework, namely, the
triune economy whereby God communicates all that he essentially is (i.e.,
his light, life and love) to the body of Christ. And so we move to my final,
constructive, 150-watt point.

THE ECONOMY OF ENLIGHTENMENT: LIGHT FROM LIGHT
THROUGH LIGHT

In setting forth what I'm calling the "economy of enlightenment," I am explicitly and dogmatically addressing the concerns of renewal and Reformed
traditions alike. What I take from the Pentecostal discussion about pneumatic hermeneutics is the importance of the community in addition to Word

[50]Kevin J. Vanhoozer, "The Spirit of Understanding: Special Revelation and General Hermeneutics,"
in *Disciplining Hermeneutics: Interpretation in Christian Perspective*, ed. Roger Lundin (Grand Rapids: Eerdmans, 1997), 156.
[51]Calvin, *Institutes* 1.13.18.
[52]Cf. Michael Horton: "The Third Person of the Trinity brings to fruition Christ's 'new creation.'
The Father speaks, the Son is spoken, and the Spirit brings about in history the effect and perfection of that speech" (*Introducing Covenant Theology* [Grand Rapids: Baker Academic, 2006], 137).
[53]See further my *Is There a Meaning in This Text? The Bible, the Reader, and the Morality of Literary
Knowledge* (Grand Rapids: Zondervan, 1998), 427–29.
[54]See also my "Triune Discourse: Theological Reflections on the Claim that God Speaks (Part 2),"
in *Trinitarian Theology for the Church: Scripture, Community, Worship*, ed. Daniel J. Treier and David
Lauber (Downers Grove, IL: IVP Academic, 2009), 50–78.

and Spirit, as well as the insistence that interpretation involves not only informing but also transforming interpreters. What I take from the Reformed discussion about the Spirit's role in hermeneutics is the notion that what the Spirit subjectively impresses on the minds and hearts of interpreters is precisely the meaning and significance of the word written, and especially its subject matter: what the Father is doing to renew all things in the Son through the Spirit. The watchword is thus "always reforming, always renewing."

God is light: the Father of Lights. Behind the economy, of course, is God in himself: "God is light" (1 Jn 1:5) and "the Father of the heavenly lights" (Jas 1:17). Why light? Kallistos Ware suggests it is because, of all the constituents of the physical world, light is "the least material. It illumines the objects upon which it falls without suffering loss or change in itself."[55] God himself "lives in unapproachable light" (1 Tim 6:16), yet Scripture also connects light with glory, the splendor of the divine presence: "in your light we see light" (Ps 36:9). And this, I take it, gets us to the heart of the nature of divine participation in the divine light. Indeed, this is precisely why I speak of an "economy of enlightenment": the whole biblical narrative is the story of how God executes in time his eternal decision to communicate the saving knowledge of himself to human creatures.

"Light from Light": the Son as the light of the Father come into the world. John of Damascus appeals to the analogy of light to illustrate the relationships among the three persons of the Trinity. The Father is the source of light, the Son an emanating ray of light and the Spirit the radiance of the ray.[56] The Son is "the radiance of God's glory" (Heb 1:3). According to John 1, the Word who was with God at the beginning is also "the true light that gives light to everyone" (Jn 1:9). This Word who was God was made flesh in order to communicate God's life-giving light and life to the world (Jn 8:12; 9:5). In the economy of enlightenment, the Son, as light of the world, communicates the light and life of God. Nicaea rightly describes the relationship of the Son to the Father as "light from light."

The Bible too is part of the economy of enlightenment, a creaturely means by which God advances the dominion of light. Your word, says the psalmist,

---

[55]Kallistos Ware, "Light and Darkness in the Mystical Theology of the Greek Fathers," in *Light from Light: Scientists and Theologians in Dialogue*, ed. Gerald O'Collins and Mary Ann Meyers (Grand Rapids: Eerdmans, 2012), 159.

[56]See Kathryn Tanner, "The Use of Perceived Properties of Light as a Theological Analogy," in *Light from Light*, 122–26.

is "a light on my path" (Ps 119:105; cf. 2 Pet 1:19). Paul speaks of "the light of the gospel of the glory of Christ" (2 Cor 4:4 ESV). Scripture contains words of life and words of light. It is not the Bible that needs illumining, but readers. And this brings us to the Spirit's role in biblical interpretation.

The Spirit of enlightenment: shining the light of Christ into hearts. "For God, who said, 'Let light shine out of darkness,' made his light shine in our hearts to give us the light of the knowledge of God's glory displayed in the face of Christ" (2 Cor 4:6). This may be the most important text for understanding the economy of enlightenment. There are several noteworthy features of this passage.

First, Calvin speaks of a "twofold enlightening" (*duplicem illuminationem*): "[God] shines forth upon us in the person of his Son by his Gospel, but that would be in vain, since we are blind, unless he were also to illuminate our minds by his Spirit."[57] It is the particular work of the Spirit to complete and bring to perfection all God's works *ad extra*. The Spirit completes the process of enlightenment—the communication of light—by removing the veil of ignorance: "And we all, who with unveiled faces contemplate the Lord's glory, are being transformed into his image with ever-increasing glory, which comes from the Lord, who is the Spirit" (2 Cor 3:18).[58]

Second, as to the nature of the light the Spirit shines, Jonathan Edwards says it communicates "a true sense of the divine excellency of the things revealed in the word of God."[59] Reason cannot see the beauty and loveliness of spiritual things, but an enlightened person not only grasps what is being proposed but also takes real delight in it. Spiritually enlightened persons do not simply have a notion of the glory of the gospel but, in addition, have a sense of the gloriousness of the gospel in their hearts: "There is a difference between having a rational judgment that honey is sweet, and having a sense of its sweetness."[60] In my terms: the Spirit's enlightenment communicates not merely the sense but also the sweetness of *what is in Christ*. This, after

---

[57]Commentary on 2 Cor. 4:6, in John Calvin, *The Second Epistle of Paul the Apostle to the Corinthians and the Epistles to Timothy, Titus, and Philemon*, trans. T. A. Small (Grand Rapids: Eerdmans, 1996), 57.

[58]See, for example, Ambrose, *The Holy Spirit* 3.12.88.

[59]Jonathan Edwards, "A Divine and Supernatural Light," in *The Sermons of Jonathan Edwards: A Reader*, ed. Wilson H. Kimnach, Kenneth P. Minkema and Douglas A. Sweeney (New Haven, CT: Yale University Press, 1999), 126.

[60]Ibid.

all, is Scripture's glorious role as a light to our path: it shows us Christ.

Third, what is in Christ—the glory of God that shines forth from his transfigured face—reflects the brightness of the new creation (2 Cor 5:17). The light the Spirit shines in our hearts "is the long awaited light of the eschaton."[61]

Fourth, in shining the light of the gospel into our hearts, the Spirit communicates the light and life that is in Christ into us, and thereby conforms us to his image.[62] The knowledge attained through what Owen called the disciplinary means cannot do that: exegesis alone cannot transform the exegete into the image of the things known.[63] Jonathan Edwards makes a similar point: "This light is such as effectually influences the inclination, and changes the nature of the soul. It assimilates the nature to the divine nature."[64] In sum, the Spirit's role in hermeneutics is to communicate what is in Christ so thoroughly that what is in Christ begins to characterize what is in us too: the natural man does not hear the things of the Spirit; but we, says Paul, "have the mind of Christ" (1 Cor 2:16). Biblical interpretation is ultimately a means of spiritual formation, of transformation unto Christlikeness.

Fifth, and finally: God does not intend his light to stay hidden in our hearts.[65] Transformation into the image of Christ "is applicable not only individually but corporately."[66] The final goal of interpretation in the economy of enlightenment is a hermeneutic aimed at cultivating a holy nation: a people of light.[67]

---

[61]Timothy B. Savage, *Power Through Weakness: Paul's Understanding of the Christian Ministry in 2 Corinthians* (Cambridge: Cambridge University Press, 1996), 126.

[62]See further, Christopher A. Beeley, *Gregory of Nazianzus on the Trinity and the Knowledge of God: In Your Light We Shall See Light* (Oxford: Oxford University Press, 2008); cf. Gary L. Nebeker: "The Spirit's role—or goal—in interpretation is to allow the interpreter to understand the text in such a way that the text transforms the interpreter into the image of Christ" ("The Holy Spirit, Hermeneutics, and Transformation: From Present to Future Glory," *Evangelical Review of Theology* 27 [2003]: 47).

[63]Owen, "Causes, Ways, and Means," 3:507.

[64]Edwards, "A Divine and Supernatural Light," 139.

[65]David Garland, *2 Corinthians: An Exegetical and Theological Exposition of Holy Scripture*, New American Commentary 29 (Nashville: B & H, 1999), 218.

[66]Nebeker, "The Holy Spirit, Hermeneutics, and Transformation," 54.

[67]I have interpreted 2 Cor 4:6 as pertaining to salvific, interpretive and transformational illumination, that is to say, to the Spirit's work in regeneration, interpretation and sanctification alike. Cf. Fred Klooster: "The Spirit's illumination is not one additional activity; rather it is an aspect of each" ("The Role of the Holy Spirit in the Hermeneutic Process," 452). See also the discussion of initial, progressive and transformative illumination in M. X. Seaman, *Illumination and Interpretation: The Holy Spirit's Role in Hermeneutics* (Eugene, OR: Wipf & Stock, 2013).

A people of light. Yes, the community is indeed part of the economy of enlightenment. Jesus says: "You are the light of the world" (Mt 5:14). Paul uses an even more intriguing phrase: "For you were once darkness, but now you are light in the Lord [*phōs en kyrios*]" (Eph 5:8). To be "in the Lord" is to be active in Christ's sphere of influence.[68] The "economy of illumination" set out in 2 Corinthians 4:6 thus encompasses everything involved in the triune communication of God's light, from the creation of the world to the re-creation of human beings in the image of his Son: "children of light." Light from light through light.

CONCLUSION: THE SPIRIT OF ILLUMINATION AND THE COMMUNITY OF BIBLICAL IMPROVISATION

God is light; the Son is the light of the world; the Spirit is the one who shines Christ's light into our hearts so that it reflects on our faces. What is the church's role in the economy of enlightenment? Paul's answer is at once simple and profound: "Live as children of light" (Eph 5:8). To live as children of light is to enact the Scriptures in ways that demonstrate both head and heart understanding of what is in Christ. The church's place in the economy of enlightenment is unique: no other interpretive community enacts what is in Christ. When the Spirit efficaciously illumines the church, it becomes a community of faithful improvisation, a sanctified flash mob.[69]

Wikipedia defines flash mob as "a group of people who assemble suddenly in a public place, perform an unusual and seemingly pointless act for a brief time, then quickly disperse."[70] I submit that the first flash mob assembled in Jerusalem, at Pentecost, and that their performance was anything but pointless. In the economy of enlightenment, wherever two or three are gathered in Christ's name, there is an opportunity to improvise God's Word, by which I mean faithfully enact what is in Christ in new and illumining ways. It is the life of the church, not the commentary, that is our most im-

---

[68]See Constantine Campbell, *Paul and Union with Christ: An Exegetical and Theological Study* (Grand Rapids: Zondervan, 2012), 371.

[69]At this point in the oral presentation of this paper, the audience viewed the following video clip of a flash mob singing in a library: "Students in Library Get Surprised with Awesome Gospel Flash Mob," *Godvine*, www.godvine.com/Students-in-Library-Get-Surprised-with-Awesome -Gospel-Flash-Mob-3436.html.

[70]*Wikipedia*, s.v. "Flash Mob," last modified August 31, 2014, http://en.wikipedia.org/wiki/Flash_mob.

portant form of biblical interpretation. And there is indeed more light yet to break forth from God's Word, especially when it is brought to life—contextualized—by a flash mob that has learned to read its world in light of the world of the biblical text. When the Spirit gathers men and women to improvise discipleship, the community becomes both living letter and commentary, not only recipients but also agents and catalysts of illumination in their own right: a holy flash mob, a brilliant parable of the kingdom of God. "In your light we *be* light." Come, illumining Spirit!

10

Creatio Spiritus and the Spirit of Christ

Toward a Trinitarian Theology of Creation

Amos Yong

The title of this volume, *Spirit of God: Christian Renewal in the Community of Faith*, is suggestive of a perspective long held across the modern Pentecostal movement, namely, that charismatic renewal will invigorate Christian faith and life as a whole, across denominational and traditional lines. The Pentecostal revival at Azusa Street in Los Angeles in the first decade of the twentieth century, for instance, was intended not to form a new denomination but to energize Christian commitment for those who felt their churches lacked such vitality. The charismatic renewal in the mainline Protestant and Roman Catholic churches in the 1960s and 1970s presumed something similar, although in practice more charismatics remained to rejuvenate their churches than did the earlier Pentecostals (who were as often dismissed from their congregations as they chose to freely move on, or "come out," as some put it). The point for our purposes is that as spiritual revitalization potentially renews the whole community of faith, so also pneumatological theology (reflection on all things related to the doctrine of the Holy Spirit) potentially contributes something of import to the broader scholarly and academic conversation.[1]

Hence the title of this essay is indicative of my overarching aspiration: to

---

[1] This has long been the burden of my work as a Pentecostal theologian, most recently and more comprehensively argued in my *Renewing Christian Theology: Systematics for a Global Christianity*, images and commentary by Jonathan A. Anderson (Waco, TX: Baylor University Press, 2014).

consider how pneumatological reflections on a theology of creation can open up to a more robust trinitarian vision of the world as divinely created. Methodologically speaking, the route to trinitarian theology was initiated with the turn to Christology in the early church (fourth and fifth centuries). While in some respects the turn to pneumatology was also navigated (especially through, although not limited to, the discussions culminating with the Council of Constantinople in A.D. 381), the conversation has not come full circle. Pneumatology has remained generally neglected, if not marginalized, in the theological quest.[2] The twentieth-century Pentecostal-charismatic renewal movement has precipitated, at least in part, the "rediscovery" of pneumatology or at least its retrieval and reappropriation in contemporary theology.[3] Pneumatological theologies of creation thus also have begun to emerge in the present theological landscape.[4] These have expanded the scope of pneumatology even as they have enriched Christian thinking about the doctrine of creation. My own work in this vein has heretofore attempted also to develop a pneumatology of creation informed by Pentecostal-charismatic spirituality and sensibilities.[5]

While in this essay I explore the possibility of a pneumatologically focused approach to the Christian doctrine of creation, its trinitarian horizons suggest that starting with the Spirit requires christological and patrological facets. More specifically, a pneumatological and thereby trinitarian theology of creation is not merely a cognitive construct but also an affective orientation and a practical task. This is because the work of the Spirit involves not just the renewing of human minds but also the transformation of human hearts and the empowerment of human lives for witness. The two parts that follow therefore lay out especially the biblical bases of a pneumatological

---

[2]See my article, "A Theology of the Third Article? Hegel and the Contemporary Enterprise in First Philosophy and First Theology," in *Semper Reformandum: Studies in Honour of Clark H. Pinnock*, ed. Stanley E. Porter and Anthony R. Cross (Carlisle, UK: Paternoster, 2003), 208–31.

[3]For example, Veli-Matti Kärkkäinen, *Pneumatology: The Holy Spirit in Ecumenical, International, and Contextual Perspective* (Grand Rapids: Baker Academic, 2002).

[4]Leading the way in this regard have been Jürgen Moltmann, *God in Creation: A New Theology of Creation and the Spirit of God*, trans. Margaret Kohl (Minneapolis: Fortress Press, 1993); Mark I. Wallace, *Fragments of the Spirit: Nature, Violence, and the Renewal of Creation* (Harrisburg, PA: Trinity Press International, 2002); Denis Edwards, *Breath of Life: A Theology of the Creator Spirit* (Maryknoll, NY: Orbis, 2004), among other works.

[5]Amos Yong, *The Spirit of Creation: Modern Science and Divine Action in the Pentecostal-Charismatic Imagination*, Pentecostal Manifestos 4 (Grand Rapids: Eerdmans, 2011); cf. James K. A. Smith and Amos Yong, eds., *Science and the Spirit: A Pentecostal Engagement with the Sciences* (Bloomington: Indiana University Press, 2010).

approach to a theology of creation and then unpack its methodological, epistemic-existential and performative implications.

Creation and the Triune God: A Pneumatological Reframing

A more narrowly expressed pneumatological theology of creation would begin with biblical references to the Spirit in relationship to the world and proceed from there to elaborate on its systematic and perhaps dogmatic features.[6] Yet a trinitarian formulation is irreducibly both pneumatological and christological. The key is to connect with major strands in the history of Christian thought that have developed a theology of creation christologically.[7] The following discussion sketches a trinitarian perspective on the doctrine of creation by following the salvation-historical drama of Scripture. How might the creation be conceived when considered with respect to God as primordial Creator, as historic redeemer and as eschatological consummator? To be sure, such is no plain biblical account if that means that the following merely proceeds straightforwardly off the surface of the scriptural narrative. Surely, a trinitarian hermeneutic is selective about how to order, interpret and renarrate the biblical data for present purposes, in this case, understanding creation. Just as surely, a pneumatological priority is here deployed. If a more effusively trinitarian vision of creation emerges on the other side, a hope this project is wagered on, then my efforts will have been justified.

God as Creator through Word and Spirit. Unmistakably, the biblical revelation proceeds from "In the beginning God created the heavens and the earth" (Gen 1:1). The New Testament is equally clear: "Through him all things were made; without him nothing was made that has been made" (Jn 1:3; cf. Heb 1:2). The author of the epistle to the Colossians puts it this way about God, Christ and the creation: "The Son is the image of the invisible God, the firstborn over all creation. For in him all things were created: things in heaven and on earth, visible and invisible, whether thrones or powers or rulers or authorities; all things have been created through him

---

[6]For example, World Council of Churches, *Come Holy Spirit, Renew the Whole Creation: Six Bible Studies on the Theme of the Seventh Assembly of World Council of Churches* (New York: Friendship, 1989).

[7]Lars Thunberg, *Man and the Cosmos: The Vision of St. Maximus the Confessor* (Crestwood, NY: St. Vladimir's Seminary Press, 1997); M. C. Steenberg, *Irenaeus on Creation: The Cosmic Christ and the Saga of Redemption* (Leiden: Brill, 2008); Noël O'Sullivan, *Christ and Creation: Christology as the Key to Interpreting the Theology of Creation in the Works of Henri de Lubac* (Oxford: Peter Lang, 2009).

and for him" (Col 1:15-16). If the ancient Hebrews (and contemporary Jews) were unabashedly theocentric in their understanding of the origins of the world and its dependence on Yahweh, Christians through the centuries have been no less christocentric in their doctrine of creation.

The scriptural witness, however, is also replete with references to the role of the Spirit of God in creation. The Genesis account actually continues to say, "In the beginning *when* God created the heavens and the earth, the earth was a formless void and darkness covered the face of the deep, while a wind [*rûaḥ*] from God swept over the face of the waters" (Gen 1:1-2 NRSV [emphasis added]). While it is certainly true that within the ancient Hebrew perspective the *rûaḥ* of God was not understood as a distinct divine and personal hypostasis, as the Holy Spirit is in post-Nicene trinitarian theology, the latter frame of reference allows for a credible connection between the breath or wind of God in the First Testament and the Spirit of God in the Christian Scriptures.[8] Pursuant to this springboard, there are other canonical indicators that link the divine breath with both the creative and providential activities of God. The psalmist, for instance, insists,

> By the word of the LORD the heavens were made,
> their starry host by the breath of his mouth. (Ps 33:6)

This is a seeming elaboration on the Genesis statement. Further, the author of the creation narrative references the divine breath of life (Gen 1:30; 2:7). This the psalmist also explicates when considering living creatures.

> When you hide your face,
> they are terrified;
> when you take away their breath,
> they die and return to the dust.
> When you send your Spirit,
> they are created,
> and you renew the face of the ground. (Ps 104:29-30; cf. Job 34:14-15;
> Eccles 12:7)

---

[8]It is in part for this reason that John R. Levison, *Filled with the Spirit* (Grand Rapids: Eerdmans, 2009), does not capitalize "spirit" in relationship to God, even when discussing the divine spirit in the New Testament; I am sympathetic to his argument exegetically but will retain capitalization in this essay as I am working intentionally as a systematician toward a trinitarian theological construct.

The Old Testament witness is clear: the breath of Yahweh is involved in the divine creation and certainly in the originating and sustaining of creaturely life.

What is the payoff for a trinitarian theology of creation and its origins? Briefly for now, the point is to insist that God creates the world through his two hands—by Word and Spirit. When applied to the theology-and-science conversation, such claims beg to be cashed out in terms of the world's properties, whether that be correlating Word and Spirit with form and energy, or with energy and information, or some other set of associations.[9] Depending on predispositions toward how theology functions symbolically, metaphorically or analogically, such claims and arguments will be more or less plausible. These need not be adjudicated for our purposes, which is only to point out that the Christian doctrine of creation is both christological and pneumatological, and hence, in that case, fundamentally trinitarian.

God as redeemer by Word and Spirit. If it is theologically not only acceptable but also imperative that God is acknowledged to be Creator through Word and Spirit, can the same be said about God as redeemer? Certainly Christian theology is founded on God revealed in and by Christ, which involves God's redemptive activities in Jesus' life, death, resurrection and ascension, minimally delimited. More accurately for our present purposes, however, God saves by Christ not just people but also the world, even the created order and what is in it. The latter part of the Colossian hymn quoted earlier proclaims, "through him [God] reconcile[d] to himself all things, whether things on earth or things in heaven, by making peace through his blood, shed on the cross" (Col 1:20). Undeniably, God who created through the Word also redeems the creation by the Word.

Can the same also be said of the Spirit? Does God who created through the breath of Yahweh also redeem the world by the Spirit? Theological categorizations that understand the work of Christ soteriologically and the work of the Spirit in terms of the doctrine of sanctification might argue that, strictly speaking, the Spirit purifies rather than saves. However, any pneumatological theology requires also a fully pneumatological soteriology (God's saving work in Christ ensues pneumatologically), even as any Christian doctrine of sal-

---

[9]Sjoerd L. Bonting, "Spirit and Creation," *Zygon: Journal of Religion and Science* 41 (2006): 713–26, prefers to see the Word as the energy of creation and the Spirit as the information of creation, analogically understood of course.

vation without the Spirit remains binitarian rather than truly trinitarian.[10] Unfolded in this way, Jesus saves as the Christ precisely through the Spirit's messianic anointing, even as the Day of Pentecost's outpouring of the Spirit is deeply soteriological, not just ecclesiological (as might have been suggested in certain streams of the theological tradition). In fact, Peter's "pentecostal sermon" (drawing from the prophet Joel, as recorded by St. Luke), proclaims the intertwining of the work of the Spirit and the salvation of the world.

> In the last days, God says,
> > I will pour out my Spirit on all people.
> Your sons and daughters will prophesy,
> > your young men will see visions,
> > your old men will dream dreams.
> Even on my servants, both men and women,
> > I will pour out my Spirit in those days,
> > and they will prophesy.
> I will show wonders in the heavens above
> > and signs on the earth below,
> > blood and fire and billows of smoke.
> The sun will be turned to darkness
> > and the moon to blood
> > before the coming of the great and glorious day of the Lord.
> And everyone who calls
> > on the name of the Lord will be saved. (Acts 2:17-21)

The Spirit's redemptive work is attained as the Spirit of Christ himself—it is Jesus who, after all, pours out the Spirit on the world from the Father's right hand (Acts 2:33)—but its soteriological character ought not be overlooked. And with regard to the specific assignment before us, note that the saving work of the Spirit has cosmic scope, involving the heavens and the earth together. This is not to minimize its effectiveness in saving "everyone who calls on the name of the Lord," but neither should the Spirit's cosmic redemption be underestimated.[11]

But what are the repercussions for a theology of creation if the redemption of the cosmos is a triune achievement? At this juncture, two preliminary

---

[10]See chap. 2 of my *The Spirit Poured Out on All Flesh: Pentecostalism and the Possibility of Global Theology* (Grand Rapids: Baker Academic, 2005).

[11]See Frank D. Macchia, *Justified in the Spirit: Creation, Redemption, and the Triune God*, Pentecostal Manifestos 3 (Grand Rapids: Eerdmans, 2010).

comments are in order. First, all created realities formed through Word and Spirit are fallen, and in need of redemption. Put otherwise, the created world is deformed, its mechanisms broken, and its processes misdirected. The two hands of the Father are thus at work to reform the world, to heal its functions and mechanisms, and to reorient its trajectories. Second, however, it could also be said that the norms of such reformation, healing and renewal are christological, according to the revelation of God in Christ, even while their means are pneumatological, through the outpouring of the Spirit on all flesh. The pneumatological corollary to the latter claim is that the many tongues of all flesh can somehow be redeemed, even to the point of being able to declare "God's deeds of power" (Acts 2:11, NRSV)—exactly what the primordial creation was designed to do. We will return in part two to flesh out other elements of this pneumatological aspect of a theology of creation.

God as consummator in Word and Spirit. If it is expected that God both creates and redeems by Word and Spirit, there should not be too much disagreement about extending the latter to considering God as bringing about the final consummation through Word and Spirit. Traditional theology has always affirmed this christologically, not least as grounded in what the Colossian hymn declares as already having been accomplished by the cross of Christ. The classical articulation, however, tended to talk about the ongoing, not-yet or eschatological scope of salvation in terms of the Spirit's sanctifying and glorifying work. The present discussion presumes both that God's redemption in Christ is pneumatological (and therefore trinitarian) even as eschatological salvation is also both christological and in the Holy Spirit (thus triunely executed).

There is abundant testimony in the Scriptures to this eschatological aspect of the Spirit's work. Our present focus, however, invites consideration of the consummating work of the Spirit as it relates to the created order. Here St. Paul's magnificent declaration in the middle of his letter to the Romans emphasizes that "the whole creation has been groaning as in the pains of childbirth right up to the present time. Not only so, but we ourselves, who have the firstfruits of the Spirit, groan inwardly as we wait eagerly for our adoption to sonship, the redemption of our bodies"; more precisely, toward this eschatological consummation, "the Spirit helps us in our weakness. We do not know what we ought to pray for, but the Spirit himself intercedes for us through wordless groans. And he who searches our hearts knows the mind of the Spirit, because the Spirit intercedes for God's people in accordance with the will of God" (Rom 8:22-23, 26-27).[12] This passage succinctly connects what are otherwise disparate threads across the New Testament witness: the redemptive work of the Spirit unleashed in incarnation and Pentecost culminates in the coming reign of God, and the salvation of saints—that people of God, the body of Christ, and the fellowship of the Spirit—is interconnected with the renovation and renewal of all creation.[13]

What then is at stake for such a conjoined christological and pneumatological approach to creation's consummation? On the one hand, the redemption of the world of people is not accomplished apart from the reclamation of all creation, and this final restoration is trinitarianly finalized in Christ and the Spirit. On the other hand, creation has a goal, the beautiful image of Christ, refracted in the Spirit of God, and it appears that what is divinely initiated and to be brought to pass nevertheless also involves human groaning, sighing and interceding. Such intercession invites responsive human intervention, understood as participation in the redemptive and consummative work of the triune God.[14]

THE SPIRIT OF CHRIST AND THE RENEWAL OF CREATION: A TRINITARIAN RECONFIGURING

The emerging thesis of this essay is that a trinitarian theology of creation is not only christological but also pneumatological and that the latter especially involves both redemptive and eschatological horizons. This pneumatological, soteriological and eschatological trajectory also contributes to, and even extends, where other theologies of creation (even christologically

---

[12]Unpacked in Amos Yong, *Spirit of Love: A Trinitarian Theology of Grace* (Waco, TX: Baylor University Press, 2012), chap. 7, esp. 121–24.

[13]See also Andrew Sung Park, *Triune Atonement: Christ's Healing for Sinners, Victims, and the Whole Creation* (Louisville, KY: Westminster John Knox, 2009); and David T. Beck, *The Holy Spirit and the Renewal of All Things: Pneumatology in Paul and Jürgen Moltmann* (Eugene, OR: Wipf & Stock, 2010).

[14]For example, Lincoln Harvey, "'The Two Hands of the Father': A Trinitarian Doctrine of Creation as a Christian Solution to the Question of How Humans Grow in Knowledge of the World" (PhD diss., King's College, London, 2008), chap. 5 ("From Garden to City: Growth in Knowledge and the Project of Creation"), where Harvey, drawing on the oeuvre of the late Colin Gunton, argues that human growth in knowledge is possible through the Spirit as part of participation in the Spirit's eschatological work of redemption in anticipation of the coming reign of God and the heavenly city.

defined ones) often fail to go. The additional argument to be developed is
that a pneumatological-eschatological approach to theology has implications not only for *what* we know about the creation but also *how* we understand and then act within it.[15] If this is the case, then a *theology* of creation
includes a creational praxis that works—even prays (as St. Paul grasped)—
for the *renewal* of creation. The following trinitarian theology of creation
thus has not only cognitive but also existential and performative dimensions.
The former existential aspect, intellectually articulated, has methodological
and theoretical applications as well, so we begin there.

*The many tongues of the Spirit of Christ: methodological and disci-
plinary implications.* I have already gestured above toward the important
role for the Day of Pentecost narrative in any pneumatological approach to
theology of creation.[16] I suggested there that the many tongues of the Day
of Pentecost event signal how the salvation of the Spirit recaptures the many
human languages for the purpose of giving glory to God. But if human
languages are constituted by and perpetuate cultural realities and traditions
as well, then the redemptive work of God involves also the redemption, renewal and sanctification of these domains. This is not to say that all cultures
and what each includes are thereby rendered pure, as if concluding toward
a universalist soteriology; it is to say that there can be no a priori demarca-
tions of the Spirit's regenerative work and that there is always the possibility
of any language and its cultural milieu being apprehended to bear the gospel
message and be reoriented toward the reign of God to come.[17]

But if the work of the Spirit involves the redemption of human tongues
and languages in various respects, what does this mean for a theology of
creation? Insofar as any understanding of the created order involves at least
some focused attention on and study of its various elements, inasmuch as
such study has evolved over the centuries into different scientific disciplines
and other fields of inquiry, and to the degree that the gaining of expertise in
such disciplines and areas of inquiry can be likened to learning new lan-

---

[15]For more extensive considerations of this claim, see my book-length *Word-Community: Theological Hermeneutics in Trinitarian Perspective*, New Critical Thinking in Religion, Theology and
Biblical Studies (Aldershot: Ashgate, 2002; repr., Eugene, OR: Wipf & Stock, 2006).
[16]See also Yong, *Spirit Poured Out on All Flesh*, chap. 7.
[17]E.g., Amos Yong, "Discerning the Spirit(s) in the Natural World: Toward a Typology of 'Spirit'
in the Theology and Science Conversation," *Theology and Science* 3 (2005): 315–29.

guages and gaining facility in a range of discursive practices (of research), might it be possible to view the various methods of investigation across the disciplines as redemptive epistemologies that by illuminating the created world for human understanding make possible, support and arouse the glorification of God?[18] Again, this is not to baptize all scientific or other forms of inquiry as redemptive in whole or in part. It is to recognize that the sciences and other fields of human knowing provide methodologies with which to understand the world and that theists in general, not to mention Christians particularly, can avail themselves of such approaches as well. When interwoven with theological commitments, what emerges are dual but complementary lenses—the two books of nature and of Scripture, as the medieval theologians put it[19]—through which the world is understood, discussed and engaged. The Day of Pentecost metaphor, I submit, invites consideration of how the many discursive practices that constitute contemporary scientific and other fields of research can also be vehicles for declaring the glory of God.

To be sure, just as not all tongues, nor all languages or all cultures, speak coherently or truthfully about God's deeds of power, so also the many disciplines may deploy faulty methods, be based on false presuppositions and communicate misleading ideas. Any trinitarian theology of creation thus holds that while it is the work of the Spirit to inspire the many tongues—and by extension here, the many disciplines—to glorify God, it is the form of Christ that provides the norm and standard for assessing all truth claims, even those related to the created world. The caveat of course is that oftentimes it is difficult to apply a christological assessment to particular claims (i.e., in mathematics, physics, geology and so on). Especially the scientific disciplines, as self-correcting paths of inquiry (when working properly), will be expected to adjudicate matters in the long run, and theologians will need to exercise the virtue of patience in order to allow the various disputes to be sorted out. On the other hand, it may also be that theologians who have some training in and are alert to what can be learned from other disciplines (languages) would be

---

[18]This is first argued in my article, "Academic Glossolalia? Pentecostal Scholarship, Multi-Disciplinarity, and the Science-Religion Conversation," *Journal of Pentecostal Theology* 14 (2005): 61–80; see also the elaborated version in my *Spirit of Creation*, chap. 2.

[19]For more on the two books in the medieval tradition, see Amos Yong, "Reading Scripture and Nature: Pentecostal Hermeneutics and Their Implications for the Contemporary Evangelical Theology and Science Conversation," *Perspectives on Science and Christian Faith* 53 (2011): 1–13, esp. 9–11.

in a good position to offer theological perspectives with the potential to advance the discussion also in such fields of research, examination and study.

The many invitations of the Spirit of Christ: existential-integrative supplications. The preceding leads us into the thorny area of faith integration.[20] Christian colleges and universities are especially concerned about these matters, and rightly so. Part of the problem with integration discourse is that it presumes two compartments—that of faith and reason (among other labels)—that logically and rhetorically already resist assimilation. This is not to give up on the project of "integration," but it does invite alternative conceptualizations. The undertaking is much more urgent given the modernist epistemology that bifurcates facts from values, that exacerbates the chasm between objectivity and subjectivity, and that separates the external realm of nature from the personal dimension of the human. There is no doubt that modern science has blossomed in part because of its capacity to ferret out hypotheses based on experimental replication across cultural-linguistic divides. However, there is also no disputing that some extreme formulations apart from faith can devolve into a methodological scientism that not only ignores the personal dimension of all human knowing but also fools itself into thinking that human knowers somehow stand apart from what is known as if from an omniscient view from nowhere.[21] Arrogant pronouncements dismissing religion according to the so-called light of science sometimes result, and this in turn has galvanized some faithful into rejecting modern science because of its perceived atheism.[22]

A pneumatological approach to theology recognizes that there can be a head-knowledge without a heart-transformation. While knowledge *of* is important and should not be dismissed, existentially meaningful knowing connects the head to the whole person and realizes that the latter response is re-

---

[20]I broach this topic in "Finding the Holy Spirit at the Christian University: Renewal and the Future of Higher Education in the Pentecostal-Charismatic Tradition," in *Spirit-Empowered Christianity in the 21st Century: Insights, Analyses, and Future Trends*, ed. Vinson Synan (Lake Mary, FL: Charisma House, 2011), 455–76 and 577–87, which argument is being expanded in my forthcoming book (with Dale Coulter), *Finding the Holy Spirit at the Christian University: Renewing Christian Higher Education* (Grand Rapids: Eerdmans, 2015).

[21]Brilliantly exposed as inaccessible by Thomas Nagel, *The View from Nowhere* (Oxford: Oxford University Press, 1989).

[22]Amos Yong, "God and the Evangelical Laboratory: Recent Conservative Protestant Thinking About Theology and Science," *Theology and Science* 5 (2007): 203–21; and "Science and Religion: Introducing the Issues, Entering the Debates—A Review Essay," *Christian Scholar's Review* 40 (2011): 189–203.

quired (see Acts 2:38). Soteriologically, this involves, at least in part, repentance and turning to Christ. With regard to a theology of creation, however, a pneumatological orientation extends such intellectual conversion to include an attentiveness to and turning toward whatever aspect of the world is desired to be understood.[23] This expands the previously delineated methodological and disciplinary commitments in a personalistic direction. It also bridges the gulf between faith and reason both personally and interpersonally in believing communities of inquiry that pursue their scholarly vocations faithfully.

What, then, is involved in such a pneumato-personalistic theology of creation? Minimally, any theological knowing *of* creation must also confess an inhabitation *amid* creation. Further, faith and reason are not thereby dualities to be bridged—there is no simple demarcation of object and subject—but two sides of the one coin of faithful knowing.[24] Within this framework, then, even theological knowing of the world—creation in its many guises—can learn not only from across the scientific disciplines but also from the interpersonal and dialogical engagements with perspectives of many other cultural and historical traditions. A theology of creation does not leave behind scientific forms of inquiry but necessarily now expands to include intercultural components and moments. The stakes are higher now, however, because knowledge of creation is no longer just objectively gained by us about something "out there" but is also about our being together interpersonally and intersubjectively in the world with those of other perspectives and even commitments.

None of this involves leaving behind scriptural foundations or compromising faith allegiances. It does complicate understanding of where biblical and theological analyses begin and leave off, where scientific, humanistic and crosscultural perspectives come in and exit, and how personally and socioculturally shaped inclinations, intuitions and sensibilities facilitate navigation of these epistemic and existential matters. An integrative the-

---

[23]I presume here a Lonerganian-Polanyian epistemology and a Kuhnian philosophy of science, all explicated via the pneumatological imagination that I develop in my book *Spirit-Word-Community*, esp. part 2.

[24]See my essays, "Sanctification, Science, and the Spirit: Salvaging Holiness in the Late Modern World," *Wesleyan Theological Journal* 47, no. 2 (2012): 36–52; "Whence and Whither in Evangelical Higher Education? Dispatches from a Shifting Frontier," *Christian Scholar's Review* 42 (2013): 179–92; and "The Holy Spirit and the Christian University: The Renewal of Evangelical Higher Education," in *Christian Scholarship in the Twenty-First Century: Prospects and Perils*, ed. Gregg A. Ten Elshoff, Thomas M. Crisp and Steve L. Porter (Grand Rapids: Eerdmans, 2014), 163–80.

ology of creation requires just that sort of interdisciplinary and intercultural approach, since what is being considered is the entirety of what is, according to the Christian understanding. A pneumatological imagination insists that such knowing cannot leave behind the subjectivity of the knower—involving aesthetic, imagistic and affective modalities of perception too—even as it also has to take into account the thick subjectivity of other knowers both within and outside of the faith.[25] The christological criterion, however, enables discernment of that which is more versus less assured as Christians see through a glass dimly (1 Cor 13:12). This pneumatological-christological flank is necessary for any trinitarian theology of inquiry into creation to emerge.

The many witnesses of the Spirit of Christ: performative applications. My claim throughout this second half of the essay is that a pneumatologically forged theology of creation involves methodological and disciplinary pluralism (the many tongues) even as it requires the existential immersion of the theologian into the very subject or object of consideration—creation itself in its complexity and diverse particularities. Certainly it is far from easy to determine or hear the christological accents clearly amid the many voices. It is here then that a trinitarian theology of creation foregrounds the teleological or eschatological vista of the Spirit's work, which is to reconcile all things to the Father through the Son.

What this means is that a theology of creation comes full circle in moving from intellectual knowledge of creation through personal knowing amid creation to practical knowing regarding creation. The goal of the Spirit's illumination and renewal of minds is both the transformation and renovation of hearts as well as the empowerment and reinvigoration of persons to bear witness to the coming reign of God. Christian scholarship about creation thus heralds the coming reign; Christian mission carried out with sensitivity to creation's ecological and environmental orders thus inaugurates the universal restoration of the age to come; and Christian vocation faithfully

---

[25]I develop this thesis with regard to the religious dimensions of culture in a few books, most recently in a volume engaging with the theology and science discussion as well: *The Cosmic Breath: Spirit and Nature in the Christianity-Buddhism-Science Trialogue*, Philosophical Studies in Science & Religion 4 (Leiden: Brill, 2012); see also, Veli-Matti Kärkkäinen, Kirsteen Kim and Amos Yong, eds., *Interdisciplinary and Religio-Cultural Discourses on a Spirit-Filled World: Loosing the Spirits* (New York: Palgrave Macmillan, 2013).

pursued in the world also anticipates the shalomic order of the triune God.[26] A trinitarian theology of creation therefore knits together knowing-being-doing in a hermeneutical spiral because it is communicated through, by and in the Spirit of the coming Christ.

Christ is the goal toward which creation culminates. Any elaborated theology of creation that fails to motivate positive christoform actions may not be submitted to the Spirit of God. Further, any alleged theology of creation that urges a set of behaviors or a way of life that is contrary to the full measure of the stature of Christ is thus detected to be anti-Christian and acted out inconsistently with the inspiration of the divine breath. These christological parameters, however, far from narrowing the range of possibilities for human thinking-being-acting, could empower innovative and liberative creational praxis. What is checked by the Spirit of Christ, for those capable of perceiving, are sinful, false and destructive notions (and their effects); what is empowered are a wider range of freedoms for others, for the world and for the creation originally declared good and now longing for liberation and final redemption. If inspection of the fruits assists in determination of the tree, so also theological truth claims will be discriminated via the consequences they underwrite.

Practically, then, one trajectory of assessing the value of theologies of creation will be how they inform Christian beliefs about, postures toward and practices regarding the created environment.[27] Any worship of creation is indefensible since by theological definition the world derives from and is dependent on God as Creator. However, theologies that either do not admonish against the exploitation of creation or fail to urge human stewardship of the environment and its resources are both defective. Both fall short of the christological criterion of incarnation that reflects the divine commitment to embrace and redeem the materiality of the created order, and hence both cannot be stimulated by the divine breath that actualized the form of Christ as the image of the eternal and living God.

---

[26]Sigurd Bergman, *Creation Set Free: The Spirit as Liberator of Nature* (Grand Rapids: Eerdmans, 2005).

[27]I am helped here by my fellow Pentecostal theologians, e.g., Steven M. Studebaker, "The Spirit in Creation: A Unified Theology of Grace and Creation Care," *Zygon: Journal of Religion and Science* 43 (2008): 943–60, and the three essays by Shane Clifton, Matthew Tallman and Peter Althouse in *The Spirit Renews the Face of the Earth: Pentecostal Forays in Science and Theology of Creation,* ed. Amos Yong (Eugene, OR: Pickwick, 2009), part 3, "Theological Explorations."

CONCLUSION: THE SPIRIT AND AN ESCHATOLOGICAL THEOLOGY OF CREATION

In some respects this essay is prolegomena to a theology of creation in general, much less to a trinitarian theology of creation in particular; it explores the methodological arcs outlined by a pneumatological approach to the topic, clarifying along the way notions of interdisciplinarity, epistemic holism and the link between beliefs and practices. On the other hand, I noted at the beginning that any pentecostally inflected theology ultimately aspires not just to further Pentecostal in-group thinking but also to renew the church, including its theological discussions. The preceding thus suggests that such a pneumatological and hence trinitarian theology of creation generates not just a new set of ideas—there is from Qoheleth's standpoint nothing new under the sun—but perhaps a reorganization of basic Christian beliefs, sentiments and practices that are nevertheless timely for trinitarian thinking about science and the material world in the present global context. God creates through Word and Spirit, redeems by Word and Spirit, and consummates the divine plans in Word and Spirit. Christian theologies of creation after the turn to pneumatology will receive impetus to not just think truthfully about the world but also to inhabit it more faithfully and to work within it more intentionally in anticipation of the coming reign of God. We are a long way from living rightly in the world, much less acting justly in it. So if these are indispensable moments of the hermeneutical spiral and crucial to the Christian theological task, we must also still be far from having thought truthfully about the creation as well. Perhaps the foregoing can contribute in some small way to linking Christian ideas, commitments and practices back together toward a trinitarian theology of creation. Come, Holy Spirit; renew us and the creation.

11

"Rooted and Established in Love"

The Holy Spirit and Salvation

Michael Welker

The Holy Spirit and salvation—this is a topic that makes us hold our breath. Should we speculate about the spiritual power of God that protects us "for a salvation ready to be revealed [only] in the last time" (1 Pet 1:5 ESV)? Should we thus try to gaze into a distant realm of eternity, far beyond our finite and mortal life? Such an approach would bring with it the problem that the few stories and images about the eternal heavenly joy and glory that we find in the biblical traditions do not offer us much substantial information on the role and work of the Holy Spirit.

The biblical traditions do not offer much information about a direct relation between the Holy Spirit and so-called end-time salvation in a general way either. Rather, they speak in a more down-to-earth way of salvation in and "through our Lord Jesus Christ" (see, e.g., 1 Thess 5:9; Rom 3:24; Heb 5:9; 2 Tim 2:10). Should we therefore, as many orthodox theologies have done, draw the talk about the Spirit into the realm of Christology?[1]

To be sure, the resurrected and elevated Jesus Christ does not come without his Spirit and without those he wants to win by the power of his Spirit for his reign and for the divine and eternal life.[2] But it requires some

---

[1]A prime example for this procedure can be found in the work of Karl Barth, esp. throughout his *Church Dogmatics*, but also the writings of Hendrikus Berkhof; cf. Oliver Crisp, "Uniting Us to God: Toward a Reformed Pneumatology," in this volume.

[2]I elaborate this in Michael Welker, *God the Revealed: Christology*, trans. Douglas W. Scott (Grand Rapids: Eerdmans, 2013), 209–50.

careful unfolding and unpacking to penetrate and to clarify these relations between Christ and the Holy Spirit in order to understand and to explain what is meant by the few biblical remarks about "The Holy Spirit of God, with whom you were sealed for the day of redemption" (Eph 4:30).

If we want to resist the temptation to simply shy away from the topic "Holy Spirit and salvation" and to focus on the realm of Christology instead— if we want to gain an adequate notion of the Holy Spirit himself—we have to avoid another problematic shift of the topic. We have to avoid a trap that led Occidental thought to confuse the biblical notions of the Spirit with Stoic and Aristotelian concepts, with a notion of the spirit as a basically mental and intellectual power, wrongly identified with the divine Spirit. Dominant thoughts in the West about this kind of spirit have focused on the cognitively steered self-referentiality of the individual person, of groups, societies and cultures. With this confusion, they have blocked an adequate understanding of the Holy Spirit and his saving work.[3]

THE ARISTOTELIAN SPIRIT AND THE BIBLICAL SPIRIT OF GOD

In the famous book 12 of his *Metaphysics*, Aristotle defines the spirit as the force that thinks itself, insofar as it participates in what is thought and becomes part of it.[4] Thus the spirit is the power that does not lose itself in a relationship with "the other," but rather receives and maintains itself in the thinking relationship to the objects of thought. Our understanding of the world and our understanding of ourselves are mediated through this spirit. The quality of all thought and understanding is the result of the heightening of self-understanding along with the simultaneous recognition and understanding of external reality. Aristotle connects this spiritual activity with self-actualization, freedom and one's own well-being. He even calls this activity "divine." For it is the perfect actualization of all knowledge about all

---

[3]Michael Welker, "The Holy Spirit," in *The Oxford Handbook of Systematic Theology*, ed. John B. Webster, Kathryn Tanner and Iain R. Torrance (Oxford: Oxford University Press, 2007), 236–48. The fixation on the self-referential activity of the Spirit also created great stress in the pious self-examining heart; see the vivid illustration with respect to the Wesley brothers and their environments by Jeffrey Barbeau, "Enthusiasts, Rationalists and Pentecost: The Holy Spirit in Eighteenth-Century Methodism," in this volume.

[4]See Aristotle, *Metaphysics, Books 10–14*, trans. Hugh Tredennick and G. Cyril Armstrong, Loeb Classical Library 287 (Cambridge, MA: Harvard University Press, 1935), 12.1072b; and Michael Welker, *God the Spirit*, new ed. (Eugene, OR: Wipf & Stock, 2013), 283–302.

reality, together with absolute self-knowledge that characterizes divinity. The best and eternal life belongs to it, and it does so in perfect freedom.[5]

Many theological notions of a faith-relation to God and of the eternal *visio beatifica*, the vision of ultimate salvation, are shaped, or we should rather say, poisoned by this line of thought. This critique of such an influential reduction of the spirit to cognitive rationality, however, should not lead us to support many conventional false oppositions of "Spirit and reason" or "faith and reason." Paul discusses speaking in tongues with the Corinthians. In 1 Corinthians 14:19 he clearly says: "I rather desire to speak five words with reason [with *nous*] in the church, that I may instruct others, rather than ten thousand in tongues." And he then argues strongly for even praying with *nous* and for doxology with *nous*.[6] The problem is not the use of reason in faith and in the church. The decisive problem is the reduction of the human spirit and even the works of the divine Spirit to powers of intellect and reason.

Aristotle's influential philosophical theory of the spirit and its correlated view of freedom and salvation have blocked the path to a biblically oriented doctrine of the Spirit of God and an understanding of freedom and salvation as mediated by the Holy Spirit. A biblically oriented alternative to Aristotelian thought about the spirit has to start from a different perspective than the self-referential cognitive and mental power. It should start, as I propose, with the great biblical image of the "outpouring of the Spirit." Talking about the outpouring of the Spirit forces us to focus on a wealth and plenitude of relations, on the constitution of a spiritual community with many interrelations, mutual effects and radiations.[7] This is a very different starting point over against the reflexive, mentalistic and often individualistic anthropomorphic concepts of spirit that have resulted from the influence of Aristotelian metaphysics and related theories.

However, the wealth of relations captured with the notion of the outpouring of the Spirit is not easily perceived as helpful exactly because the generated diversity and plenitude is not easy to control in imagination. This approach

---

[5]See Aristotle, *Metaphysics* 12.1072b.19–32.

[6]See my argument in "Spirit Topics: Trinity, Personhood, Mystery, and Tongues. A Response to Frank Macchia on *God the Spirit*," *Journal of Pentecostal Theology* 10 (1997): 29–34, with reference to Welker, *God the Spirit*.

[7]Sandra Richter, "What Do I Know of Holy? On the Person and Work of the Holy Spirit in Scripture," in this volume, illuminates this with reference to several phenomena, especially the life of worship.

then leads many people to assume that we cannot really know anything about the Holy Spirit at all—that the Spirit is just a numinous power. And it seems to follow that, when we want to focus on the divine Spirit, we had rather remain piously silent in the face of the divine apophatic mystery.

Over against an intellectualistic reductionism in the Aristotelian vein on the one side and over against the—only seemingly pious—will to opacity and vagueness on the other side, the biblical classics about the pouring of the Spirit provide us with illuminating insights. In the foremost classic, the prophet Joel tells us that God's Spirit will be poured out on men and women, on the old and the young, and on male and female slaves (Joel 2:28-29). The other great classic, the Pentecost narrative in Acts 2, quotes Joel and adds that the Spirit of God comes down on human beings of different nations, cultures and languages.

The consequences of this outpouring of the Spirit are indeed understood to be salvific. The human beings who are gifted and filled by the Spirit gain cognition of God, the power of proclamation and spiritual communication, and related, orienting ethical powers for their lives.[8] At this point it should be emphasized that the biblical traditions do not regard each and every pouring of the Spirit as salvific. Rather, God can pour out a "spirit of distortion" (Is 19:14 NASB) or a negative "spirit of deep sleep" that blinds even the prophets (Is 29:10 NASB). Over against this negative effect, the salvific pouring of the Spirit of which not only Joel and Acts speak, but also Isaiah (32:15), Ezekiel (39:29), Zechariah (12:10) and Paul's letter to the Romans (5:5), constitutes a lively spiritual plural and polyphonic communality and community.

In the light of the biblical classics, this polyphony appears to be loaded. It can be regarded as subversive and even as revolutionary. According to the prophet Joel not only the men but also the women are overcome by the Spirit— and this is said in patriarchal environments. The young people are overcome by the Spirit—and this is said in gerontocratic contexts. And even the "men-servants and maidservants," most likely slaves, are overcome and gifted by the Spirit of God—and this is said in slaveholder societies. Finally the account of Acts challenges all ethnocentric and exclusivist perspectives on the work of

---

[8]See Michael Welker, ed., *The Work of the Spirit: Pneumatology and Pentecostalism* (Grand Rapids: Eerdmans, 2006); and Frank Macchia, *Baptized in the Spirit: A Global Pentecostal Theology* (Grand Rapids: Zondervan, 2006).

the Spirit by its emphasis on the fact that people from many nations, many cultures and many languages are overcome by the Spirit of God.

The idea of such a polyphony and of the multitude of interrelations in the community of the Spirit easily raises the fear that we have nothing but chaos.[9] To be sure, the emergent reality of the working of the Spirit and the emergent reality of the coming of the reign of God that the biblical traditions envision present multifarious cognitive difficulties for our attempts to grasp this process and event.[10] However, the outpouring of the divine Spirit gains clarity by its connection with the gifts of the Spirit (*charismata*) that are especially emphasized by Paul (1 Cor 7:7; 12:4-13; 13:1-3; 14:4-19; Rom 12:4-8). According to Paul, the Spirit and the gifts of the Spirit serve the edification, enlivenment and vivification of a structured community—of the "body of Christ" (Rom 12; 1 Cor 12). The church as the body of Christ has to be seen as a pluralistic and organismic unity of a distinct and limited number of members. These members are all related to Jesus Christ as their head, but among themselves they live in only relative and functional hierarchical relations. Sometimes the eyes are particularly important, sometimes the hands, sometimes the feet (see 1 Cor 12:12-26). The lively polyphonic "unity of the body" is constituted and maintained by the pouring of the Spirit and the multitude of the gifts of the Spirit.[11]

Since so many established monohierarchical, patriarchal, ageist, classist, nationalistic and culture-chauvinistic guidelines are thus questioned and challenged by the outpouring of the Spirit, we should ask again: How is it that Paul can claim that the "Spirit of freedom" is not actually a Spirit of disorder, even of chaos (see 1 Cor 14:33)?

SPIRIT AND LAW

The first answer to that question deals with the form and efficacy of the Spirit and with the work of the Spirit. It helps us to clearly address the concerns

---

[9]Estrelda Y. Alexander, "The Spirit of God: Christian Renewal in African American Pentecostalism," in this volume, gives examples of how these fears are evoked today.

[10]See Michael Welker and Michael Wolter, "Die Unscheinbarkeit des Reiches Gottes," in *Reich Gottes, Marburger Jahrbuch Theologie XI*, ed. W. Härle and R. Preul (Marburg: Elwert, 1999), 103–16; Welker, *God the Revealed*, 223–34.

[11]See John Zizioulas, *Being as Communion: Studies in Personhood and the Church* (New York: St. Vladimir's Seminary Press, 1997), 110–14; Welker, *The Work of the Spirit*, 221–32.

that the Spirit of God is not a "numinous being" and that the outpouring of the Spirit does not lead to religious and cultural chaos and confusion. This answer is also important for theological discourse between different religions and for theological discourse with other worldviews. It says that the efficacy of the Spirit of God stands in continuity and discontinuity with the law traditions—with regard to the Old Testament they stand in continuity and discontinuity with the Torah.

The Spirit, too, cares for justice, mercy and the cognition of truth before God—for true worship. In the most important messianic promises in the book of Isaiah (Is 11; 42; 61), which the New Testament expressly and explicitly associates with the person and work of Jesus Christ, we find mention of "the Chosen One of God" on whom *the Spirit of God rests*.[12] It is said that this Chosen One of God will bring justice among the nations, protection and rescue for the poor and the weak, and knowledge of God both for the Jews and for the Gentiles. Justice, compassion and the knowledge of God— here we have the fundamental goals of the biblical law. Matthew 23:23 identifies "the more important matters of the law [as] justice, mercy and faithfulness." One can hardly overestimate the incredible influence on Western cultures of these normative powers and their interconnections.

Even today the connection between justice and the protection of the weak continues to shape the dynamics of the evolution of a just and humane law and society. Correspondingly, the connection between the protection of the weak and the law has led to the institutionalization of a "culture of aid" not only in the social work of the churches and other religious communities but also in the form of basic legal, societal, cultural and political interests in many nations on earth: interests in general education, in basic economic welfare for all people and in a dependable health-care system. It was hardly coincidental that after the fall of the Nazi regime Germany sought to regain international trust and recognition by portraying itself as a "state under the rule of law" and as a "welfare state."[13]

Within the topic of this chapter we cannot examine the complex normative dynamics of the biblical legal traditions which have been power-

---

[12]Welker, *God the Spirit*, 108–24.
[13]See Douglas Peterson, "Stories of Grace: Pentecostals and Social Justice," in this volume, on these dynamic relations in today's spiritual movements.

fully effective up to the modern era.[14] If we want to focus on the relation of the Spirit to the law with respect to salvation, we have to focus on the *limits* the law has despite its wonderful inner dynamics. Even God's good law can fall under the power of sin. The law can indeed take on highly dangerous forms and even degenerate into a "law of sin" (Rom 8:2). But it is very important to see that Paul does not operate with some primitive dichotomy between law and Spirit, or he could not have spoken of a "law of the Spirit" (Rom 8:2), a "law of faith" (Rom 3:27 NASB) or a "law of Christ" (Gal 6:2). Rather what is characteristic of the work of the Spirit of God is the further development of the most impressive yet vulnerable ethos of the law into an ethos of love, hope and faith. The intentions of the law—namely, to promote justice, mercy and the knowledge of God (or perceptions of truth)—remain intact. In a positive sense they have been "elevated" by the power of the Spirit.

This elevation also applies to the Spirit of Christ. However, for many people, even within the church, the "Spirit of the Lord" is still connected with the model of a monarchical "royal rule of Christ" or of a "Christocratic brotherhood" in the sense of Barmen III,[15] the hierarchical-patriarchal tones of which cannot easily be associated with a convincing understanding of freedom. It is Calvin who offers a helpful alternative in going back to the biblical understanding that Jesus Christ, on whom the Spirit of God (the Spirit of justice, mercy and knowledge of God) rests, pours out this Spirit on all "those who are his."[16]

In his great work the *Institutes of the Christian Religion*, Calvin emphatically notes that Christ the Messiah was not anointed with oil but with the Holy Spirit so that those who belong to him might have a share in his power.

---

[14]See Michael Welker, "Theologie und Recht," *Der Staat* (2010): 573–85; Welker, "The Power of Mercy in Biblical Law," *Journal of Law and Religion* 29, no. 2 (2014): 1–11; in the following I take up some of the insights gained in these contributions.

[15]While the Barmen Declaration was in its own time, and still is today, a highly laudable and in many respects exemplary theological text, it does display significant pneumatological deficits; see Michael Welker, "Barmen III: Woran orientieren? Die Gestalt der Kirche in gesellschaftlichen Umbrüchen," in *Begründete Freiheit—Die Aktualität der Barmer Theologischen Erklärung. Vortragsreihe zum 75. Jahrestag im Berliner Dom*, ed. Martin Heimbucher, Evangelische Impulse 1 (Neukirchen-Vluyn: Neukirchener, 2009), 59–75.

[16]James Dunn, "Towards the Spirit of Christ: The Emergence of the Distinctive Features of Christian Pneumatology," in *The Work of the Spirit: Pneumatology and Pentecostalism*, ed. Michael Welker (Grand Rapids: Eerdmans, 2006), 3–26.

Therefore the anointing of the king is not with oil. . . . Rather he is called "Anointed" [*Christus*] of God because "the spirit of wisdom and understanding, the spirit of counsel and might . . . and of the fear of the Lord have rested upon him" [Is 11:2] . . . he did not enrich himself for his own sake [*privatim*], but that he might pour out his abundance upon the hungry and thirsty.[17]

Here Calvin stresses the so-called baptism of the Spirit through anointing "by the Spirit," and this same baptism became a groundbreaking spiritual experience for the early church.[18] The half a billion Christians of the global Pentecostal movement and twentieth-century charismatic renewal have made it the center of their piety.[19]

THE SPIRIT OF LOVE AND THE POWERS OF SALVATION

The power of the Spirit of God and of the elevated Christ in his kingly office and in the kingly dimension of the coming reign of God is most often inconspicuous, but it has an enormous creativity. Jesus Christ is the King—this means the true King is also a brother and a friend, even poor and an outcast. This humble and merciful King wins his witnesses for his reign and for the divine life. A look at the dynamics of love discloses the enormous creativity of this power. In a loving relationship, we respond to the depth and potential richness of the other person's identity, and we rejoice in sharing and discovering ever-new dimensions of the beloved; respectively we feel passionately any deficiencies and lack of opportunities for this person and strive for compensation and healing. The mathematician and philosopher Alfred North Whitehead captured this in his brilliant insight that love might be understood on the basis of parent-to-child love or love between spouses and dear friends as a "self-devotion where the potentialities of the loved object are felt passionately as a claim that it find itself in a friendly Universe. Such love is really an intense feeling as to how the harmony of the world should be realized in particular [persons or] objects."[20]

---

[17]John Calvin, *Institutes of the Christian Religion*, ed. John T. McNeill, trans. Ford Lewis Battles (Louisville, KY: Westminster John Knox, 2006), 2.15.5, 499–501; cf. 2.15.2. Calvin continues: "The Father is said to have given the Spirit to his Son without measure" (Jn 3:34). The reason is expressed as follows: "That from his fullness we might all receive grace upon grace" (Jn 1:16) (cf. 2.15.5, 500).

[18]See Dunn, "Towards the Spirit of Christ," 10–17.

[19]Frank Macchia, *Baptized in the Spirit*; Peter Zimmerling, *Die charismatischen Bewegungen* (Göttingen: Vandenhoeck & Ruprecht, 2001).

[20]Alfred North Whitehead, *Adventures of Ideas* (New York: Free Press, 1967), 289.

The kingdom of Christ and his Spirit is marked by the praxis of loving and forgiving acceptance, by healing, and by liberating teaching and education. In continuity and discontinuity with the Torah traditions, love and forgiveness are defined through the power of *free and creative self-withdrawal for the benefit of others.*[21] The freedom-promoting power that arises from this type of free, creative—and in love also joyous—self-withdrawal for the benefit of one's neighbor is tremendous. The goal of love—which can be defined only unsatisfactorily through the triad of *eros, agape* and *philia*[22]—is that "all things work together for the good" (Rom 8:28) of the one who is loved; to set his or her feet "in a broad place." When it comes to the kingdom of God, it is vital to realize that we are *not primarily aiming to propagate in ourselves a responsibility* toward freedom-promoting action or behavior, but rather to promote *a joyous and thankful recognition of the experience of free self-withdrawal that is done for our own good.* It is for this reason, as recipients of the free self-withdrawal of their favor, that children are said to have a particular closeness to the kingdom of God (Mt 10:14).[23]

A grateful sensitivity for the enormous potentials within free and creative self-withdrawals in family contexts, among friends and in civil and societal organizations can open our eyes to these powers of love. A further sensitivity to today's tremendous global, educational, therapeutic, constitutional, ecclesiastical and intercultural challenges can open our eyes to the incredible formative and freedom-promoting forces of the *munus regium Christi and his Spirit*—for the coming of which we pray. The kingdom of God and the kingdom of Christ are shaped by many, often seemingly insignificant acts of love and forgiveness.

It is not only the direct witnesses who receive a share in this often inconspicuous yet incredibly powerful reign. A "Christian humanism," as William Schweiker and others have named it,[24] also finds equivalent and similar

---

[21]Welker, *God the Revealed*, 235–43.

[22]See John Polkinghorne, ed., *The Work of Love: Creation as Kenosis* (Grand Rapids: Eerdmans, 2001), 127–36.

[23]Michael Welker, "The 'Reign' of God," *Theology Today* 49 (1992): 500–515; see also the moving witnesses in Douglas Peterson's contribution to this volume ("Stories of Grace: Pentecostals and Social Justice").

[24]See David E. Klemm and William Schweiker, *Religion and the Human Future: An Essay on Theological Humanism* (Oxford: Blackwell, 2008); William Schweiker, "Flesh and Folly: The Christ of Christian Humanism," in *Who Is Jesus Christ for Us Today? Pathways to Contemporary Christology,* ed. Michael Welker, Andreas Schuele and Günter Thomas (Louisville, KY: Westminster John Knox, 2009), 85–102.

expressions in other religious and secular forms of practiced love and compassion, while also receiving strong impulses from them. The boundaries of the freedom-promoting kingdom of Christ are more encompassing than those set by the churches of all times and all regions. "Whatever you did to one of the least of these who are members of my family, you did for me," whether you recognized me in them or not (Mt 25:34-40).[25] Those who limit the reign of Christ to only "word and sacrament" fail to recognize the breadth of Christ's liberating presence in the power of the Spirit.

As impressive as these dimensions of the reign of Christ and of his Spirit in the power of love may be, can we really associate the Spirit and love already with the notion of *salvation*? The first step to opening our eyes to the depth of salvation is the observation that love as joyful, free and creative self-withdrawal in favor of the others turns in a strange way against the basic tendency of natural life (on earth): the tendency to assert oneself, to promote oneself, to sustain and extend oneself at the cost of other life. All natural life has to live at the expense of other life. In a counterintuitive way, however, we strangely *gain and enhance life* in love and forgiving by creatively withdrawing the basic interests of our self-preservation in favor of others. The even deeper intensions of salvation come further into view when we include the other dimensions of Christ's reign and the other dimensions of the power of his Spirit, namely, the prophetic and the priestly radiation of his life.

The priestly dimensions of Christ's work should not, under the influence of the voice of the letter to the Hebrews, be limited to sacrifice and atonement.[26] They rather encompass the whole realm of the spiritual life of his witnesses, the whole life of worship, prayer and spiritual communication of faith, love and hope before God and in relation to God. This opens up dimensions of serious searching for God in faith- and truth-seeking communities in the churches and beyond them. The priestly dimensions of Christ's work and of the work of his Spirit overlap with the prophetic dimensions that we encounter as creative forces in serious proclamation, in teaching and in ethical work that cares for justice, mercy and love in the faith communities and beyond them.

At first glance, the priestly and prophetic dimensions of Christ's presence

---

[25]John Hoffmeyer, "Christology and Diakonia," in Welker, Schuele and Thomas, *Who Is Jesus Christ for Us Today?*, 150–66.

[26]For the following, see Michael Welker, *God the Revealed*, 209–16 and 277–303.

in the power of his Spirit can be closely associated with his kingly office and the works of love in all their rich dimensions. The topic of salvation, however, comes in view more clearly when we realize that in love, finite human beings leave their drive toward mere self-sustenance behind them. Rather, they experience an enrichment that is nothing less than a share in the identity and truth of God. Even in this life here on earth and in the midst of fragility and finitude, they are ennobled to experience the full powers of salvation. In their faithful search for truth and justice in the fellowship of Christ they participate in his Holy Spirit and become connected with the divine and eternal life.

Different voices of the biblical canon coincide in illuminating this perspective. Paul says that the love of Christ "controls us" and enables us to regard no one from a human point of view any longer (2 Cor 5:16). In the love of Christ we are able to discover that "If anyone is in Christ, the new creation has come: The old has gone, the new is here!" (2 Cor 5:17). The letter to the Colossians sees the goal of those who are "encouraged in heart and united in love" to "have the full riches of complete understanding, in order that they may know the mystery of God, namely, Christ, in whom are hidden all the treasures of wisdom and knowledge" (Col 2:2-3). Finally, and even more strongly, the letter to the Ephesians stresses the message of salvation: Those who "being rooted and established in love, may have power, together with all the Lord's holy people, to grasp how wide and long and high and deep is the love of Christ, and to know this love that surpasses knowledge— that you may be filled to the measure of all the fullness of God" (Eph 3:17-19).

To be filled with the fullness of God already here on earth—this is exactly the experience of salvation, "the seal of the Holy Spirit" that connects us to Christ, to the powers of the Spirit, to the powers of new creation even under the conditions of the frail and finite life of this creation. The biblical remarks about "the Holy Spirit of God, with whom you were sealed for the day of redemption" (Eph 4:30), no longer appear as utterances of a vague hope. They gain a great experiential clarity in a firm and transparent trust.

12

The Spirit of God and Worship

The Liturgical Grammar of the Holy Spirit

Geoffrey Wainwright

Questions concerning the ontological origin, doxological status and salvific functions of the Holy Spirit famously reach back at least as far as the fourth century of the Christian era. What became recognized as the orthodox answers to these questions were theologically argued by Basil of Caesarea in his treatise *On the Holy Spirit* and liturgically settled in terms of what became the Nicene-Constantinopolitan Creed. Among Greek-speaking Christians, Basil established the propriety of addressing the doxology to God the Father not only "through [*dia*] the Son in [*en*] the Holy Spirit," as the more familiar formula had it, but also now to God the Father "with [*meta*] the Son," "together with [*syn*] the Holy Spirit"—and this on the grounds of the second and third persons' inner-trinitarian origins.[1] He pointed out that Syriac Christians had no other linguistic way of coordinating the three persons than by "and," which was also the form used throughout "the entire West, almost from Illyricum to the boundaries of the empire" in the worshipful address to the Trinity: *Gloria Patri et Filio et Spiritui Sancto*. As to the creed, this governed the faith of Christians regarding the deity and liturgical roles of the Holy Spirit, finally confessed as "Lord, and Giver of life," "who proceeds from the Father [and the Son]," and "with the Father and the Son to-

---

[1]The Greek text and a French translation are contained in Benoît Pruche, *Basile de Césarée. Sur le Saint-Esprit*, Sources chrétiennes 17 (Paris: Cerf, 1968); cf. St. Basil, *On the Holy Spirit*, trans. Stephen Hildebrand, Popular Patristics 42 (Crestwood, NY: St. Vladimir's Seminary Press, 2011).

gether is worshiped and glorified." From the divine side it is affirmed that the Spirit "spake by the prophets," and the Holy Spirit is recounted as speaking and acting salvifically in narratives of the New Testament.

For our part we shall be reflecting on the Holy Spirit as the goal or as the location and instrument of praise and prayer; that is, the moral, practical and intellectual functions of the Holy Spirit in relation to creation and the creatures as liturgically expressed in linguistic and gestural interaction with these latter. I shall draw examples both from the Scriptures and from the classical prayers of the Christian churches. Right from the start, St. Basil's justification of the coordinated form of doxology means that there is no immediate need for suspicion of subordinationism when we encounter or employ the more differentiated form of address or function in connection with the Holy Spirit. Guided by the scriptural principles and the firm creedal (and matching dogmatic) traditions of Christianity, I will examine several of the historically proven examples of genuinely pneumatic worship with a view to discerning "the liturgical grammar of the Holy Spirit" and thereby help our own communities to frame and practice—in praise and petition—recognizably authentic encounters with the triune God "in the Spirit and in truth" (Jn 4:23).

PAULINE PNEUMATOLOGY

For a strong scriptural example of the Holy Spirit's salvific standing and liturgical roles, we may appropriately turn to St. Paul's letter to the Romans, and notably Romans 8 and Romans 15. Of people who are joined to Christ by faith (Rom 3:21-26) and baptism (Rom 6:1-4), it may be said that they are "in Christ" (Rom 8:1) and that "Christ is in [them]" (Rom 8:10) and/or that they are "in the Spirit" and "the Spirit of God lives in [them]" (Rom 8:9). To be led by the Spirit is to be a son or daughter of God (Rom 8:14); it is to "have received the Spirit of adoption, whereby we cry Abba, Father" (Rom 8:15 KJV). We have, says the apostle, "the firstfruits of the Spirit" (Rom 8:23); and while we are—with the whole creation—awaiting the redemption of our bodies, the Spirit "helps us in our weakness" and "intercedes for us through wordless groans" (Rom 8:26); and God "searches our hearts knows the mind of the Spirit, because the Spirit intercedes for God's people in accordance with the will of God" (Rom 8:27).

Advancing to Romans 15, we may detect a pneumatological watermark underlying the opening verses. The clue occurs in Romans 15:5, with the reference to the "God of *steadfastness* and *encouragement*" (RSV; emphasis added). The apostle prays for his recipients thus: "May the God of stead-fastness and encouragement grant you to be of one mind among yourselves, according to the will of Christ Jesus, that you may with one heart and one mouth glorify the God and Father of our Lord Jesus Christ." Now, stead-fastness (*hypomonē*) is often mentioned in a pneumatic context, almost as though it were a gift of the Spirit (Rom 5:1-5; 8:23-27; 2 Cor 6:1-10; 12:12; 1 Thess 1:2-7), and encouragement (*paraklēsis*; see 1 Cor 14:3, 31; Phil 2:1) sug-gests the Paraclete (Jn 14:16, 26; 15:26; 16:7), so that the Holy Spirit may ap-propriately be considered as the divine source to which Paul looks in asking on behalf of the Romans that they may be of one mind (*to auto phronein*), one heart or will (*homothymadon*) and one mouth or voice (*heni stomati*), in their glorification of the God and Father of our Lord Jesus Christ. Moreover, the phrase in Romans 15:4—*dia tēs paraklēseōs tōn graphōn* ("through the encouragement of the Scriptures")—suggests that, in the creation of unity among the believers, which is necessary to the proper worship of God, a part is played by the reading of the inspired Scriptures—now of the New Tes-tament as well as of the Old.

In the rest of Romans 15, the Holy Spirit surfaces four times explicitly. The Holy Spirit is mentioned by name in Romans 15:13 as the source of hope directed toward the time when all the Gentiles would come to praise and glorify God along with his people of the old covenant (Rom 15:8-12). Paul speaks in liturgical or priestly terms of his own evangelical mission among the nations toward that end: by the "grace God gave [him]," he is a minister (*leitourgos*) of Christ Jesus to the Gentiles, serving as a priest (*hierour-gountos*) the gospel of God, so that the offering (*prosphora*) of the Gentiles may be acceptable (*euprosdektos*) and sanctified (*hēgiasmenē*) by the Holy Spirit (Rom 15:16). (It matters little whether the genitive be taken as objective or subjective—whether "the offering of the Gentiles" be Paul's offering of them or their own offering.) What Christ wrought through the apostles in winning the obedience of the Gentiles was done "by what I have said and done—by the power of signs and wonders, through the power of the Spirit of God" (Rom 15:18-19). Finally, Paul appeals to the Romans "by our Lord Jesus Christ and by the love of the Spirit, to join me in my struggle by praying to God for me" (Rom 15:30), that he may emerge safely from Judea and visit them on his journey to Spain (Rom 15:24, 28). The interweaving between mission, praise and prayer, between evangelistic witness and the worship of God is striking—and it all takes place "in the Spirit."

THE ANGLICAN COLLECT FOR PURITY OF HEART

As our first concrete example of a liturgical prayer, we may turn to the beautiful prayer that traditionally figures at the opening of "The Order of the Administration of the Lord's Supper or Holy Communion" in the Church of England's Book of Common Prayer and has spread more widely.

> Almighty God, unto whom all hearts be open, all desires known, and from whom no secrets are hid: Cleanse the thoughts of our hearts by the inspiration of thy Holy Spirit, that we may perfectly love thee, and worthily magnify thy holy Name; through Christ our Lord. Amen.

That prayer would, in fact, be substantially appropriate at the start of any service of Christian worship.

Similarly, a passage from the thirteenth century by St. Bonaventure would be generally applicable as a principle for any service of preaching, since the aid of the Holy Spirit has to be petitioned both for preachers and for their hearers.

> We preachers do nothing unless He works in the heart by his grace. Therefore in order that we may hear and understand his voice, we will ask the Holy Spirit to help us by his grace—help me to speak, and help you to hear.[2]

The same principle of mutual intelligibility applies also to the practice of Spirit-inspired "speaking in tongues" after the pattern of 1 Corinthians 14.[3] Here I may perhaps recount anecdotally how I was once invited to preach in a Pentecostal church in Johannesburg, and I began my sermon by saying how honored I felt to have been asked to preach there on Pentecost Sunday; but the South African congregation didn't tumble to that one. "Every Sunday is Pentecost Sunday," they told me.

---

[2]"Nihil facimus nos praedicatores et doctors extra clamantes, nisi ipse interius operetur in corde per gratiam suam. Ut igitur possimus istam linguam intelligere et audire, rogabimus Spiritum sanctum, ut invet nos per gratiam sua, me ad loquendum, vos ad audiendum etc." Bonaventure, De S. Andrea Sermo in Opera Omnia (Ad Claras Aquas [Quaracchi]: Typographia Collegii S. Bonaventurae, 1901), 463.

[3]See Geoffrey Wainwright, "The One Hope of Your Calling? The Ecumenical and Pentecostal Movements After a Century," Pneuma: Journal of the Society for Pentecostal Studies 25 (2003): 7–28.

SEASONAL PRAYERS FOR THE SPIRIT

Now we should look more specifically at pneumatologically marked prayers in specific services of the Eucharist, beginning again with texts that figure as standard in any such celebration and then coming to seasonal prayers appointed for festivals on which the Holy Spirit is prominently named on account of some highlights in salvation history, and where the event or episode will have been recalled perhaps in the prayer or collect of the day, and certainly in the Scripture readings of the day (for example, the Annunciation to Mary: "The Holy Spirit will come on you, and the power of the Most High will overshadow you" [Lk 1:35]; or the baptism of Jesus himself: "heaven was opened and the Holy Spirit descended on him in bodily form like a dove" [Lk 3:22]). On "ordinary Sundays" in most churches, the standard prefaces of the Eucharistic Prayers—addressed to the Father—make only a passing mention, if any, of the Holy Spirit. For our purposes we may turn rather to the preface of a Eucharistic Prayer for the feast of Pentecost and another for Trinity Sunday.

In the Book of Common Prayer of the Episcopal Church in the USA (1990), the "Proper Preface" for Pentecost runs thus: "Through Jesus Christ our Lord. In fulfillment of his true promise, the Holy Spirit came down [on this day] from heaven, lighting upon the disciples, to teach them and to lead them into all truth; uniting peoples of many tongues in the confession of one faith, and giving to your Church the power to serve you as a royal priesthood, and to preach the Gospel to all nations." The Episcopal Church's Preface for Trinity Sunday runs thus: "For with your co-eternal Son and Holy Spirit, you are one God, one Lord, in Trinity of Persons and in Unity of Being; and we celebrate the one and equal glory of you, O Father, and of the Son, and of the Holy Spirit."

EUCHARISTIC EPICLESES

In our consideration of the Eucharistic Prayer we come next to a feature that dates back to early Christian days and attracted a new measure of attention from liturgists in the twentieth century, namely, the "epiclesis" whereby the Holy Spirit is "called upon" to consecrate the sacramental elements and energize those who will partake of them.[4] Perhaps the earliest developed epi-

---

[4]For the scriptural and patristic history of the sacramental service in its entirety, see Paul F. Bradshaw, *Eucharistic Origins*, Alcuin Club Collections 80 (London: SPCK, 2004). For a wider view of worship in the first centuries of our era, see Maxwell E. Johnson, *Praying and Believing in Early*

clesis is that variously found in the so-called *Apostolic Tradition* of Hippolytus (ca. 220) and much noticed in the twentieth century.

> Mindful therefore of his [Christ's] death and resurrection, we offer this bread and wine to you [Father], thankful that you have judged us worthy to stand in your presence and serve you. And we pray that you send your Holy Spirit upon the offering of your holy Church: gathering together in unity all those who partake of these holy mysteries so that they may be filled with the Holy Spirit unto the strengthening of the faith in truth. Thus may we praise and glorify you through your child Jesus Christ, through whom be glory and honour to you Father and Son with your Holy Spirit in your Holy Church now and forever. Amen.[5]

Coming quickly into present times, we may look first at the current Roman Missal (2010). There the Second Eucharistic Prayer encloses the narrative of Christ's institution of the Lord's Supper within a two-part Epiclesis: "You are indeed Holy, O Lord, the fount of all holiness. Make holy, therefore, these gifts, we pray, by sending down your Spirit upon them like the dewfall, so that they may become for us the Body and Blood of our Lord Jesus Christ."[6] Following the institution narrative, the Second Eucharistic Prayer notably continues: "Humbly we pray that, partaking of the Body and Blood of Christ, we may be gathered into one by the Holy Spirit." In the Third Eucharistic Prayer, the Epiclesis runs thus: "Look, we pray, upon the oblation of your Church and, recognizing the sacrificial Victim by whose death you willed to reconcile us to yourself, grant that we, who are nourished by the Body and Blood of your Son, and filled with his Holy Spirit, may become one body, one spirit in Christ." And in the Fourth Eucharistic Prayer, a developed form:

Christianity: The Interplay Between Christian Worship and Doctrine (Collegeville, MN: Liturgical, 2013). For the earlier history of the epiclesis throughout Christendom, see E. G. Cuthbert F. Atchley, *On the Epiclesis of the Eucharistic Liturgy and in the Consecration of the Font* (London: Oxford University Press, 1935). The story is continued in John H. McKenna's *Eucharist and Holy Spirit: The Eucharistic Epiclesis in Twentieth Century Theology (1900–1966)*, Alcuin Club Collections 57 (Great Wakering, UK: Mayhew-McCrimmon, 1975), where the second part is significantly headed "The Interpretations of Twentieth-Century Liturgists and Theologians: The Epiclesis in the Shadow of the 'Moment of Consecration' Problem."
[5]See McKenna, *Eucharist and Holy Spirit*, 19–20.
[6]*Roman Missal*, New English Translation, 2010; widely accessible, but see Eamon Duffy, ed., *The Heart in Pilgrimage: A Prayerbook for Catholic Christians* (London: Continuum, 2013), 420.

And that we might live no longer for ourselves but for him who died and rose again for us, he sent the Holy Spirit from you, Father, as the first fruits for those who believe, so that bringing to perfection his work in the world, he might sanctify creation to the full. Therefore, O Lord, we pray: may this same Holy Spirit graciously sanctify these offerings, that they may become the Body and Blood of our Lord Jesus Christ for the celebration of this great mystery, which he himself left us as an eternal covenant. . . . Look, O Lord, look upon the Sacrifice which you yourself have provided for your Church, and grant in your loving kindness to all who partake of this one Bread and one Chalice that, gathered into one body by the Holy Spirit, they may become a living sacrifice in Christ to the praise of your glory.

In these prayers, the Holy Spirit consecrates the elements and revitalizes those who partake of the sacrament.

As a Methodist, I now jump back to the formative works of John and Charles Wesley. We may find examples of epiclesis among the 166 Wesleyan *Hymns on the Lord's Supper*.[7] Most straightforward is hymn number 72.

Come, Holy Ghost, Thine Influence shed,
And realize the Sign.
Thy Life infuse into the Bread,
Thy Power into the Wine.

Effectual let the Tokens prove,
And made by Heavenly Art
Fit channels to convey Thy Love
To every Faithful Heart.

The Wesleyan hymn number 16 from the same source draws directly on *Apostolic Constitutions* 8.12.39 with its designation of the Spirit as "Witness of the Sufferings of Christ" and now their "Remembrancer Divine."

Come, Thou everlasting Spirit,
Bring to every thankful Mind
All the Saviour's dying Merit,
All his Suffering for Mankind:

---

[7]A facsimile of the first edition of John and Charles Wesley's *Hymns on the Lord's Supper* (Bristol: Felix Farley, 1745) has been produced by the Charles Wesley Society (Madison, NJ, 1995) via its Archives and History Center at Drew University.

True Recorder of his Passion,
Now the living Faith impart,
Now reveal his great Salvation,
Preach his Gospel to our Heart.

Come, Thou Witness of his Dying,
Come, Remembrancer Divine,
Let us feel thy Power applying
Christ to every Soul and mine;
Let us groan thine inward Groaning,
Look on Him we pierc'd, and grieve,
All receive the Grace Atoning,
All the Sprinkled Blood receive.

In the current *Book of United Methodist Worship* (1992) and *United Methodist Hymnal* (1989), the first "Service of Word and Table" contains in its "Great Thanksgiving" (addressed to God the Father) the hint toward an epiclesis before the institution narrative ("When the Lord Jesus ascended he promised to be with us always in the power of your Word and Holy Spirit"); and then the Epiclesis proper follows on the "anamnesis and oblation."

Pour out your Holy Spirit on us gathered here, and on these gifts of bread and wine. Make them be for us the body and blood of Christ, that we may be for the world the body of Christ, redeemed by his blood. By your Spirit make us one with Christ, one with each other, and one in ministry to all the world, until Christ comes in final victory and we feast at his heavenly banquet. Through your Son Jesus Christ, with the Holy Spirit in your holy church, all honor and glory is yours, almighty Father, now and for ever. Amen.

The recognition of the Holy Spirit's work in the United Methodist "Service of Word and Table" continues the earlier Wesleyan emphasis on the Spirit's witness to the work of Christ and infusion of life through participation in the elements.

Prayers to All Three Persons of the Trinity

I hinted at the start that prayers might be addressed simultaneously to all three persons of the Trinity. Early—and still current—examples may be given. That is obviously the case with the *Gloria Patri*: "Glory be to the Father, and to the Son, and to the Holy Ghost: As it was in the beginning, is now, and ever shall be, world without end. Amen." Another example occurs in the *Te Deum Laudamus*: "The holy Church throughout all the world doth acknowledge thee: The Father of an infinite majesty; Thine honourable, true, and only Son; Also the Holy Ghost the Comforter." Or, slightly less evenly, the *Gloria in Excelsis Deo*: "We give thanks to thee for thy great glory, O Lord God, heavenly King, God the Father Almighty. O Lord, the only begotten Son Jesu Christ; O Lord God, Lamb of God, Son of the Father, that takest away the sins of the world. . . . Thou only, O Christ, with the Holy Ghost, art most high in the glory of God the Father. Amen."

PRAYERS ADDRESSED SPECIFICALLY TO THE THIRD PERSON OF THE TRINITY

On the other hand, prayer may be addressed specifically to the third person of the Trinity, with other or broader themes than the eucharistic Epiclesis. According to Basil the Great, the Holy Spirit "completes" or "strengthens" the works of God toward the world, which are all begun from the will and command of the Father and are mediated through the Son or the Word.[8] The Byzantine Pentecostarion provides one of the most familiar hymns from the Orthodox tradition, dating from around the eighth century, the *Basileu ouranie, Paraklēte*.

> O King enthroned on high,
> Thou Comforter divine,
> Blest Spirit of all truth, be nigh
> And make us thine.
>
> Thou art the source of life,
> Thou art our treasure store;
> Give us thy peace, and end our strife
> For evermore.
>
> Descend, O heavenly Dove,
> Abide with us alway;
> And in the fullness of thy love,
> Cleanse us, we pray.[9]

---

[8]Basil, *On the Holy Spirit* 16.38.
[9]John Brownlie, trans., *Hymns of the Greek Church* (Edinburgh: Oliphant, Anderson, & Ferrier, 1900), 24.

Thus the third person may be invoked in his capacity as "Creator Spirit," as in the medieval hymn for Pentecost, where the cosmic and the anthropological dimensions of the Spirit's work are brought together: *Veni, Creator Spiritus.* Thus runs the seventeenth-century translation into English by John Dryden:

> Creator Spirit, by whose aid
> The world's foundations first were laid,
> Come, visit every waiting mind;
> Come, pour thy joys on humankind;
> From sin and sorrow set us free,
> And make thy temples worthy thee.
>
> O source of uncreated heat,
> The Father's promised Paraclete!
> Thrice holy fount, thrice holy fire,
> Our hearts with heavenly love inspire;
> Come, and thy sacred unction bring
> To sanctify us while we sing.
>
> Plenteous of grace, descend from high,
> Rich in thy sevenfold energy;
> Make us eternal truths receive.
> And practice all that we believe;
> Give us thyself, that we may see
> The Father and the Son by thee.
>
> Immortal honor, endless fame,
> Attend the almighty Father's name:
> The Savior Son be glorified,
> Who for lost man's redemption died:
> And equal adoration be,
> Eternal Paraclete to thee.[10]

Attributed to Rabanus Maurus, the *Veni, Creator Spiritus* dates from the ninth century and was translated by the seventeenth-century bishop John Cosin; it is sung at Anglican ordinations.

> Come, Holy Ghost, our souls inspire,
> And lighten with celestial fire;

---

[10]John Dryden, "Veni, Creator Spiritus, Mentes," in *The Handbook to the Lutheran Hymnal* (St. Louis: Concordia, 1942), 176.

Thou the anointing Spirit art,
Who dost thy sevenfold gifts impart.

Thy blessèd unction from above
Is comfort, life, and fire of love;
Enable with perpetual light
The dullness of our blinded sight.

Anoint and cheer our soilèd face
With the abundance of thy grace;
Keep far our foes, give peace at home;
Where thou art guide no ill can come.[11]

Veni, Sancte Spiritus (the "Golden Sequence") dates from the thirteenth century and was translated into English by John Mason Neale.

Come, thou holy Paraclete,
And from thy celestial seat
Shed thy light and brilliancy:
Father of the poor, draw near;
Giver of all gifts, be here;
Come the soul's true radiancy.

What is soilèd, make thou pure;
What is wounded, work its cure;
What is parchèd fructify;
What is rigid, gently bend;
What is frozen, warmly tend;
Strengthen what goes erringly.

Fill thy faithful, who confide
In thy power to guard and guide,
With thy sevenfold mystery.
Here thy grace and virtue send;
Grant salvation to the end,
And in heaven felicity.[12]

Then there is the *Discende, Amor santo* (by the Italian Bianco da Siena), which we Anglophones have set to Ralph Vaughn Williams's lyrical tune "Down Ampney."

---

[11]The Book of Common Prayer (1990).
[12]John Mason Neale, *Collected Hymns, Sequences, and Carols of John Mason Neale* (London: Hodder and Stoughton, 1914), 130–31.

Come down, O Love divine,
Seek thou this soul of mine,
And visit it with thine own ardor glowing.
O Comforter, draw near,
Within my heart appear,
And kindle it, thy holy flame bestowing.[13]

These prayers, each addressed specifically to the Holy Spirit, express the
Christian belief that the Spirit strengthens God's works in the world.

A Soteriological Hymn from Charles Wesley

Stanzas from one of Charles Wesley's many Spirit hymns—rooted in salvation history and now appropriate to invocation by the assembled worshiping community—run thus:

Lord, we believe to us and ours
The apostolic promise given;
We wait the pentecostal powers,
The Holy Ghost sent down from heaven.

To every one whom God shall call
The promise is securely made:
To you far off—he calls you all;
Believe the word which Christ hath said:

The Holy Ghost, if I depart,
The Comforter shall surely come,
Shall make the contrite sinner's heart
His loved, His everlasting home.

Assembled here with one accord,
Calmly we wait the promised grace,
The purchase of our dying Lord:
Come, Holy Ghost, and fill the place.

If every one that asks may find,
If still Thou dost on sinners fall,

[13]Bianco of Siena, "Come Down, O Love Divine," trans. Richard F. Littledale, in *The United Methodist Hymnal: Book of United Methodist Worship* (Nashville: United Methodist, 1989), 475.

Come as a mighty rushing wind;
Great grace be now upon us all.[14]

The hymn demonstrates the Wesleyan emphasis on the Spirit. The Wesleys transformed the promise of Christ into a testimonial hymn shared among the community gathered "in one accord."

PRAYERS IN (THE UNITY OF) THE HOLY SPIRIT

I previously noted Basil of Caesarea's justification of the "older" form of praise and prayer addressed *to* the Father, *through* Jesus Christ his Son, *in* the Holy Spirit. Over the centuries that invocation of the Spirit became frequently expanded to "*in* (the unity of) the Holy Spirit." There the Holy Spirit's status and role figure perhaps more obviously as the locus and enablement of unity. We shall correspondingly find the Spirit prominently invoked in the various causes of ecumenism, even before that term itself became fashionable. Readers will, in fact, already have noticed in the aforementioned texts various hints toward ecclesial unity and worldly mission. These themes, of course, bear a pneumatological dimension, not only in the worship of the churches but also wherever they occur in the reflection and practice of the churches.

When we have been talking about the invocation of the Holy Spirit in the liturgy of the Eucharist, we have quietly been assuming that the people who were voicing those prayers in the particular service were living and worshiping in a state of mutual "*koinōnia*," a condition that would indeed be maintained, deepened and extended by their common participation in "the holy communion" of the sacrament. Of course, that is sadly far from always being the case; and the ecumenical questions are unavoidable already under the heading of the Holy Spirit and baptism.

THE HOLY SPIRIT AND BAPTISM

Not surprisingly, orders of service for baptism contain ample reference to the Holy Spirit. Take for example those in the Book of Common Prayer of the Episcopal Church in the USA (1990). As is usual in liturgical services in

---

[14]Charles Wesley, *A Collection of Hymns: For the Use of the People Called Methodists* (London: Wesleyan Conference, 1877), 351. All italics orginal.

that church, the celebrant begins with a trinitarian invocation: "Blessed be God, Father, Son, and Holy Spirit," to which comes the response, "Blessed be his kingdom, now and for ever." The celebrant then quickly opens up the baptismal theme, inviting an appropriate response from the people.

> Celebrant: There is one Body and one Spirit;
> People: There is one hope in God's call to us;
> Celebrant: One Lord, one Faith, one Baptism;
> People: One God and Father of all.

As the service progresses, all participants are expected to affirm the tripartite Apostles' Creed, with, of course, the third article and its pneumatological scope. The celebrant's "Thanksgiving over the Water" runs as follows:

> We thank you, Almighty God, for the gift of water. Over it the Holy Spirit moved in the beginning of creation. Through it you led the children of Israel out of their bondage in Egypt into the land of promise. In it your Son Jesus received the baptism of John and was anointed by the Holy Spirit as the Messiah, the Christ, to lead us, through his death and resurrection, from the bondage of sin into everlasting life.
>
> We thank you, Father, for the water of Baptism. In it we are buried with Christ in his death. By it we share in his resurrection. Through it we are reborn in the Holy Spirit. Therefore in joyful obedience to your Son we bring into his fellowship those who come to him, baptizing them in the name of the Father, and of the Son, and of the Holy Spirit.

At the following words, the celebrant touches the water.

> Now sanctify this water, we pray you, by the power of your Holy Spirit, that those who are here cleansed from sin and born again may continue for ever in the risen life of Jesus Christ our Savior.
>
> To him, to you, and to the Holy Spirit, be all honor and glory, now and for ever, Amen.

The baptism then takes place.

> N[ame], I baptize you in the Name of the Father, and of the Son, and of the Holy Spirit. Amen.

After this action has been completed for all candidates, the bishop or priest prays over them.

Heavenly Father, we thank you that by water and the Holy Spirit you have bestowed upon *these* your servants the forgiveness of sin, and have raised *them* to the new life of grace. Sustain *them*, O Lord, in your Holy Spirit. Give *them* an inquiring and discerning heart, the courage to will and to persevere, a spirit to know and to love you, and the gift of joy and wonder in all your works. *Amen*.

Then the bishop or priest places a hand on the person's head, marking on the forehead the sign of the cross (using chrism if desired) and saying to each one: "*N[ame]*, you are sealed by the Holy Spirit in Baptism and marked as Christ's own for ever. Amen."

THE HOLY SPIRIT AND ECUMENISM

During the twentieth century, a movement toward the mutual recognition of baptism developed among some churches that were otherwise divided from one another. In its long-developed and much-noticed "Lima document" of 1982—*Baptism, Eucharist and Ministry*—the Faith and Order Commission of the World Council of Churches could describe baptism as performed in water and "administered in the name of the Father, the Son, and the Holy Spirit."

> The Holy Spirit is at work in the lives of people before, in and after their baptism. It is the same Spirit who revealed Jesus as the Son (Mark 1:10-11) and who empowered and united the disciples at Pentecost (Acts 2). God bestows upon all baptized persons the anointing and the promise of the Holy Spirit, marks them with a seal and implants in their hearts the first installment of their inheritance as sons and daughters of God. The Holy Spirit nurtures the life of faith in their hearts until the final deliverance, when they will enter into its full possession, to the praise of the glory of God (2 Cor. 1:21-2; Eph. 1:13-14).[15]

The initially unitive power of baptism could thus be affirmed, as also in paragraph 7—but again, not without a forward look.

> Baptism initiates the reality of the new life given in the midst of the present world. It gives participation in the community of the Holy Spirit. It is a sign of the Kingdom of God and of the life of the world to come. Through the gifts of faith, hope and love, baptism has a dynamic which embraces the whole of

---

[15]World Council of Churches, *Baptism, Eucharist and Ministry*, Faith and Order Paper 111 (Geneva: World Council of Churches, 1982), "Baptism," §5.

life, extends to all nations, and anticipates the day when every tongue will confess that Jesus Christ is Lord to the glory of God the Father.[16]

Clearly, much strongly unitive work of the Holy Spirit could already be recognized. But the authors of the document had to confess, however gently, an as yet partially unrecognized or—at least—unachieved future.

> Administered in obedience to our Lord, baptism is a sign and seal of our common discipleship. Through baptism, Christians are brought into union with Christ, with each other, and with the Church of every time and place. Our common baptism, which unites us to Christ in faith, is thus a basic bond of unity. We are one people and are called to confess and serve one Lord in each place and in all the world. The union with Christ which we share through baptism has important implications for Christian unity. "There is . . . one baptism, one God and Father of us all . . ." (Eph. 4:4-6). When baptismal unity is realized in one holy, catholic, apostolic Church, a genuine Christian witness can be made to the healing and reconciling love of God. Therefore, our one baptism into Christ constitutes a call to the churches to overcome their divisions and visibly manifest their fellowship.[17]

The ecumenical cause of restored unity among the churches naturally turned to the Holy Spirit in search of prayerful help. We may, for instance, read thus in Pope John Paul II's encyclical letter of May 25, 1995, *Ut Unum Sint* ("On Commitment to Ecumenism"):

> The unity of all divided humanity is the will of God. For this reason he sent his Son, so that by dying and rising for us he might bestow on us the Spirit of love. On the eve of his sacrifice on the Cross, Jesus himself prayed to the Father for his disciples and for all those who believe in him, that they *might be one*, a living communion. . . . The Lord of the Ages wisely and patiently follows out the plan of his grace on behalf of us sinners. In recent times he has begun to bestow more generously upon divided Christians remorse over their divisions and a longing for unity. Everywhere, large numbers have felt the impulse of this grace, and among our separated brethren also *there increases from day to day a movement*, fostered by the grace of the Holy Spirit, *for the restoration of unity among all Christians*. Taking part in this movement, which is called ecumenical, are those who invoke the Triune God and confess

---

[16]Ibid., §7.
[17]Ibid., §6.

Jesus as Lord and Savior. . . . The Catholic Church embraces with hope the commitment to ecumenism as a duty of the Christian conscience enlightened by faith and guided by love. Here too we can apply the words of Saint Paul to the first Christians of Rome: "God's love has been poured into our hearts through the Holy Spirit"; thus "our hope does not disappoint us" (Rom. 5:5). This is the hope of Christian unity, which has its divine source in the Trinitarian unity of the Father, the Son and the Holy Spirit.[18]

The slogan "One Baptism, one Church"—recently developed in many ecumenical circles—leaves issues to be resolved and works to be attained in matters of both "faith" and "order" before full unity can be declared in doctrine and discipline.[19]

THE SPIRIT, THE SAINTS AND THE MARTYRS

One final, even eschatological connection may be detected between the Holy Spirit and those Christians whose faithful witness has been sustained by the Spirit to the point of sainthood and even martyrdom. They may be invoked not only for the sake of their example in the past but also for their continuing personal help from within the heavenly community as enabled by the Holy Spirit—a pneumatically conveyed unity in prayer.[20] At that point, we have perhaps summarized the theme of the entire present essay: What—through all the constancies and varieties of history, geography, culture and the human condition—are the ritual, liturgical and symbolic forms under which the Father may be worshiped in Spirit and in Truth (Jn 4:23-24)?

[18]John Paul II, *Ut Unum Sint*, §§6–8, Vatican website, www.vatican.va/holy_father/john_paul_ii/encyclicals/documents/hf_jp-ii_enc_25051995_ut-unum-sint_en.html. Italics original.

[19]See Geoffrey Wainwright, "One Baptism, One Church? Agreements, Differences, Resolutions," in *The Oxford Handbook of Sacramental Theology*, ed. Hans Boersma and Matthew Levering (Oxford: Oxford University Press), forthcoming.

[20]See Geoffrey Wainwright, "The Holy Spirit, Witness, and Martyrdom" in the booklet *The Spirit in the New Millennium* (Duquesne University Annual Holy Spirit Lecture and Colloquium, July 7–8, 2005), 3–30; and Wainwright, "The Saints and the Departed," in *Embracing Purpose: Essays on God, the World and the Church* (Peterborough, UK: Epworth, 2007; repr., Eugene, OR: Wipf & Stock, 2012), 222–47.

13

Stories of Grace

Pentecostals and Social Justice

Douglas Petersen

INTRODUCTION

From its origins in the Azusa Street Revival in Los Angeles in 1906, the Pentecostal movement has expanded from humble beginnings into a global phenomenon. According to the Pew Research Center's Study on Global Christianity, Pentecostals now constitute nearly 600 million (27 percent) of the world's Christian population of 2.2 billion people.[1] However, it is only in the past couple of decades that Pentecostals have wholeheartedly embraced social action as an integral element of holistic mission.

In an article in *Christianity Today* titled "A New Kind of Pentecostal," Robert Crosby celebrates the blossoming social efforts of Pentecostals engaged in a broad range of social compassion projects.[2] Similarly, in the most comprehensive overview of Pentecostal social endeavors to date, Donald E. Miller and Tetesunao Yamamori document the outcomes of a four-year empirical research study encompassing twenty countries and four continents, calling these ever-growing social endeavors "the new face of Christian social engagement."[3] In 2009 the Assemblies of God, the largest of the Pentecostal

---

[1]Pew Forum on Religion and Public Life, *Global Christianity: A Report on the Size and Distribution of the World's Christian Population* (Washington, DC: Pew Research Center, 2011); see also Allan Anderson's essay "The Dynamics of Global Pentecostalism: Origins, Motivations and Future," in this volume.

[2]Robert C. Crosby, "A New Kind of Pentecostal," *Christianity Today*, August 2011, 50–54.

[3]Donald E. Miller and Tetsunao Yamamori, *Global Pentecostalism: The New Face of Christian Social Engagement* (Berkeley: University of California Press, 2007).

denominations and affiliated groups, formalized their commitment to social ministries by adding "compassion" as the fourth element of its reason for being "in recognition that Jesus came to glorify God . . . save the lost, make disciples, [and] also serve human need." A recent statement from Dr. George O. Wood, general superintendent of the Assemblies of God, reflected the desire of millions of Pentecostals who are committed to addressing the needs of hurting people:

> The Assemblies of God is deeply concerned for the poor. Partnering with national Assemblies of God churches, our missionaries worldwide are engaged in helping orphans, widows, and the victims of human trafficking. They dig wells for those without access to adequate water and provide mosquito nets to those in danger of malaria. They provide food and education for children in Latin America, Africa, and Asia. Moreover, we partner with and are grateful for organizations that reach out to alleviate suffering and meet human need.[4]

As Robert Crosby correctly points out in his *Christianity Today* article, it would be inaccurate to suggest that Pentecostals have never been involved in caring for the physical and social needs of hurting people. They have. Crosby highlights the work of two organizations as long-standing examples of Pentecostal social concern focused on "whole life transformation":[5] Teen Challenge—one of the oldest, largest and most successful drug recovery programs of its kind—has over two hundred centers in the United States and one thousand centers in ninety countries;[6] and Latin America ChildCare (LACC), a faith-based network of elementary and secondary schools, provides education, food and medical assistance to one hundred thousand impoverished children in three hundred schools in twenty-one countries throughout Latin America and the Caribbean.[7]

Nonetheless, even as Pentecostals offered social assistance to the most needy, they were often ambivalent about their own actions. For many,

---

[4]George O. Wood, "Statement of Assemblies of God General Superintendent George O. Wood Regarding World Vision Decision to Reverse Same-Sex Marriage Policy," March 27, 2014, AGwebservices.org, http://agchurches.org/Sitefiles/Default/RSS/AG.org%20TOP/Gen%20 Supt/World_Vision_Statement_Reversal.pdf.
[5]Crosby, "A New Kind of Pentecostal," 52–53.
[6]Teen Challenge USA, http://teenchallengeusa.com, and Global Teen Challenge, http://globaltc .org (accessed April 24, 2014).
[7]Latin America ChildCare, http://lacc4hope.org (accessed March 24, 2014). The author was the cofounder and president of Latin America ChildCare for twenty-three years.

limited resources precluded even the simplest relief efforts. Since the over-whelming majority of Pentecostals were to be found near the bottom of the social and economic scale, it could be argued, they didn't need a social program—they were a social program. Others believed that an emphasis on social needs would dull the focus of their primary message, namely, that the multitudes were "lost" forever without the saving message of Jesus Christ. Everyone agreed that they should avoid a "social gospel" (the idea that Christians could reform society by doing good deeds, as propagated by Walter Rauschenbusch and the religious mainliners of his day).

In the 1970s, when I first started working in the social-concern arena, Pentecostals were still not quite convinced that the good news of the gospel involved an integral balance of both "words and deeds." Thankfully in recent years, for the most part, the concept that people "are souls with ears" is in the past. Pentecostals' obvious efforts to reflect God's heart in caring for people—body and soul—is a refreshing emphasis. Indeed, younger generations of Pentecostals have taken hold of the message of "word and deed" and run with it.

In spite of amazing progress, however, it would be fair to say that Pentecostals still struggle to intentionalize their social efforts or articulate theologically a rationale for what they are doing. In many cases, Pentecostal social-concern efforts could be best characterized as ad hoc in nature, failing to recognize the importance of a systematic approach that treats immediate needs and confronts the structural realities of injustice that are inevitably at the root of the problem. For most Pentecostals, no matter how well-intentioned, there remains a substantial disconnect between theological underpinnings firmly grounded in the biblical text and actual practices that a coherent approach to social concern requires.[8]

---

[8]Most of my own work has been in this area. In short, a Pentecostal theology of social concern is a trinitarian-based praxis theology intended to produce a dynamic hermeneutic that links the biblical text with social and ethical practices. In constructing a Pentecostal social doctrine, faith and action are rooted both in God's self-revelation in Scripture and in the value and worth of all persons because they are created in his image. These foundational truths fulfilled in the words and deeds of Jesus Christ in his kingdom mission, carried out by the church and evidenced by the dynamic work and empowerment of the Holy Spirit provide an integral framework for holistic ministry. For further discussion, see Douglas P. Petersen, *Not By Might, Nor By Power: A Pentecostal Theology of Social Concern* (Oxford: Regnum, 1996), and, more recently, Petersen, "A Moral Imagination: Pentecostals and Social Concern in Latin America," in *The Spirit in the World: Emerging Pentecostal Theologies in Global Contexts*, ed. Veli-Matti Kärkkäinen (Grand Rapids: Eerdmans, 2009), 53–68.

In this essay I encourage a direct association between theological reflection and ethical action in at least two aspects. First, and somewhat surprisingly, there is at times (even among Pentecostals) a decreasing devotion
to the proclamation of the explicit message of salvation that must be integral
to all of our social justice efforts. The popular dictum, usually attributed to
St. Francis of Assisi—"Preach the gospel at all times, and when necessary
use words"—mutes the message of the gospel when understood simplistically to mean that right actions speak so loudly that there is no need to use
words to explain those actions. When the story of the cross and resurrection
is absent, there is little left that is "Christian" about these social efforts.
Second, it is a challenge to discover what is distinctly "Pentecostal" about
many Pentecostal social ministries. Just "being" Pentecostals who practice
social concern does not make those efforts necessarily "Pentecostal." Indeed,
one is hard-pressed to distinguish the social action of some Pentecostal
groups from the good work done by many NGOs.

The question arises: How does Pentecostal experience define and inform
Pentecostal social justice endeavors? To put the question another way: Is
the work and power of the Holy Spirit evident in the midst of our social
justice endeavors? In response to this question, I will examine three topics
relevant to the development of a distinctly Pentecostal approach to social
justice. First, for social-action endeavors to be redemptive there must be
an intentional emphasis on the dynamic interplay between word (verbal)
and deed (action); each interprets the other. Second, for social justice endeavors to be Pentecostal, these efforts should be permeated by two defining spiritual experiences: salvation and Spirit baptism. "Experiences of
the divine" exemplify the presence of the risen Lord and the normative
work of the Holy Spirit in our daily lives. When social justice endeavors
and "experiences of the divine" are wedded together, the consequence is a
transformation of the whole person. Third, sacred stories told by those
whom Pentecostals serve—in my case, children—interpret the meaning of
divine experiences and provide a lens through which one may discern the
Spirit at work in the daily lives of the "least of these." Sacred stories may
also function as an assessment tool to evaluate the Pentecostal distinctiveness that is integral to the success of social action. Perhaps it is best to
begin with a functional definition of terms.

Pentecostalism. Any attempt to define Pentecostalism according to a precise confession of faith faces a challenging task.[9] In spite of enormous diversity, however, most Pentecostals agree that theological thinking and social action spring from the transforming spiritual experience of conversion followed, sometimes immediately, by a distinctive second work of the Spirit—usually evidenced by speaking in tongues—known as Spirit baptism or "being filled with the Spirit" (not to be confused with being "born of the Spirit" at conversion). Through this experience, participants receive an endowment of "spiritual power," often characterized by signs and wonders equipping them to be active participants in God's mighty works. Pentecostals believe that God's miraculous actions are continuous and normative and that, through the operation of the Spirit, they are empowered to do everything that Jesus said and did.

Social justice. Social justice signifies the creation of societies where all persons receive their due and essential needs as human beings are met. The focus is on service both to the individual and to the community where a person's basic needs are met and societies are created where people flourish. While terms like *social justice, social concern, social action* and *social service* each have unique meanings, for the purposes of this essay I will use the terms interchangeably to encompass a broad range of social endeavors (individual and collective) in service of the poor and oppressed.

WORD, DEED AND SALVATION HISTORY

As I have already noted, in order for our social action to be redemptive there must be an intentional interplay between word (verbal) and deed (actions). One interprets the other.[10] My own thinking on this topic has been profoundly shaped by an article written by George Eldon Ladd more than four decades

---

[9]Compare my thoughts with the essays in this volume by Estrelda Alexander, "The Spirit of God: Christian Renewal in African American Pentecostalism," and Anderson, "The Dynamics of Global Pentecostalism."

[10]Elsewhere, I have treated the more traditional "word and deed" argument of holistic mission; see, e.g., the "Brussels Statement on Pentecostal Mission and Social Concern," published in a variety of books and journals including *Mission as Transformation,* ed. Vinay Samuel and Chris Sugden (Oxford: Regnum, 1999), 112–17; and more recently, *All the Gospel to All the World: 100 Years of Assemblies of God Missiology,* ed. Paul W. Lewis (Springfield, MO: Assemblies of God Theological Seminary, 2014), 93–99.

ago: "The Search for Perspective."[11] Salvation history, Ladd wrote, describes the biblical story of God's redemptive work in the events of human history. Ladd's perspective is best understood within the context of prevailing hermeneutical controversies in his day—dominated by scholars like Rudolf Bultmann, who were committed to a purely historical-critical approach to the interpretation of the biblical text. Bultmann had contended that history and transcendence were mutually exclusive, and the stories found in the Gospels, especially the miracles, must be considered more as theological representations reflecting the faith of the early church than as stories depicting actual historical events. Ladd argued that the presuppositions inherent to the scientific approach advocated by Bultmann promoted the belief that history was a "closed continuum of an unbroken series of historical causes and effects" and ignored the supernatural, namely, that God had actually broken into human history.

For Ladd, such an approach refused to interpret the biblical record based on its own terms.[12] The New Testament, wrote Ladd, contains not only "an historical account of what God had done in Jesus Christ" (the events), but also the interpretation of those divine events.[13] Christ's death and resurrection were historical events even though they transcended ordinary historical experience. But even such momentous events were not self-revelatory. Christ died for our sins and rose again in victory over sin—the in-breaking of transcendent reality into human affairs—was the word of interpretation that made the events revelatory.[14] Therefore, Ladd asserted, the biblical record is an account of God's saving acts in history, but it is also the prophetic interpretation of what those redemptive acts mean.

It is not a stretch for believers to appropriate and apply Ladd's understanding of the dynamic nature of redemptive history to our own acts of Christian social justice. Our actions alone are not self-interpretive, and they cannot be a substitute for words. Just as the redemptive acts of God recorded in the biblical account only have meaning when they are accompanied by the word, our actions in pursuit of social justice are redemptive only when accompanied by an explanation that includes the transcendent. We cannot

---

[11]George Eldon Ladd, "The Search for Perspective," *Interpretation* 25 (1971): 41–62.
[12]Ibid., 51.
[13]Ibid., 57–58.
[14]Ibid.

simply act in a generous or caring manner and expect people to know or understand anything about God unless at some point we interpret our deeds as being from a God who is motivated by love, gets involved with us and desires a response. Social actions must be explained in light of the story of the incarnation, cross, resurrection, Pentecost and return of Christ.

THE HOLY SPIRIT AND EXPERIENCES OF THE DIVINE

For Pentecostals, the words and deeds of the early church constitute a living history filled with the continued, creative work of the Holy Spirit—a work that moves beyond rational logic, calculation or strategy. The Holy Spirit was capable of doing the new, the unexpected and even the "impossible" in and through God's servants. For all, access to the sources of power flowed from two foundational spiritual experiences: salvation and Spirit baptism.[15]

Salvation through the power of the Holy Spirit marked entrance into the community of faith (Acts 2:38-41; 8:12-17; 10:47-48; 19:5-6). The historical reality that Christ died for our sins, was buried and was raised on the third day was of first importance (1 Cor 15:3-8). The experience of salvation generated a sense of the continuing presence of a personal, transcendent and transforming power. The experience was given further expression in Jesus' promise to the disciples, "I am going to send you what my Father has promised; but stay in the city until you have been clothed with power from on high" (Lk 24:49), and in the fulfillment of the promise on the day of Pentecost, "All of them were filled with the Holy Spirit and began to speak in other tongues as the Spirit enabled them" (Acts 2:4).[16] This "baptism" or "infilling" of the Holy Spirit, as Pentecostals call it—an intense, direct and overwhelming experience centering on the person of Christ—was the initial indicator that the community of faith collectively and individually had become the dwelling place of God for the purpose of participating in the divine mission, the reconciliation of all things and, ultimately, God's plan for the world.

The experience of baptism in the Holy Spirit in Acts 2:4 was accompanied by "signs and wonders." The first of these signs, glossolalia, or "speaking in

---

[15]For a splendid overview, see Frank Macchia, "The Kingdom and the Power: Spirit Baptism in Pentecostal and Ecumenical Perspective," in *The Work of the Spirit: Pneumatology and Pentecostalism*, ed. Michael Welker (Grand Rapids: Eerdmans, 2006), 109–25.

[16]Luke Timothy Johnson, *The Writings of the New Testament: An Interpretation*, rev. ed. (Minneapolis: Fortress, 1999), 113–15.

tongues," was visible, empirical evidence that Jesus was the resurrected Lord and that the Holy Spirit was present in the experience to empower believers. Healing, another sign of the presence and power of the Spirit (besides demonstrating the Lord's compassion and mercy), was also testimony that the resurrection of Jesus was real, present and powerful (Acts 3:1-7; 5:12-16; 8:4-7; 14:8-13; 27:7-10); healing offered a sense of empowerment over the uncertainties of life. Miracles, divine guidance and divine interventions, all unmediated, were equally markers of divine encounters.

Prayer, too, provided a channel to divine power (Acts 4:23-32; Jas 5:16-18). The intersection of human agency and divine action represented the conviction that God was at work in the world and that he intervened in daily life. Because the mode of access and the experience were both unmediated, virtually anyone had access to the source of all power, diffusing any sense of ecclesiastical hierarchy. And, as with tongues, God would and did use anyone!

The book of Acts, from which Pentecostals draw considerable authority for their theologically distinctive understanding of Holy Spirit baptism and empowerment, provides fertile ground for theological reflection on what could be described as a veritable agenda for social justice. From Luke's review of Jesus' ministry of "doing good and healing all who were under the power of the devil" (Acts 10:38), to the resuscitation of Dorcas, who was "always doing good and helping the poor" (Acts 9:36), to the provision for the widows' needs (Acts 6:1-3), to Paul's collections for the impoverished saints in Jerusalem (Acts 20:35), the early church linked ethical concerns with the postresurrection story. Within their own communities, through the power of the Spirit, the early church overcame the entrenched gender, economic, cultural and religious barriers of a divided world. These actions of social justice, infused with the power of the Spirit, were profoundly redemptive and wholly transformative.[17]

Similar to the New Testament accounts of social change, Pentecostals believe that social justice efforts become redemptive and transformational when we explain those actions in light of the resurrection story and encourage people to turn toward a divine source of power. Intentionality opens

---

[17]The most compelling argument that connects a Pentecostal social ethic with the work of the Holy Spirit has been made by Murray W. Dempster, "The Structure of Christian Ethics Informed by Pentecostal Experience: Soundings in the Moral Significance of Glossolalia," in *The Spirit and Spirituality*, ed. Wonsuk Ma and Robert P. Menzies (New York: T & T Clark, 2004), 108–40.

access to experiences of the divine such as salvation and Spirit baptism—experiences so powerful that mind and body are wholly transformed. Such experiences, in themselves, require further explanation.

Most Pentecostals recognize that spiritual experience, by its nature, cannot be analyzed using the tools of scientific investigation.[18] Joachim Wach, a sociologist of religion, describes religious experience as the response of the whole person—emotion, will, mind and body—to what is perceived as ultimate. Working from the premise that all power organizes reality around it, Wach argues that the more intense the experience, the greater the capacity to profoundly organize every aspect of one's life in response to ultimate power. For example, after Paul's encounter with the risen Lord on the Damascus Road, his life changed completely, as Paul puts it, "by the power of the resurrection."

Experience, in all cases, remains individual and subjective. It is sometimes difficult to identify the specifically "religious" in the experience (e.g., "I saw an angel") and impossible to verify. Experience can be faked or counterfeited. In spite of these substantial challenges, however, we must find ways to take religious experience seriously or forfeit critical knowledge about the central power that can change a person's destiny and around which people organize their lives into coherent wholes.[19] Spiritual experience can change lives like no other power.

SACRED STORIES

Stories of spiritual experience are central to Pentecostalism. The only access we have to the meaning of spiritual experiences is through the story or testimony of participants. Stories explain God's redemptive action in us. They show how our lives are organized in response, for example, to the spiritual experience of salvation, Spirit baptism and physical healing. A story allows us to see the Spirit at work in the life of a person or even in the daily activities of ministry. Indeed, story or testimony can function like the "word." It gives meaning to the "deed." In fact, stories may be the most important indicators of the efficacy of Pentecostal social work and its transformational effect on the whole person—body, soul and spirit.

---

[18]Joachim Wach, *The Comparative Study of Religions* (New York: Columbia University Press, 1958), 27–58.
[19]I am indebted for this argument on the "experience of the divine" to Luke Timothy Johnson, *Religious Experience in Earliest Christianity: A Missing Dimension in New Testament Studies* (Minneapolis: Fortress, 1998), 39–68.

Sacred stories or testimonies of "the least of these"—the children and recipients of our efforts at Latin America ChildCare—are one of the best ways to appreciate the work of the Spirit in our midst. The children I write about in this essay are the ones who live in the urban slums, shantytowns and the poorest barrios in Latin America; they live in places where the most basic necessities of life—clean water, medical care and a decent and safe place to sleep—are too often beyond their reach. There is never enough to eat. They are among the 1.2 billion people in our world who live in abysmal, soul-destroying poverty.

Upon entering one of our schools, most of the children are putting a foot in a religious institution or church for the first time. They are completely bereft of religious information or instruction, but they are quick to ask spiritual questions: Who is God? Why am I here? What about devils and angels? Do you believe in miracles? What is heaven like? Will I go to heaven when I die? Most of all, they want to know if God is real and, if he is, what difference he will make in their lives. The door to divine power begins to open. Soon, children experience the good news of the gospel for themselves. Now they have stories to tell.

Children's stories are framed by context—the world and vocabulary of the child—and the tools they use to tell their stories. Their language of expression corresponds to their age, as does their understanding and capacity to interpret complex (and often adult) moral problems. The stories tell us about how children interpret spiritual experiences. Children ask universal questions about God while they try to figure out a world that is complex, inconsistent and contradictory. They build their own versions of faith and tell us about them. They might speak about the mystery of God and a game of hopscotch or marbles all in the same story. Their minds soar to heaven in one moment and then dive-bomb into the hell of their real-life context in the next. Still, they are convinced that God has broken into their lives. They believe they have access to divine power; they are participants in God's mission. There are no go-betweens or mediators—only them and God.[20]

---

[20]I recognize that a series of testimonies does not prove that something is either *always* the case or *never* the case. Rather, I argue that, on the whole, in the daily lives of Pentecostals, the regularity of the appearance of divine encounters as evidenced in the stories and testimonies of the participants is one important indicator of the nature and work of the Holy Spirit in our activities, including social action.

Certainly, from these stories we cannot be too quick to make inferences and extrapolations, but we do have opportunities to see theology done from the bottom up when children respond to questions they actually care about. Children's stories offer us a peek into a rich tapestry of divine experiences that have changed lives forever.

Dulce. Dulce's story is about the power of prayer. Dulce lived in one of the poorest barrios in Santo Domingo with her mother and three younger brothers. Her mother had a live-in boyfriend who was abusive. One day, nine-year-old Dulce prayed to God: "If you are real, all I want is peace in our home!" Just like that, the boyfriend left!

But now the family had lost their sole source of support. Dulce's mother had to move the family to an abandoned house with a leaky roof. She sold candy on a street corner to get enough money to buy food. Dulce, the oldest, became the substitute mother.

One day, while sweeping the floor of their little shack, Dulce decided to ask God for one more thing. She prayed, "God, if you are real, all I want is to go to school." That week some women from a local Assemblies of God church invited Dulce and her mother to a women's revival service. On Saturday night, Dulce and her mother formally accepted Christ, and the next morning Dulce's brothers did too. On Sunday afternoon, the pastor came to visit and told Dulce's mother that her children could attend the church's school. By Monday morning, Dulce and her brothers were in school, wearing new uniforms, enjoying a nutritious lunch and meeting their teacher. Talk about sudden transformation!

Dulce's mother, overwhelmed with gratitude, volunteered to clean the school in the late afternoons after she finished selling candy on the street corner. Soon the school hired her. A widowed deacon from the church came to repair the leaky roof of their house. He fell in love with and married Dulce's mother.

Dulce testified that she had received a "mighty answer to prayer." She and her family now lived in a home filled with peace and love. Dulce grew up, studied at university and eventually married. "Just look around you," Dulce told us years later. "See what God has done."

Dulce's account—a lesson in the power of prayer—is a story of word, deed and spiritual experience. Greater than the sum of its quantifiable parts, the consequence is profoundly transformative.

Sara. Sara's story gives us a glimpse into the transformative power of God to heal in answer to prayer. Children make few distinctions between God's ability to help them with unspectacular daily decisions and dramatic acts of healing and miracles. They have confidence that God can and does intervene in any area of life, big or small.[21] That's what happened in the life of Sara, a third-grade student in one of our schools who was getting sicker by the week. Her teacher told her mother that she needed to take Sara to the doctor. The x-rays brought horrible news. Sara's liver, infected by a parasite, had abscessed. The doctor knew that medically there was not much more he could do. After a few weeks, it became obvious that Sara was going to die. Sara was sent home to die in the familiar surroundings of her family.

At school, Sara learned that God was powerful and had the ability to heal people, even children. Sara decided that she wanted a miracle for herself. "I am not going to die," she announced to her mother, *porque Dios me va a sanar* ("because God is going to heal me"). Her classmates began to pray with Sara for a miracle.

Within days she improved. New x-rays clearly indicated that Sara's liver was completely normal. Because of the healing, Sara's mother was converted and became a member of the Assemblies of God church located next to the school.[22]

Sara's healing provides a dramatic illustration of the outcomes of social justice endeavors when they intersect with divine experience. Access to divine power opened the door for something human action alone could never accomplish. The supernatural healing of a little girl and the salvation of her family were parts of a living testimony to the entire community of what life can look like when God gets involved in human history. It is around that kind of power that people organize their lives.

Luis. Luis was just six when he began attending one of our schools—located in one of the worst slums in San Jose, Costa Rica. Neither of his parents were Christians. His clothes were little more than rags. Years later, Luis recalled that two of his most vivid memories of childhood were the food he received at school each day (often his only meal for the day) and the

---

[21]For an excellent discussion of the holistic worldview integral to Pentecostal teaching about healing, see Margaret M. Poloma, "Divine Healing, Religious Revivals, and Contemporary Pentecostalism," in Kärkkäinen, *The Spirit in the World*, 21–39.

[22]Carmela Rodriguez (mother of Sara) and Rev. Carlos Bermudez (Sara's pastor), interview by the author, September 25, 1990.

time the director of the school gave him a new pair of shoes.

Yet the "the most meaningful and life-changing moment in my life," Luis said, "was the day my third-grade teacher led me to Christ." Later that same year, during a chapel service, God spoke to his heart about dedicating his whole life to the Lord in service. Luis was filled with a strong desire to serve God with his whole being.

Luis started to memorize the Scriptures, and though he was still a child he began to preach in his local church. After graduation from high school, he attended university and Bible school in preparation for a life of service as a teacher in the very place he had found the Lord. Besides his work at the school, Luis is also the youth pastor of the local church next door to the school.

Christian education, new shoes and daily food were essential components of the church's participation in genuine social justice, but it was the experience of God's personal presence that generated the power around which Luis organized his life. Pentecostal social action addresses the whole person—body and spirit.

Emmanuel. The story of a boy named Emmanuel is embedded within a full range of divine experiences and encounters. The country of Costa Rica heard his story during a national *evento de gala* ("gala event") organized by then-president Rafael Angel Calderon. The intent of the gala was to celebrate and honor the children of Costa Rica. In the providence of God, the president's office called the director of one of our schools, Doña Coralia, and asked her to select a child to speak at the gala on behalf of all the children of the country. Doña Coralia selected Emmanuel López Navarro, an eight-year-old child in the second grade.

Emmanuel had never been out of the barrio where he lived. Government officials seated the little boy between the president and the first lady. The event was filmed. Here is what Emmanuel said:

> My name is Emmanuel López Navarro. I am eight years old and in the second grade. . . . Every day I give thanks to the Lord for allowing me to study in a school as beautiful as mine. The Lord has done great and marvelous things in my life and in the life of my family. I want to tell you my testimony.
>
> Since I was little, I have been abused and mistreated by my father. My mother told me that when I was a baby, when she would try and feed me, my father would become angry and hit her. I remember one time when I was

taking a bath that my father became so angry that he began to hit me with the buckle of his belt until I started to bleed. I wasn't fortunate like other children to have my own bed. I slept on a few sacks of cement. . . . I never understood why my father could be so violent. . . . My family was a complete disaster.

When I came to the Christian school, I found out for the first time that the Lord loved me. The teacher told us that the Lord loved children and that we could speak to him. That is how I learned to pray.

One day the pastor of the church came to my class, and after talking with us he said that there were some of us who had been abused and mistreated—that we had problems at home. He told us to come to the front of the class, and he would pray with us. It was then when the Holy Spirit touched me for the first time in my life. I fell to the floor. When I got back up, I began to pray until my shirt was wet with sweat—asking the Lord to change my suffering and the suffering of my family.

The Lord began to do a work in my family. Now my father doesn't smoke or mistreat my mama or me. My brothers and sisters who were out doing bad things were converted, and today we are a happy family. . . . I give glory and gratitude to the Lord for his mercy and love. How wonderful is the Lord Jesus!

And then, Emmanuel addressed the president directly, "Mr. President, if you follow God's commandments and do what he says, you have nothing to fear!"

Enrique. Lest we think that Pentecostal social work must always result in miraculous healing or guidance or intervention, consider the example of Enrique. His story shows that while Pentecostals anticipate the miraculous, there are countless times when God does not miraculously heal, ardent prayer does not seem to be answered or God's response is inexplicable.

Enrique was an energetic younger teenager who attended one of our schools during the day and worked the evening shift at a local restaurant, doing his share to support the family. Enrique loved his classes, and no matter how late in the evenings he worked, he always appeared on time for school the next morning.

Enrique wrote a letter to his American sponsor one morning. He wanted to make the letter perfect, and his teacher waited for him to put on the finishing touches. As soon as he was finished, Enrique left the class on the run, wanting to take a catnap before he began his evening work shift. When his grandmother came to wake him up to go to his job, she found that his heart had stopped while he slept. Enrique was in the presence of the Lord.

The next morning, upon hearing the news, the teacher went to find the last letter Enrique had written. It read:

> It is a joy to greet you through this letter. Thank you for writing me . . . your words encourage me and give me strength. It is very important to keep a close relationship with God. . . . I thank and praise God because he helps me do well in my job.
>
> In the book of Revelation, chapter 2, verse 10, it reads: "Fear none of these things that you shall suffer . . . be faithful unto death, and I will give you a crown of life."
>
> I'll say goodbye to you in the name of the Lord.

Enrique's family and classmates did not need to witness a miracle of healing to justify their belief in the supernatural intervention of God. Enrique's letter was evidence of the active and personal presence of the Holy Spirit. God knew all about Enrique.

Reiniega. Religious experience can transform the life of even the youngest child. Reiniega, a little girl from Cuba, wrote a letter to her sponsor.

> God bless you richly and may our Lord Jesus Christ keep you. I write to thank you for the help you have given me. God has been so good to me and I have received his love and goodness through your help. I don't have words to thank you. . . . I ask Jesus to help me read and write better and to be able to read the Bible.
>
> I am only seven years old and in the first grade, but with the help of God I am going to be a missionary.

The stories children tell have the power to shine a light on our own souls.

Wendy. I conclude with a story that is personal. It was thirty years ago. I was walking through one of the poorest sectors of San Salvador. I saw her on the side of a path. Seven years old. I knelt down. Her name was Wendy. Her father was blind, she told me. The conversation was short.

> Do you have a mommy and daddy?
>
> *Just a daddy.*
>
> Where is your mommy?
>
> *I don't know. I live with my daddy and my little brother.*
>
> What does your daddy do?

He sells lottery tickets and cigarettes.

What do you want to do when you grow up?

I want to sell lottery tickets and cigarettes like my daddy.

I couldn't get Wendy's story off my mind. Maybe it was because she was seven—at the time, about the same age as my own three children. When I thought of her, I thought of them.

I want to sell lottery tickets and cigarettes like my daddy.

With those words, Wendy invited me to comprehend the tragedy of her own circumstances. The story wasn't just about Wendy anymore or even about children like her. It was about me. The story pointed a searchlight on my own narrow vision, on my moral values, on my assumptions. Her story was affecting. Every time I thought about Wendy, I thought about my own kids.

I want to sell lottery tickets and cigarettes like my daddy.

What did my kids think about when they went to bed at night? What did they dream about? I knew they each had a marvelous imagination. There was no limit to what they might dream about or what they would like to do when they grew up. I realized that I was now involved in this story. There was something I could do about the injustice. I could make a difference. I could give a million kids just like Wendy a chance to dream. All I had to do was decide. I would never be the same.[23]

Conclusion

The above stories probably would not have occurred in a social service program where children were not told about God's grace, how he gets personally involved in our lives and that he empowers ordinary people, even children, to be participants in his mission. As these children's stories demonstrate, Pentecostals would do well to recognize the need to establish an "essential connectedness" between the core spiritual experiences of salvation and Spirit baptism and social justice practices. When social actions are infused by the power of divine experience, the outcomes are effective, redemptive and pentecostal.

---

[23]As of August 2013, more than 1,700,000 children had attended a school sponsored by Latin America ChildCare.

14

"In All Places and in All Ages"

The Holy Spirit and Christian Unity

Timothy George

On New Year's Eve, December 31, 1961, the Third Assembly of the World Council of Churches met in New Delhi, India. It was an important meeting, not least because it witnessed the long-negotiated assimilation of the International Missionary Council into the World Council of Churches. One of the chief architects of that convergence was the great missionary, bishop and ecumenical theologian Lesslie Newbigin. The assembly at New Delhi also adopted an important statement on Christian unity, which contains what has been called "the greatest run-on sentence in ecumenical history."[1] It says:

> We believe that the unity which is both God's will and his gift to his church is being made visible as all in each place who are baptized into Jesus Christ and confess him as Lord and Savior are brought by the Holy Spirit into one fully committed fellowship, holding the one apostolic faith, preaching the one gospel, breaking the one bread, joining in common prayer, and having a corporate life reaching out in witness and service to all and who at the same time are united with the whole Christian fellowship in all places and all ages in such wise that ministry and members are accepted by all, and that all can act and speak together as occasion requires for the tasks to which God calls his people.

---

[1]World Council of Churches, "New Delhi Statement on Unity, and Orthodox Response," World Council of Churches website, 2000, www.wcc-coe.org/wcc/who/crete-02-e.html.

"It is for such unity," the assembly concluded, "that we must pray and work."[2]

Even today one could hardly craft a better statement of the basis, aims and means of Christian unity than that one. However, when I read it I am reminded of what Archbishop William Temple once said: "I believe in one, holy, catholic and apostolic church but regret that it doesn't exist."[3] Could it be that one reason for the ecumenical malaise acknowledged today by almost everyone (except those bureaucrats who are paid not to acknowledge it) is the sidelining of the Holy Spirit and his distinctive office of unity in building up the body of Christ?

It was just one week prior to that meeting in New Delhi that Pope John XXIII issued an apostolic constitution called *Humanae Salutis*, which convoked Vatican Council II. In that statement, John concluded with a prayer to the Holy Spirit. He prayed: "Renew your wonders in our time, as though for a new Pentecost, and grant that the holy Church, preserving unanimous and continuous prayer, together with Mary the Mother of Jesus, and also under the guidance of St. Peter, may increase the reign of the divine Savior, the reign of truth and justice, the reign of love and peace. Amen."[4]

Despite such beautiful sentiments, one has to ask, when assessing the Catholic-Protestant divide over the last half century, whether the Holy Spirit has really been taken seriously ecumenically and theologically. To illustrate: When we look a little further into the documents of that council, Vatican II, we come to one on the church titled *Lumen Gentium*, which contains five references to the Holy Spirit. These references, however, were not in the original draft of *Lumen Gentium*. They were added later and, although they fit in quite well, still feel like a bit of an afterthought when read today.

Albert Outler—who was present as a Protestant observer at all four sessions of Vatican II and who, along with Geoffrey Wainwright, has been one of the greatest gifts of world Methodism to the modern ecumenical movement— pointed some years ago to the diminution of the Holy Spirit in the ecumenical movement. He did so by reviewing the central themes of the several assem-

---

[2]John H. Leith, ed., *Creeds of the Churches: A Reader in Christian Doctrine from the Bible to the Present*, 3rd ed. (Louisville, KY: John Knox, 1982), 583.
[3]Cited in George Carey, *A Tale of Two Churches* (Downers Grove, IL: InterVarsity Press, 1985), 147.
[4]Pope John XXIII, *Humanae Salutis, Constitutio Apostolica qua SS. Oecumenicum Concilium Vaticanum II Indicitur, 25 Decembris 1961, Ioannes PP. XXIII*, Vatican website, www.vatican.va/holy_father /john_xxiii/apost_constitutions/1961/documents/hf_j-xxiii_apc_19611225_humanae-salutis_lt.html.

blies of the WCC going back to the First Assembly, which met at Amsterdam in 1948. The theme of the First Assembly was "Man's Disorder and God's Design." Karl Barth, one of the main speakers, appropriately protested that the wording was wrongly ordered, as it put the fall, "man's disorder," before divine election, "God's design."[5]

Nonetheless, the emphasis was clearly *theocentric*. This assembly was followed, in turn, by a series of decidedly *christocentric* themes, such as "Christ, the Hope of the World" (Evanston, 1954); "Jesus Christ, the Light of the World" (New Delhi, 1961); and "Jesus Christ, the Life of the World" (Uppsala, 1968). Only in 1991, at the Seventh Assembly in Canberra, did the third person of the Holy Trinity take center stage with the theme "Come, Holy Spirit, Renew the Whole Creation."

Outler, writing just prior to the assembly in Canberra, predicted that the result would be either "a new ecumenical landmark" or "a cacophony of disparate hopes."[6] To avoid the cacophony, Outler admonished, "Canberra will have to begin and end with a trinitarian perspective and thus avoid the narcissist temptation to confound the Spirit's presence with a variety of emotional exaltations."[7] Was Canberra the turning point toward the ecumenical cacophony and narcissism that Outler feared? This is not the place to pursue that question, but judging from the reactions of Eastern Orthodox and evangelical participants after the assembly it is fair to say that the grand hopes for a new, landmark ecumenical pneumatology were not realized.[8]

I have begun in the weeds of contemporary ecumenical discourse, but I want to take my bearings from the Scriptures and the earlier Christian tradition, keeping in mind the statement of New Delhi that the one fully committed fellowship into which we are brought by the Holy Spirit includes the whole Christian koinonia "in all places and all ages." I will return to several examples of ongoing ecumenical dialogues that advance the cause of Christian unity, but first I begin with a biblical reflection on the coinherence of Jesus Christ and the Holy Spirit.

---

[5]Albert C. Outler, "Pneumatology as an Ecumenical Frontier," *Ecumenical Review* 41 (1989): 363.
[6]Ibid., 363.
[7]Ibid., 369.
[8]For a sampling of reactions, see Valerie Zahirsky, "Are the Orthodox That Far Apart?" *Ecumenical Review* 43 (1991), 222–25; and "Evangelicals Find Inroads, Remain Cautious," *Christianity Today,* April 1991, 68–71.

On the night before his death, Jesus prayed to the heavenly Father for his disciples, both for those who were with him at the time and for all others who would become his disciples through their witness across time. He prayed that they might all be one, even as he and the Father are one, so that the world might believe (Jn 17:20-21). This locus classicus for Christian unity from the Gospel of John is located, not coincidentally, in the context of Jesus' promise not to abandon his disciples as orphans once he was gone. He promised to send them the Holy Spirit, the Spirit of truth, as another *paraklētos*, another "advocate" or "counselor," another "encourager." Here we have a preview of the ascension (Acts 1) and Pentecost (Acts 2): the lifting up of the Son, his return to the Father and the sending down of the Spirit.

Read in isolation and taken out of context, it might seem that the promised Paraclete is a new force or power or energy—to be created de novo and ex nihilo—to care for the disciples once Jesus has gone in order to prevent their being left as orphans. But we have read our Bibles, in particular the first part of John's Gospel, and we know that this is the same Spirit who has already descended on Jesus at his baptism (Jn 1:32-34), the same Spirit of whom Jesus had also spoken and named the life-giver (Jn 6:63), the medium of rebirth (Jn 3:5) and the one who will give flowing "rivers of living water" (Jn 7:38 ESV) to all who are thirsty even as Jesus has done for the Samaritan woman at Jacob's Well (Jn 4:7-15). And even if we did not have at hand Matthew's Gospel or Mark's or Luke's to read about Jesus' Spirit-anointed healings, exorcisms and other miracles, we do have the Hebrew Scriptures. We know about the brooding Spirit of God at creation, the Spirit of the covenant, the Spirit of prophecy and the Spirit of counsel and understanding who rested on the servant of the Lord in Isaiah.

The Spirit that Jesus promises to send is, above all, a person. He does things that only a person can do: he abides and indwells, teaches, reminds, testifies, adjudicates and convicts, guides, speaks, declares and glorifies Jesus Christ. His job, Jesus said, will be to "take what is mine and declare it to you" (Jn 16:14 ESV). All of these acts are in service to the Holy Spirit's mission as the unifier of God's people. So Paul, in writing to the sect-ridden Corinthians, reminds them that there should be no divisions (*schismata*) among them, for the Holy Spirit dwells within them as in a temple, and they have all been baptized by one Spirit into one body through the cross. Hence the scandalous implications of his rhetorical question: "Is Christ divided?" (1 Cor 1:13). The Greek word is *memeristai*, which literally means to cut up into little pieces, just as you might go to a butcher shop and buy a chunk of meat and then dice it up on a tray to serve as hors d'oeuvres. How preposterous! Yet this is how we are treating Christ when we violate the Spirit's presence within us and in our midst. Is Christ divided? Is Christ partisan? Is Christ sectarian? God forbid! The Spirit has made us members of the church of the undivided Christ.

When Clement of Rome wrote to this same church at Corinth a generation or so after St. Paul, he made the same point: "Why are there strifes, and tumults, and divisions, and schisms, and wars among you? Have we not all one God and one Christ? Is there not one Spirit of grace poured out upon us? And have we not one calling in Christ?"[9] It has often been said that in the early church, pneumatology was abstracted from Christology, that the Spirit was identified christologically in a way that obscured his own divine person, mission and reality. While there might be some basis for this charge, it stands in stark contrast to many modern conceptions of the Spirit in which the Holy Spirit is distanced not only from Jesus Christ but also from the Trinity itself. In such a construal, the Spirit is identified with creation, not as its Lord or sustainer but rather as the generic presence of God—a God of radical immanence. Thus the Spirit is not a distinct, divine person, but an all-pervading reality more suited to panentheism than to the historic Christian doctrine of God. This indeed is a long way from Irenaeus, who wrote, "Where the church is, there is the Spirit of God; where the Spirit of God is, there is the church."[10]

Jesus Christ, Israel's Messiah, is the bearer of the Spirit and not merely one instance in the history of religions when the Spirit may be seen to be present. As Thomas Torrance once put it, "We cannot speak of the operation of the Spirit in the world as if the Incarnation had not taken place . . . or as if he may now operate as it were behind the back of Jesus Christ."[11] This is to simply echo what would be recognized as a salient feature of the *consensus fidelium*: where the Spirit is, Christ is. Where one person of the Trinity is present, the whole

---

[9]Alexander Roberts and James Donaldson, eds., *Ante-Nicene Fathers: The Writings of the Fathers Down to A.D. 325*, vol. 1, *The Apostolic Fathers, Justin Martyr, Irenaeus* (Peabody, MA: Hendrickson, 1994), 17.

[10]Irenaeus, *Against Heresies* 3.24.1 (Ibid., 458).

[11]Thomas F. Torrance, *Theology in Reconstruction* (Grand Rapids: Eerdmans, 1966), 230.

Trinity is present. Nonetheless we must give an account not only of the church's way to Nicaea (325) but also of the church's road to Constantinople (381).

It is undoubtedly true that the church stumbled and made many missteps on the way to the Council of Constantinople in 381. I suggest that there were at least two things at work here. First, there was a kind of reticence or modesty in speaking directly about the Holy Spirit. In his communication with Serapion, Athanasius is reluctant to speak so explicitly of the Holy Spirit's ineffability and transcendence.[12] Gregory of Nazianzus, the first of the Cappadocian fathers, said, "If ever there was a time when the Father was not, then there was a time when the Son was not. If ever there was a time when the Son was not, then there was a time when the Spirit was not. If the one was from the beginning, then the three were so too. If you throw down the one, I am bold to assert that you do not set up the other two. . . . Is the Spirit God? Most certainly. Well, then, is he consubstantial? Yes, if he is God."[13] Even St. Gregory the Theologian, as he was called, felt woozy scaling the heights of such supernal realities: "What, then, is procession? Well, you tell me what the unbegottenness of the Father is, and I will explain to you the physiology of the generation of the Son, and the procession of the Spirit, and we shall both of us be frenzy-stricken for prying into the mystery of God."[14] Here, I think, we see some of the patristic roots of what will later come to flower in Eastern hesychasm.[15]

Yet following in the steps of Athanasius and his good friend Basil the Great, Gregory of Nazianzus defended the equality of the Spirit with the Father and the Son over against the *pneumatomachoi*, the "fighters against the Spirit." Their argument against these Spirit-detractors boiled down to this: we can tell what the Spirit *is* by observing what he *does*: "If the Holy Spirit is not to be worshipped, how can he deify me by baptism? But if he is

---

[12]Athanasius the Great and Didymus the Blind, *Works on the Spirit*, trans. Mark DelCogliano, Andrew Radde-Gallwitz and Lewis Ayres (Crestwood, NY: St. Vladimir's Seminary Press, 2011).

[13]Gregory of Nazianzus, *The Theological Orations*, in *Christology of the Later Fathers*, ed. Edward R. Hardy (Louisville, KY: Westminster John Knox, 1954), 195, 199.

[14]Gregory of Nazianzus, *Theological Orations*, 198.

[15]Hesychasm is the Eastern Orthodox belief that by means of strict asceticism, disinterest in worldly affairs, discipleship, prayer and a state of stillness within one's body and spirit a believer will subsequently undergo a mystical experience uniting him or her intimately with God (see Jaroslav Pelikan, *The Christian Tradition: A History of the Development of Doctrine*, vol. 2, *The Spirit of Eastern Christendom (600–1700)* [Chicago: University of Chicago Press, 1974], 254–70).

to be worshipped, surely he is an object of adoration, and, if an object of adoration, he must be God; the one is linked to the other, a truly and golden saving chain."[16] What Bernard Lonergan has argued with reference to the *homoousios* of the Son is also true of the church's recognition of the Spirit's deity: it was a move from the inchoate pneumatology and "undifferentiated consciousness," to use his term, of the early Christian community to the differentiated and liturgically formed consciousness of the fourth century.[17]

Before the church could recognize the Holy Spirit not only as he who gives life but also as he who brings unity, it had first to recognize the eternal *perichōrēsis* of the Spirit with the Father and the Son in what Jonathan Edwards would later call the "sweet and holy society" of the divine Trinity.[18] In the East, the distinction of the persons was clarified and made a priority, while in the West, especially through the influence of Augustine, the unity of the divine essence (or *substantia*, to use the earlier Latin word of Tertullian) was the starting point. There are many implications of this spelled out by Augustine in his *De Trinitate*, but the most important of these is his emphasis on the Holy Spirit as the *viniculum amoris*, or the bond of love, uniting the Father and the Son.[19]

Augustine's concept of the Holy Spirit as the bond of unity between the loving Father and the beloved Son has been criticized on various grounds, especially from the East, because in some constructions it tends to depersonalize the Spirit, to "thingify" the Spirit as a mere instrument or conductor between the Father and the Son. This was certainly not Augustine's intent, as we can see from his so-called psychological doctrine of the Trinity. In the triad of memory, understanding and will, the Holy Spirit is the dynamic, active agent—the executive, we might say—who draws on the Father's great storehouse of memory, informed by the *Logos* of the eternal Word, to accomplish the eternal purposes of God within history and within the church. Combining these two schema, perhaps we can say that the Holy Spirit for Augustine is the

---

[16]Ibid., 211.

[17]See Bernard Lonergan, *The Way to Nicea: The Dialectical Development of Trinitarian Theology* (Philadelphia: Westminster, 1976).

[18]Jonathan Edwards, "Christ's Sacrifice an Inducement to His Ministers," in *The Works of Jonathan Edwards*, vol. 25, *Sermons and Discourses, 1743–1758*, ed. Wilson H. Kimnach (New Haven, CT: Yale University Press, 2006), 662.

[19]Augustine, *De Trinitate* 6.7.

agency of love. Not only is he the bond of love within the eternal Trinity, but he is also the one who sheds the love of God abroad in the hearts of forgiven sinners (Rom 5:5), fulfilling the trinitarian promise of salvation in St. Paul: "Because you are his sons, God has sent the Spirit of his Son into our hearts, the Spirit who calls out, 'Abba, Father!'" (Gal 4:6). (This might be, in my opinion, the one verse in the entire New Testament that brings together the dynamic emphasis of the divine Trinity: The Father sent the Spirit of his Son into our hearts crying, "Abba, Father.")[20] In other words, the office of unity that the Holy Spirit exercises within the divine Godhead is also extended to those he has baptized into the body of Christ, the church.

The Holy Spirit is unique, and although his work cannot be duplicated, it can be imitated. Thus the New Testament admonishes believers to test the spirits through the process of discernment (dokimazō). In 1 Corinthians 12, the "discerning of spirits" is listed among the diversity of gifts that are given by the same spirit to the community of faith alongside gifts of faith, healing, miracles, prophecy and speaking in tongues. For lack of this gift, or rather for lack of the right use of it, the church has come to grief again and again. There are many spirit substitutes and pseudo-spirits along the way, and we are told that their numbers will increase as the parousia approaches.

Perhaps the greatest, most momentous decision ever made in the history of the church was the excommunication of Marcion from the church in Rome in 144. We forget that Marcion was not just a lonely heretic croaking out there all alone on his lily pad. Rather, he was a powerful church leader, and "Marcionism," if we can call it that, was a church movement with its own ecclesial structure and bishops. There were places where Marcionism was in the majority. Some of the followers of Marcion, who had no real doctrine of the Holy Spirit at all, were teaching that the apostle Paul was the Holy Spirit! The church had to come to a parting of the ways and had to make a fundamental decision about Marcion. Marcion's theology severed creation from redemption because it denigrated and finally excised the entire Hebrew Scriptures from the Christian Bible. But the church decided that there could be no Christian Bible without the Hebrew Scriptures.

Why was Marcion's dismissal the most fundamental decision ever made

---

[20]See Gerald Bray, "Out of the Box: The Christian Experience of God in Trinity," in *God the Holy Trinity*, ed. Timothy George (Grand Rapids: Baker Academic, 2006).

in the church? Everything else—including the Arian and the Pelagian controversies—stemmed from that fundamental decision. In the twentieth century, even the effort of Hitler's Third Reich to take away the Hebrew Scriptures and to omit from Christian songs and hymns words such as "hallelujah" and "hosanna" (both Hebrew terms) is rooted in the Marcionite tradition.[21]

Throughout the history of the church there have always been spirit substitutes. The most important twentieth-century Catholic theologian on the Holy Spirit, Yves Congar, lists at the end of his magnificent three-volume work, *I Believe in the Holy Spirit*, three substitutes that Catholics have sometimes been guilty of substituting for the Holy Spirit. One of them is the Virgin Mary. Another is the Eucharist. Still another is the pope. Congar is not saying that the pope himself is claiming to be a substitute for the Holy Spirit but rather that he is being treated and understood this way at the level of popular piety. Congar thus warns against substituting anyone or anything else for the Holy Spirit.[22]

The other big "M" in the second and early third centuries was Montanism. It was said by his many enemies that Montanus, the movement's figurehead, claimed for himself that he was the Paraclete. Moreover, one of his followers, Maximilia, once said (shades of the late Harold Camping) that once she was gone the world would surely come to an end. Both Maximilia and Brother Camping are gone, and yet the world still stands.

While the New Prophecy pursued its own trajectory outside the centrist orthodoxy of Irenaeus and (perhaps) the early Tertullian, its premature suppression came at a great loss. Paul Tillich lists four such losses from the premature suppression of the New Prophecy, the first of which is the closure of the canon and cessationism. The Montanists put pressure on the church to close the canon in an opposite way from Marcion. Marcion, on the one hand, had wanted a radically reduced Christian canon so that at the end of the day all of the Old Testament would be gone, leaving only what he called the *Evangelium* and the *Apostolium*. This was a slender, expurgated version of the Gospel of Luke and selected parts of Paul. Montanism, on the other hand, went in the other direction. It opened wide the bounds of inspiration so that the new prophecies were regarded in seamless continuity with the many

---

[21]See Doris L. Bergen, *The Twisted Cross: The German Christian Movement in the Third Reich* (Chapel Hill: University of North Carolina Press, 1996), 21–43.

[22]Yves Congar, *I Believe in the Holy Spirit*, trans. David Smith (New York: Crossroad, 1997), 1:161–65.

books that were proliferating already and claiming to be inspired. With the closure of the canon, though, a shutting down of the manifestation of the gifts of the Holy Spirit in the life of the church took place. Although the closure does not necessarily imply the cessationist view, the correlation of the two in church history has provoked speculation along this line. Cessationism is still held and defended today.

The second loss Tillich notes is the victory of order over prophecy, or the victory of institutional, juridical Christianity over often erratic, but nonetheless anointed, Christianity. Near the end of Vatican II, the delegates voted on *Dignitatis Humanae*, the decree on religious liberty. It was very controversial, and several hundred bishops voted against it. Of those who voted for it, one bishop said, "I know this is what the Holy Spirit wills, but this is going to cause a lot of trouble." It did, and it still does in some circles of Catholic thinking. Sometimes even the evident lack of the Spirit provokes resistance, even turmoil, in the church. The victory of order over prophecy in the early church did not squelch the continuing struggle, which continues to this day, between these two poles of Christian identity.

The third loss stemming from the suppression of the New Prophecy is the diminution of eschatology and loss of apocalyptic verve. It is often noted that in the Apostles' Creed there is only one line given to the Holy Spirit. At the beginning of the third article, we read: "I believe in the Holy Spirit." That is it. Yet there is a kind of forward momentum in the third article that comes from the opening statement of "I believe in the Holy Spirit": the communion of saints, the forgiveness of sins, the resurrection of the body—in other words, there is a close correlation between pneumatology at the head of the third article and what follows immediately after. Ecclesiology and eschatology necessarily flow from pneumatology. If you read figures such as Justin Martyr, Irenaeus or Tertullian, there is an expectation among them for the return of Jesus Christ, an urgency in the way they look for the parousia. Unfortunately, the shutting down of Montanism prematurely led to the diminution of eschatology as a driving concern in the life of the church. It led to a loss of apocalyptic verve.

The fourth loss is the loosening of discipline, which led to accommodation and laxity. If Tertullian is to be believed in the things he wrote about Montanus's practice of fasting, Montanus conflated asceticism and legalism. Discipline can be carried to extremes, and the Montanists exemplified this tendency. But there is an opposite danger: to swing to the other extreme, namely accommodation, laxity and ultimately no discipline at all. Accommodation and laxity are reactions to overlegalism and overdiscipline, and sadly, this characterizes many evangelical churches today.

Given such vexations, schisms, heresies and religious upheavals from the apostolic age right up to our own time, where does the Spirit make present the unity for which Jesus prayed to the heavenly Father in John 17:20-23? There is no way I can read that text and not think Jesus is there praying in a palpable way for the full, visible unity of the church here on earth. This is, after all, proper to the ecumenical project prompted by the Holy Spirit. And yet I think back to Archbishop Temple, who asked, in spite of all that we confess and affirm, where do we find it? Where do we see it? Although I accept the goal of full visible unity as proper to the ecumenical project prompted by the Holy Spirit himself, we will seek in vain for such results in plans for church union, new ecumenical pneumatologies or the seeking of a lowest-common-denominator togetherness. Fresh ecumenical dialogue has a role to play, but it is crucial to remember a statement by the Orthodox ecumenical theologian Nikos Nissiotis: "Unity is not an attribute of the church, but its very life."[23] The unity we seek, the unity for which Jesus prayed, we will find in the *embodiment* of the Holy Spirit in the life of the church. To spell this out in any detail would require exposition of at least three elements in the worship of the church—each understood in terms of missiology and pneumatology. They are (1) the liturgy of the Word, especially the office of preaching, (2) baptism, and (3) the Eucharist, or Lord's Supper. Put otherwise: the book, the bath and the bread.

Unlike the modernist/ultramodernist assumption that sees the Bible as a collection of disparate documents from late antiquity that can, and ought to be, read "just like any other book," the church knows the sacred Scriptures as a unique, Spirit-inspired treasury of divine wisdom encompassing both the Tanak of Israel and the apostolic testimony that we commonly call the New Testament. To say that the Bible is the inspired Word of God is to make a claim about the larger economy of the Holy Spirit in the origin, preser-

---

[23]Nikos Nissiotis, "The Witness and Service of Eastern Orthodoxy to the One Undivided Church," in *The Orthodox Church in the Ecumenical Movement*, ed. Constantin Patelos (Geneva: World Council of Churches, 1978), 231.

vation and contemporary application of the written Word of God. As David Yeago has put it, "Through the Scriptures, the Spirit bears witness to the Father and the Son *in* the church, in order to make *of* the church a sign that glorifies the Father and the Son before the nations."[24]

One of the most encouraging things about what we call the theological interpretation of Scripture today is how the Spirit is using the Bible to build up the church across all kinds of confessional and denominational lines. This is something relatively new in the history of Christianity. The Spirit's present work makes it all the more important that we read the Bible not in lonely isolation from the wider community of faith—"me and Jesus, we got a good thing going; me and him, we got it all worked out," as the gospel ditty by George Jones has it—but rather as part of the body of Christ extended through both time and space. That wonderful statement from New Delhi talks about the church in "every time" and "every age." We are part of it. We belong to it. Therefore, as we read the Holy Scriptures it is important that we do not simply have the New Testament—even in Greek—or the most recent commentary on it. No matter who the exegete or the commentator is, there is a community of faith extended across time as well as space to whom we belong, and so we read the Scriptures in the company of our fellow pilgrims.

To this end, InterVarsity Press has undertaken the publication of two major commentary series: the Ancient Christian Commentary on Scripture, which is under the general editorship of Tom Oden, and the Reformation Commentary on Scripture, with which I am pleased to be associated. Both of these series, which together will consist of nearly sixty volumes when completed, assume that the Christian church is the primary reading community within which and for which biblical exegesis is done. It is "the Church's Bible," to borrow the title of another fine series of historic biblical interpretation, edited by Robert Wilken.

The prominence of contextual theologies today reminds us that the Holy Spirit through the Bible speaks in fresh ways to every church in every time and every place. When Jaroslav Pelikan, with the help of Valerie Hotchkiss, brought together his definitive collection of the creeds and confessions of the church, he included a summary of the gospel message by the nomadic Masai

---

[24]David S. Yeago, "The Bible," in *Knowing the Triune God*, ed. James J. Buckley and David S. Yeago (Grand Rapids: Eerdmans, 2001), 63.

tribe in Kenya. The Masai Creed is an example of the indigenization of the Christian message. Here is the Masai version of the second article of the creed:

> We believe that God made good his promise by sending his Son, Jesus Christ, a man in the flesh, a Jew by tribe, born poor in a little village, who left his home and was always on safari doing good, curing people by the power of God, teaching about God and man, showing the meaning of religion is love. He was rejected by his people, tortured and nailed hands and feet to a cross, and died. He lay buried in the grave, but the hyenas did not touch him, and on the third day, he rose from the grave. He ascended to the skies. He is the Lord.

This is not a case of decontextualizing God's work. He was a Jew by tribe! He had a place in history. Now, here is the third article:

> We believe that all our sins are forgiven through him. All who have faith in him must be sorry for their sins, be baptized in the Holy Spirit of God, live the rules of love and share the bread together in love, to announce the good news to others until Jesus comes again. We are waiting for him. He is alive. He lives. This we believe. Amen.[25]

Such a creed, of course, is not a new artifact of revelation but rather (as the *regula fidei* has always been) a summary of the overarching storyline of God's dealings with the world, Israel and the church. The creed did not replace the Bible, much less sit in authority over it, but it made the Bible's central trinitarian message clear, memorable and deliverable. The Bible itself was meant to be not only read, studied, translated, memorized and meditated on, but also to be embodied in the life and worship of the church. Such embodiment includes baptism—both baptism in water in the name of the triune God and baptism in the Holy Spirit (neither of which, as I read the New Testament, is complete without the other)—along with "the sacrament of the altar," as Lutherans call the Eucharist, or the Lord's Supper.

While preaching was not invented by the Reformation—think instead of St. Francis, Bernard of Clairvaux and John Chrysostom—the ministry of preaching was given new prominence in the worship and theology of the Reformation traditions, one with important ecumenical implications for the church today. The sermon was made the centerpiece of the regular worship

---

[25]Cited in J. Todd Billings, *The Word of God for the People of God: An Entryway to the Theological Interpretation of Scripture* (Grand Rapids: Eerdmans, 2010), 121.

of the church and correlated with the visible words of God in the Eucharist—
pulpit and table were together. We forget that in the late Middle Ages many
great sermons, such as those preached by the Dominican friars, were
delivered outdoors and in the town marketplace. What the Reformers did
was to take the sermon and move it back into the church and make it central
to the worship of the gathered community.

The church is the community of the faithful gathered by the Spirit to hear
the preaching of the Word, believing, as Heinrich Bullinger put it in the
Second Helvetic Confession of 1566, that "the preaching of the Word of God
is the Word of God." God truly speaks and is truly present in judgment and
grace whenever his Word is proclaimed. With reference to John Calvin's
thought, Thomas J. Davis has written: "God has chosen preaching, and God
invigorates the preaching of ministers by the power of God's Spirit so that
Christ truly comes in the spoken word to reside with his people. Or to reverse
the direction, as Calvin so liked to do, preaching lifted the congregation to
Christ, to participate in Christ and thus gain all the benefits he offers."[26]

In closing, I want to mention two documents dealing with Christian
unity that encourage me when I look at ecumenical dialogue today. The first
is the fifth in a series of dialogues, which began in 1972, between classical
Pentecostal churches and the Roman Catholic Church. This particular dialogue is titled "On Becoming a Christian: Insights from Scripture and the
Patristic Writings."[27] The method employed by the Pentecostals and Catholics is amazing: they began by reading the Bible together and then reading
the church fathers together. They certainly made it clear that the latter is not
on the same level as the former. Nevertheless, both parties felt that they each
had something to learn to share with one another as they pondered together
the text of the Bible, the Fathers and their application to the life of faith today.

The other document I will mention comes from "Evangelicals and Catholics Together" (ECT), an ongoing theological discussion that began some

---

[26]Thomas J. Davis, *This Is My Body: The Presence of Christ in Reformation Thought* (Grand Rapids:
Baker Academic, 2008), 102.

[27]Pontifical Council for Promoting Christian Unity, *On Becoming a Christian: Insights from Scripture
and the Patristic Writings with Some Contemporary Reflections: Report of the Fifth Phase of the International Dialogue Between Some Classical Pentecostal Churches and Leaders and the Catholic Church
(1998–2006)*, Vatican website, 2006, www.vatican.va/roman_curia/pontifical_councils/chrstuni
/eccl-comm-docs/rc_pc_chrstuni_doc_20060101_becoming-a-christian_en.html.

two decades ago. ECT's first statement, "Evangelicals and Catholics Together: The Christian Mission in the Third Millennium" (ECT), was published in 1994.[28] In 2002, ECT published a statement titled "Your Word Is
Truth," which deals with the problematic issue of Scripture and church traditions. ECT had much in common with the aforementioned Pentecostal-
Catholic dialogue, in that we began with the Scriptures, reflected together
and prayed for the guidance of the Holy Spirit before working toward a joint
conclusion. To my knowledge, it had never been said by both sides before
this particular ecumenical dialogue that the "Supreme Magisterium" of the
church is the Holy Spirit. Yet we were able to affirm together that

> during the past five hundred years, the Holy Spirit, the Supreme Magisterium
> of God, has been faithfully at work among theologians and exegetes in both
> Catholic and Evangelical communities, bringing to light and enriching our un-
> derstanding of important biblical truths in such matters as individual spiritual
> growth and development, the mission of Christ's Church, Christian worldview
> thinking, and moral and social issues in today's world. We praise God for His
> faithful work within each community as He has provided instruction and
> guidance in these and other important areas of Christian faith and life.[29]

The Pentecostal-Catholic dialogue and ECT represent two forms of ecumenical engagement: the former an official bilateral dialogue, the latter an
ad hoc gathering of theologians who speak from and to but not for their
churches. Both methods have been productive in nudging the church
forward toward "the unity of the Spirit through the bond of peace" (Eph 4:3).

---

[28]"Evangelicals and Catholics Together: The Christian Mission in the Third Millennium," *First
Things*, May 1994, 15–22.
[29]"Your Word Is Truth," *First Things*, August-September 2002, 38–42.

15

Come, Holy Spirit

Reflections on Faith and Practice

Jeffrey W. Barbeau and Beth Felker Jones

"How could you discuss the Holy Spirit for an entire semester?" The student's question reveals far more than a naive perception of Christianity. Who could cast blame on such a student? Survey the nearest theological volume—take any systematic theology off the shelf—and chances are the doctrine of the Holy Spirit doesn't have a single chapter devoted to it. The formal term *pneumatology*, the study of the Spirit, sounds sterile, disengaged and inactive. Shouldn't rather, students and laity ask, the Spirit be felt and experienced? Shouldn't we know the Spirit more than we understand the Spirit?

In fact, many systematic theologies leave readers pneumatologically malnourished, frequently subsuming the Spirit under the Trinity and closing a section on the relation between the Father and the Son with an exploration of the Spirit as the one who brings unity to the Godhead. Other textbooks used in college and seminary classrooms briefly introduce the Holy Spirit as a preliminary to the important work of sanctification—a necessary precursor to the more expansive themes of Christian life and final glorification. Far too often, the Spirit remains hidden and unknown, while Christians long for an understanding of the powerful hand of God in their lives.

The experience of reading a volume of essays on biblical, historical and doctrinal perspectives related to pneumatology could leave readers rather overwhelmed. Instead of malnourishment, the risk is that the reader will leave overstuffed—uncertain of the dizzying array of biblical passages that directly relate to the Spirit, unsure of the range of historical witnesses that call into question contemporary assumptions about the alleged inactivity of the Spirit in the world and unable to move forward in practices that reflect life in the Spirit's presence. What began in sweetness ends with a bellyache. Once introduced to such possibilities, readers naturally ask, "what difference does this make for how I live?"

In this essay, we present a way forward for readers looking for pneumatologically informed, practical-theological guidance for Christian life in the Spirit. Rather than making a study of a single idea, we present three proposals for scholars and laity alike toward the formation of a fully trinitarian vision of Christian living: what Christians believe, how Christians think and how Christians should act. In all, they constitute a challenge for this generation of Christian scholars, ministers and laity.

PROPOSAL 1—THE CHRISTIAN LIFE SHOULD REFLECT OUR WORSHIP OF THE TRIUNE GOD.

Reflection on the Holy Spirit draws us deeper into reflection on the doctrine of God, deeper into knowledge of God's character and nature. Christians have repeatedly affirmed the belief that God is neither a transcendent, absentee landlord nor an impersonal, immanent force. Rather, as Jeremiah maintains,

> "Do not I fill heaven and earth?"
>> declares the Lord. (Jer 23:24)

The God who fills heaven and earth is the very same God who created the stars in the sky, brought life into the world and renews creation with each passing day. This God is the same one who called Abraham to obedience, required Moses to take off his sandals before the fiery bush and moved the prophets to speak words of judgment and mercy. God's own Son took on flesh by the Spirit who came to rest on Mary, ministered liberation from oppression among the people in the anointing of the Spirit and died and rose again through the power of the Spirit of God. Christians confess that God has acted from the beginning of creation to the end of the age through the personal work of the Holy Spirit, who came on the judges of Israel, inspired the prophets, empowered Jesus for ministry and filled the disciples powerfully with his divine presence.

The day of Pentecost proves essential for Christian reflection on right worship of the triune God. When the people gathered together in the wake of the ascension—in what Kevin Vanhoozer calls "a community of faithful improvisation"[1]—they found the Spirit of Christ uniquely present among them: "Suddenly a sound like the blowing of a violent wind came from heaven and filled the whole house where they were sitting. They saw what seemed to be tongues of fire that separated and came to rest on each of them. All of them were filled with the Holy Spirit and began to speak in other tongues as the Spirit enabled them" (Acts 2:2-4). The same God who fills heaven and earth moved as a violent wind among the people. No longer was the Spirit reserved as a mark for the prophet or taken as the unique authority of Israel's judges. Now the Spirit was on "all of them" and rested on "each of them." Without regard for nation or race, sex or class, people from "every nation under heaven" (Acts 2:5) began to declare—in different languages—"the wonders of God in our own tongues" (Acts 2:11).

Where is God? God is all around us, filling the heavens and the earth. Yet Pentecost makes it clear that God is personally present too. Peter declares that the particular presence of God is available for all people: "Repent and be baptized, every one of you, in the name of Jesus Christ for the forgiveness of your sins. And you will receive the gift of the Holy Spirit" (Acts 2:38). The Pentecost event, which distinctly combines both the communal and the personal, challenges Christians across denominations to this day. Peter's words are directed at the thousands of people who gathered to witness the spectacle—gathered from so many nations—and yet he maintains that the promise is for "every one of you." Even more surprising is that the personal presence of God is promised to all who would ask and not only for those present in Jerusalem: the Spirit is "for you and your children and for all who are far off—for all whom the Lord our God will call" (Acts 2:39). The same God who may be found throughout the entire earth may be found personally present to all who believe.

What begins in repentance and baptism finds fulfillment in a life of worship. The Westminster Shorter Catechism (1646–1647) explains the matter in language as simple as it is profound: "Man's chief end is to glorify God, and to enjoy him forever." Once again, we discover that right worship

---

[1]Kevin J. Vanhoozer, "The Spirit of Light After the Age of Enlightenment: Reforming/Renewing Pneumatic Hermeneutics via the Economy of Illumination" (chap. 9).

of God begins and ends in God. Since God has loved us and given grace to each of us, we are able, in turn, to respond in kind: "This is how we know that we live in him and he in us: He has given us of his Spirit" (1 Jn 4:13). The life of worship is a life that glorifies and enjoys God, and such a life can only be possible because of the gift of God that Acts and 1 John each describe. Christian worship requires, by definition, a Spirit-filled life. All who believe are given the gift of the Spirit and are enabled to worship God with their entire lives. Worship of the triune God involves love of God and love of neighbor because love marks the people of God: "God lives in them and they in God" (1 Jn 4:15).

The Christian life, therefore, is a life lived in union with Christ by the Spirit of Christ. Clark Pinnock's mystical language evokes something of the mystery of the union Christians have sought throughout the centuries: "God invites creatures to participate in this divine dance of loving communion. . . . Union with God is the unimaginable fulfillment of creaturely life, and the Spirit is effecting it in us."[2] Fear hinders love of God. This is why undue worry about the so-called blasphemy of the Spirit (Mk 3:28-29) frequently distorts the gospel; when we grow anxious about some particular, unforgivable act or words of slander against God, we miss the point entirely. Blaspheming the Spirit is not a mistake accidentally made. That blasphemy marks the final denial of our true end: union with God. Fear limits our willingness to surrender to the consuming fire. Union, as Oliver Crisp reminds us, "does not imply fusion," but it does imply that we are drawn into an organic communion with the divine.[3]

As Christians, we believe that union does not occur "in the Spirit," if such a claim implies the denial of our bodily existence. Rather, union occurs in time and space. To be united to God means that we are called out of isolation and selfishness and brought into communion with believers. We gather together to hear pastors preach the word of God. We share together in meals of thanksgiving and celebrate the sacrament because God has ordained the community as a means of receiving grace that renews, sustains and accomplishes final union and the perfection of love. We repeat ancient prayers,

---

[2]Clark H. Pinnock, *Flame of Love: A Theology of the Holy Spirit* (Downers Grove, IL: InterVarsity Press, 1996), 153–54.
[3]Oliver D. Crisp, "Uniting Us to God: Toward a Reformed Pneumatology" (chap. 6).

sing hymns of praise and thanksgiving, and utter sighs and groans all by the Spirit, who draws us into the one body of Christ.[4]

The Christian life is, at its height, a life consumed with love, lived in worship and enjoyment of the triune God. Our entire lives are bound up in God the Father, Son and Holy Spirit. Since God has reached out to us, we are drawn into his life, renewed by his refining fire and sent forth in his power. The doctrine of pneumatology bears fruit in intimacy with the triune God as, through Christ, we come to the Father in the power of the Spirit.

PROPOSAL 2—CHRISTIAN THEOLOGY MUST BE FULLY PNEUMATOLOGICAL THEOLOGY.

In light of this stance on the meaning of right Christian worship, Christian theological reflection is renewed. We discover a theology that refuses to shrink back from the Spirit's power and looks for ways to embrace and cooperate with that power even as Christianity continues to grow dramatically in its new, global phase. The expansion of Christianity around the world calls older churches to renewed reflection and a rejection of stagnant thinking. Evangelical theology after the emergence of Pentecostalism must account for the Spirit's presence and power in the explosive growth of Pentecostal and charismatic Christianities, and it must account for that presence and power, not as a concession, but in full recognition of the enormous shared space between evangelical Christianities and charismatic Christianities. Only an enormous act of hubris—one that may well be tainted by ethnocentrism—could imagine otherwise. Historians have made it clear that evangelicalism and Pentecostalism are, at least, close cousins. The time has come for evangelical theologians to claim that family relationship in a way that allows parties on all sides to recognize one another as family and to live in fruitful and mutually edifying relationships that are appropriate to the sons and daughters of God. This family, empowered by the Spirit, needs to listen to Paul's call to "live in harmony with one another" (Rom 12:16). Paul goes on to warn, "Do not be proud, but be willing to associate with people of low position. Do not be conceited." Such miracles are possible among those who are empowered by the Spirit, who is God.

---

[4]Geoffrey Wainwright, "The Spirit of God and Worship: The Liturgical Grammar of the Holy Spirit" (chap. 12).

Through biblical, historical and doctrinal perspectives, we recognize that truly trinitarian theology productively develops from thoughtful pneumatological reflection. The essays in this volume encourage Christians to engage in hopeful, new theological directions. The essays demand the rejection of christomonist theology that fails to acknowledge the triune work of God. To attend not only to the Son but also to the Spirit, who proceeds from the Son's Father and from the Son is, in no way, to denigrate the person of Jesus. The Spirit who, in the language of the creed, is worshiped and glorified is the same Spirit who is *together with* that Father and that Son. Scripture bears testimony to the will and the action of the one triune God from Genesis to Revelation. The Spirit, we are reminded, is no new player on the scene. The Spirit is not an upstart, a worrisome troublemaker who challenges Western theology. The Spirit is the same eternal one who was before creation, hovering over those waters; who was before the incarnation, working the conception of Jesus in Mary's womb; who is now, before the kingdom comes in its fullness, the burning one who prepares us for that day when God will reveal the truth "with fire" (1 Cor 3:13). The Spirit who filled Jesus in the past (Mt 4:1) is the very one who fills us in the present (1 Cor 3:16).

Pneumatology, too, must necessarily transform our thinking about the whole of God's work from creation to eschatology. The one, eternal God is only and always the triune God, and this presses us to acknowledge that the Spirit of God has always been at work, from the very onset of creation, and will always be at work. "To be created," Colin Gunton explains, "is to have a direction, a dynamic, which derives from the createdness of all things by the triune God."[5] The Spirit is the same from creation to the eschaton, and the Spirit warrants our attention as we consider the whole of God's work and all of the Christian doctrines. The Creator Spirit we met in Sandra Richter's essay is the same Spirit Amos Yong points us to in his essay, as he asks us to see creation through eschatological eyes. Reflection on the Spirit can renew our understanding not only of God's past redemptive works but also our knowledge of the world through interdisciplinary perspectives and practices. From Eden to the new Jerusalem, the Spirit is present and powerful among God's people, and the Spirit points us to the future in hope.

---

[5]Colin E. Gunton, *The One, the Three, and the Many: God, Creation, and the Culture of Modernity* (Cambridge: Cambridge University Press, 1993), 230.

Likewise, we become more and more aware that Christian hope is founded on the Spirit's seal. Pneumatology demands a kind of eschatological realism that expects the reality of the kingdom: even now, even today. We should expect the Spirit to make God's kingdom real among us, and we should expect that to happen in ways that are appropriate to who the Spirit is. Notably, pneumatological eschatological realism won't be an "overrealized" eschatology; it will be a realism that respects the "not-yet" of the kingdom, a realism that doesn't pretend to remove the dark glass that obscures our full vision of God's future (1 Cor 13:12). This is important to stress given abuses associated with some groups that claim the Spirit's kingdom power in the present—abuses that would twist the gospel into a "health and wealth" lottery ticket or would deny the reality of sin in the believing community. Pneumatological eschatological realism will dwell in the biblical space between the "already" and the "not-yet" of the kingdom, but it will stretch the bounds of what some of us might think possible or appropriate in the present. This is important to stress in the face of a fatalism that would seem to deny the Spirit's power. What could be more appropriate to expect of the Spirit who is God, than the very work of God? What could be more appropriate to hope for in the work of the Spirit, than actual holiness, actual transformation, actual kingdom living in the here and now? The Spirit, who is God, will not allow us to diminish what is possible in his presence and power.

When we know the Spirit, we know the already of the kingdom. We are those who are able to "stand firm in Christ" (2 Cor 1:21) because "he anointed us, set his seal of ownership on us, and put his Spirit in our hearts as a deposit, guaranteeing what is to come" (2 Cor 1:21-22). To take up Paul's financial metaphor, the Spirit's deposit or seal is God's earnest money on the kingdom. The God we know in Scripture is faithful to his promises. God will not default on his promised future, yet he wants us to be involved in the interim—in the time between the Spirit's deposit and the fullness of the future. In biblical perspective, we discover an eschatology that demands we get to work in the present. The eschatological kingdom is that reality which is "like a man going on a journey" (Mt 25:14) who has put earnest money down *in* us—a Spirit-indwelled people who have been given "bags of gold" (Mt 25:15). By the Spirit's presence and power, we, like the man with the five talents, can go and put that earnest money "to work" (Mt 25:16). To expect the kingdom to expand among us is not to put undue confidence in humans. It is to put appropriate confidence in the Spirit, who has made a deposit on us and who—as God—is present and powerful among us. When the Spirit empowers us to put eschatology into action, we will expect that action to be shaped by the very particular character of the Spirit of Jesus Christ. This means that we will have to guard against the sinful desire to work for some sinful, selfish version of the kingdom and will need to learn, instead, in and of the Spirit who makes us Christlike (which is what the kingdom of God looks like). Again—to name a contemporary abuse of pneumatology—the kingdom will not be about human versions of "health and wealth," it will not be about obvious prosperity in this time between the first and second comings of Christ, and it will not be a cult of personality shaped around human leaders. The Father's kingdom, as we learn of it through Christ in the power of the Spirit, is a kingdom of sacrificial love.

PROPOSAL 3—CHRISTIAN PRACTICE SHOULD BE CHARACTERIZED BY LOVE.

Theology in pneumatological perspective will not only be faithful and truthful but also practical. The study of pneumatology encourages us to recognize and respond to the Spirit's active presence and power among us. The Spirit is here, immanently and intimately involved in our otherwise mundane lives. That same Spirit is mighty and powerful and makes possible the personal presence of God among us as believers. When we embrace the reality of the Spirit, then, we will be—must be—moved to action, and that action will be characterized by the Spirit's own character. In the Spirit's presence, we can expect great things.

Life after Pentecost begins a life consumed by love. The familiar words of 1 Corinthians 13 resonate with a call to faithful Christian practice: "If I speak in the tongues of men or of angels, but do not have love, I am only a resounding gong or a clanging cymbal" (1 Cor 13:1). The love of God and neighbor should fill our lives because the Spirit of God has drawn us into love. John Wesley recognized the challenge that faces each one of us: "The necessary fruit of this love of God is the love of our neighbour, of every soul which God hath made; not excepting our enemies, not excepting those who are now 'despitefully using and persecuting us'; a love whereby we love every man *as ourselves*—as we love our own souls. Nay, our Lord has expressed it still more strongly, teaching us to 'love one another even as he hath loved us.'"[6] Loving our enemies—even those whose acts leave us shaken in the darkness of night—requires a supernatural work of God. Still, love can flourish even as light shines in the darkness.

The Spirit works even among those who do not know him. Calvin rightly challenges all those who question the work of God among all people. He not only recognizes that the Spirit of God is the only fountain of truth—thereby elevating lawgivers, philosophers, physicians and mathematicians (among others)—but also clarifies that the special presence of the Spirit among God's own people is the gift of holiness: "For what is said as to the Spirit dwelling in believers only is to be understood of the *Spirit of holiness*, by which we are consecrated to God as temples. Notwithstanding of this, He fills, moves, and invigorates all things by the virtue of the Spirit, and that according to the peculiar nature which each class of beings has received by the Law of Creation."[7]

A pneumatological foundation for right practice is thereby different from a strictly rationalist one. The basis of right action is not some common understanding or recognition of right, but the universal prompting of the Spirit, who restrains wickedness and draws all people toward good.[8] When we acknowledge God's prior work in creation—albeit incomplete and not yet fulfilled—we begin to see the Spirit's cultivation of life in unexpected places. Where war has resulted in death, we may see signs of peace and new life. Where poverty has choked the seeds of hope for the future, we may discern the renewal of community in unexpected moments. Where the abuse of power has left the weak vulnerable to injustice, we may discover the hand of God making right. By the power of the Spirit, we may begin to recognize God's work where we might not have before.

How much more among those who have received the down payment of the Spirit? The Spirit works universally, but the divine work of love among those who are "in Christ" constitutes a renewal of life and an investiture of divine

---

[6]John Wesley, Sermon 18, "The Marks of the New Birth," §3.3, in *The Works of John Wesley*, vol. 1, *Sermons I*, ed. Albert C. Outler (Nashville: Abingdon, 1984), 426.

[7]John Calvin, *Institutes of the Christian Religion*, trans. Henry Beveridge (Grand Rapids: Eerdmans, 1989), 1:236 (emphasis added).

[8]While some appeal to reason alone as the basis of right action, others claim that the work of the Spirit reveals the necessity of grace without diminishing the profound impact of sin (see John Paul II, *Fides et Ratio*, §§55, 104, Vatican website, www.vatican.va/holy_father/john_paul_ii/encyclicals/documents/hf_jp-ii_enc_15101998_fides-et-ratio_en.html).

power. The gift of the Spirit to the children of God profoundly shapes the practice of faith and everyday life. Talents are transformed from natural abilities into God-given gifts for the benefit of the body. That which we think of as signs of weakness and disability may also come to be recognized as signs of divine presence and renewal within creation. The Spirit's power and character may be countercultural and counterintuitive. They will certainly be counter to the sinful nature, "corrupted by its deceitful desires" (Eph 4:22). The Spirit's power and character will be known in that new community wherein, by a miracle of grace, we "get rid of all bitterness, rage and anger, brawling and slander, along with every form of malice" (Eph 4:31) and are enabled to "be kind and compassionate to one another, forgiving each other, just as in Christ God forgave you" (Eph 4:32). We act, therefore, as members of the community of love.

In conclusion, we encourage the entire Christian community to respond to the guidance of the Holy Spirit. The Spirit calls theologians to continue to explore the riches of biblical wisdom. The project of recovering biblical pneumatology remains incomplete, but what is needed is not only study but also the wisdom that comes from the self-revelation of the Spirit. Biblical revelation remains open to further study and discussion among scholars asking questions about the Spirit's sometimes strange and always surprising work throughout time. Historical investigation of the Spirit's work, too, remains underrepresented in the literature. One aspect of continued insistence on cessationism among some Christians is a lack of knowledge of the past. Historical theologians can help uncover the past for the understanding of churches in the present. Finally, systematic theologians can draw on the resources of biblical and historical literature to develop fully trinitarian theologies that place the person and work of the Spirit fully in view.

The Spirit calls clergy and those called to pastoral vocations to care for people through the cultivation of renewed communities. As those whose vocation is primarily service to others seeking God's presence and power in their daily lives, they will see people through God's eyes and care for them as God's hands. However, too often, membership in the body leads to a confusion tantamount to the eradication of individuality. Pastors, led by the Spirit of Christ, can help the community to recognize the individual value of each member, encourage the use and growth of distinct spiritual gifts and ensure that talk of unity does not result in exploitation.[9] Further, as the Spirit empowers the body, pastors can create space for the laity to care for others around them. The people of God may care for the broken as those who have known brokenness, even as Christ has taken on brokenness. Pastors can cultivate holy conversations in their communities, reaching beyond the walls of the churches to enhance life and looking within the churches to hear the voice of God.

Laypeople, too, should look for signs of the Spirit's work everywhere. Ever mindful that the Spirit of Christ works in unexpected ways, the laity may see signs of life and acts of grace as symbols of divine presence. Jürgen Moltmann rightly speaks of the endowment of life in the Spirit when he takes up the language of charisms to explain the activity of the Spirit: "Call and endowment, *klesis* and *charisma*, belong together, and are interchangeable terms. This means that every Christian is a charismatic, even if many people never live out their gifts. The gifts which the one or the other person brings or receives are at the service of their calling; for God who calls, takes people at the point *where* he reaches them and *as they are*."[10] In the exercise of our gifts and the sharing of ourselves, we become agents of the Spirit's power in the midst of brokenness. To this end, laity are called to form friendships and cultivate small groups that care for the needs of others, encourage mutual learning and edification, and offer accountability and ethical guidance through acts of confession and forgiveness. Through community, life is renewed by the Spirit, who draws people into meaningful relationships. The Spirit calls us to accountability for acts that violate the love of God and neighbor. Distortions of human relationship—discrimination based on racial, sexual, age and cultural factors (among others)—can be addressed in communities of understanding. Shared study of the Bible can lead to new perspectives on faith and plans for mission and service in the community. The Spirit empowers the people of God for the work of the kingdom.

More work remains. As Christianity continues to grow at an unparalleled rate in the non-Western world, believers must continue to seek out the Spirit in experience and study alike. Western Christians must learn from our brothers and sisters, even as we share our own stories.

---

[9]On the Spirit and "the constitution of particularity," see Gunton, *The One, the Three, and the Many*, 205–6.

[10]Jürgen Moltmann, *The Spirit of Life: A Universal Affirmation* (Minneapolis: Fortress, 2001), 180.

Assembled here with one accord,
Calmly we wait the promised grace,
The purchase of our dying Lord:
Come, Holy Ghost, and fill the place.[11]

If we share together—our stories, songs, sorrows and lives—we will no doubt come face-to-face with the person and work of God the Holy Spirit in our midst. Empowered by the Spirit who is God, we can expect great things.

---

[11]Charles Wesley, *A Collection of Hymns: For the Use of the People Called Methodists* (London: Wesleyan Conference, 1877), 351; cf. Wainwright, "The Spirit of God and Worship" (chap. 12).

List of Contributors

Estrelda Y. Alexander (PhD, Catholic University of America) is president of William Seymour College in Maryland. Her publications include *Black Fire: One Hundred Years of African American Pentecostalism* (IVP Academic, 2011), *The Women of Azusa Street* (Seymour, 2005) and *Limited Liberty: The Ministry and Legacy of Four Pentecostal Women Pioneers* (Pilgrim, 2008).

Allan Heaton Anderson (DTh, University of South Africa) is professor of mission and Pentecostal studies at the University of Birmingham. His publications include *An Introduction to Pentecostalism: Global Charismatic Christianity* (Cambridge University Press, 2014), *To the Ends of the Earth: Pentecostalism and the Transformation of World Christianity* (Oxford University Press, 2013) and *Spreading Fires: The Missionary Nature of Early Pentecostalism* (SCM and Orbis, 2007).

Jeffrey W. Barbeau (PhD, Marquette University) is associate professor of theology at Wheaton College. His publications include *Sara Coleridge: Her Life and Thought* (Palgrave Macmillan, 2014) and *Coleridge, the Bible, and Religion* (Palgrave Macmillan, 2008).

Oliver D. Crisp (PhD, University of London) is professor of systematic theology at Fuller Theological Seminary. His publications include *Jonathan Edwards on God and Creation* (Oxford University Press, 2012), *Revisioning Christology: Theology in the Reformed Tradition* (Ashgate, 2011) and *Divinity and Humanity: The Incarnation Reconsidered* (Cambridge University Press, 2007).

Timothy George (ThD, Harvard University) is dean and professor of divinity, history and doctrine at Beeson Divinity School, Samford University. His publications include *Reading Scripture with the Reformers* (IVP Academic, 2011), *Amazing Grace: God's Pursuit, Our Response* (Crossway, 2011) and *Theology of the Reformers* (Broadman & Holman, 1988; 2nd ed. 2013).

Beth Felker Jones (PhD, Duke University) is associate professor of theology at Wheaton College. Her publications include *Practicing Christian Doctrine: An Introduction to Thinking and Living Theologically* (Baker Academic, 2014) and *The Marks of His Wounds: Resurrection Doctrine and Gender Politics* (Oxford University Press, 2007).

Gregory W. Lee (PhD, Duke University) is assistant professor of theology at Wheaton College. Recent publications include scholarly articles and a coedited volume titled *Christian Political Witness* (IVP Academic, 2014).

Matthew Levering (PhD, Boston College) is the Perry Family Foundation Professor of Theology at Mundelein Seminary of the University of Saint Mary of the Lake. Recent publications include *Engaging the Doctrine of Revelation* (Baker Academic, 2014) and *Jesus and the Demise of Death* (Baylor University Press, 2012).

Douglas Petersen (PhD, Oxford Centre for Mission Studies) is the Margaret S. Smith Distinguished Professor of World Mission and Intercultural Studies and director of the Judkins Institute for Leadership at Vanguard University. His publications include *Not by Might, Nor by Power: A Pentecostal Theology of Social Concern* (Hendrickson, 1991).

Sandra L. Richter (PhD, Harvard University) is professor of Old Testament at Wheaton College. Her publications include *The Epic of Eden: A Christian Entry into the Old Testament* (IVP Academic, 2008) and *The Deuteronomistic History and the Name Theology: lešakkēn šemô šām in the Bible and the Ancient Near East* (Walter de Gruyter, 2002).

Kevin J. Vanhoozer (PhD, Cambridge University) is research professor of systematic theology at Trinity Evangelical Divinity School. His publications include *Faith Speaking Understanding: Performing the Drama of Doctrine* (Westminster John Knox, 2014), *Remythologizing Theology: Divine Action, Passion, and Authorship* (Cambridge University Press, 2010) and *The Drama of Doctrine* (Westminster John Knox, 2005).

Geoffrey Wainwright (DTh, University of Geneva; DD, Cambridge University) is Robert Earl Cushman Professor Emeritus of Christian Theology at Duke Divinity School. His publications include *Lesslie Newbigin: A Theological Life* (Oxford University Press, 2000), *For Our Salvation: Two Approaches to the Work of Christ* (Eerdmans, 1997) and *Doxology: The Praise of God in Worship, Doctrine, and Life* (Oxford University Press, 1984).

Michael Welker (PhD, University of Tübingen; PhD, University of Heidelberg) is senior professor of systematic theology and director of the Research Center for International and Interdisciplinary Theology at the University of Heidelberg, Germany. His publications include *God the Revealed: Christology* (Eerdmans, 2013), *God the Spirit: Pneumatology* (new ed.; Wipf & Stock, 2014) and *Creation and Reality* (Fortress, 2000).

Amos Yong (PhD, Boston University) is professor of theology and mission and director of the Center for Missiological Research at Fuller Theological Seminary. His publications include *Spirit of Love: A Trinitarian Theology of Grace* (Baylor University Press, 2012), *The Spirit of Creation: Modern Science and Divine Action in the Pentecostal-Charismatic Imagination* (Eerdmans, 2011) and *The Bible, Disability, and the Church* (Eerdmans, 2011).

General Index

Scripture Index

Finding the Textbook You Need

The IVP Academic Textbook Selector
is an online tool for instantly finding the IVP books
suitable for over 250 courses across 24 disciplines.

ivpacademic.com